THE WORK OF
HANNA SEGAL

THE WORK OF HANNA SEGAL

A Kleinian Approach to Clinical Practice

Hanna Segal, M.D.

JASON ARONSON INC.
Northvale, New Jersey
London

Library of Congress Cataloging in Publication Data

Segal, Hanna.
     The work of Hanna Segal.

     (Classical psychoanalysis and its applications)
     Bibliography: p.
     Includes index.
     1. Psychoanalysis 2. Klein, Melanie. I. Title.
II. Series. [DNLM: 1. Psychoanalytic theory. 2. Psychoanalytic therapy.
WM 460.6 S454w]
RC506.S43   616.89'17   81-7877
ISBN 0-87668-422-3   AACR2
ISBN 978-0-87668-422-1

Manufactured in the United States of America. Jason Aronson Inc. offers books
and cassettes. For information and catalog write to Jason Aronson Inc., 230
Livingston Street, Northvale, New Jersey 07647.

For Michael and Agnes

Contents

Foreword

As is evident in this volume of her clinical and theoretical papers, Hanna Segal has established herself as one of the most productive and sensitive clinical psychoanalysts in the field today. Using techniques based on the work of both Freud and Klein, she has shown a consistent interest in working with patients presenting the most severe types of psychopathology. Her techniques stress the analytic and insightful resolution of these disturbances rather than avoidance based on anxiety in the therapist. As an analyst who has thereby come to grips with many of the dimensions of primitive mental states, she has produced a significant body of work yielding profound insights and important contributions to therapeutic technique. In addition, her articles on phantasy, creativity, and symbol formation stand as landmarks in the literature on these important subjects, not so much essays in applied psychoanalysis as integral elaborations of her clinical-theoretical perspective.

Robert Langs, M.D.

Preface

This volume is the fruit of thirty years of psychoanalytic work. It contains the bulk, though not all, of my papers.

I qualified as a psychoanalyst at the British Psychoanalytical Society in 1947. I was analyzed by Melanie Klein and, after the end of my analysis, had the good fortune to work with her as a student and a colleague for a number of years. She supervised my first child analysis. I had as supervisors during my training Paula Heimann and Joan Riviere. They were both acute clinicians and I owe a great deal to both of them. Working with Joan Riviere, a person of immense culture as well as a great analyst, was a particular inspiration. She did a lot to introduce me to English literature and helped me to grapple with what was to me a new culture. I started my psychoanalytic work at a most exciting time. In 1946, Melanie Klein had just published her seminal paper, "Notes on Some Schizoid Mechanisms." This paper had a double significance. First, it enabled her to formulate a comprehensive theory based on her concepts of the paranoid-schizoid and depressive positions and enabled us to see and investigate the infinite complexities of the interplay of those two positions. Second, it opened up the whole area of investigation of schizoid and schizophrenic phenomena. It is not surprising that both Herbert Rosenfeld's and my own membership papers were based on the analysis of a schizophrenic. Rosenfeld's paper,

"Analysis of a Schizophrenic State with Depersonalisation," was read in 1947; my paper, "Some Aspects of the Analysis of a Schizophrenic" (1950), in 1949. It appears as chapter 8 of this volume. I believe this paper was the first account of the analysis of an acute schizophrenic carried out without parameters. Apart from the analysis of psychotics, Melanie Klein's paper drew our attention to the importance of schizoid mechanisms in the neurotic or normal personality. This is reflected in one of my early papers, "Schizoid Mechanisms Underlying Phobia Formation" (1954), which appears as chapter 11.

Early in my practice, my attention was forcibly drawn to problems of symbolism. I was lucky in that among my very first patients I had both psychotics and artists inhibited in their work. Both these categories of patients made necessary the understanding of their symbolic process—the psychotics, because I had to understand the peculiarities of their symbol formation to communicate with them; and the artists, because they were forever struggling for symbolic expressions and any disturbance of the symbolic function was an interference with their work. Once these two groups of patients made me aware of the problem, I realized its importance to all psycho-analytic work, and my interest in it continues. The postscript to my 1957 paper on symbol formation (chapter 4) is an extract of a paper presented at the Psychoanalytical Congress in 1977. My interest in symbolism was linked with an interest in the broader aspects of the intricate relationship and differentiation between the psychotic and creative processes. I attempted to tackle this problem in the paper "Delusion and Artistic Creativity" (1974), chapter 17 of the present volume.

I have sometimes been asked who, apart from Melanie Klein, influenced my work. Working in the variegated psychoanalytic community of the British Psychoanalytical Society, I must have been influenced one way or another by the work of many colleagues. I am, however, explicitly aware mostly of the influence of W. R. Bion, in particular of his papers dealing with psychotic processes. His early work, for instance his papers "Differentiation of the Psychotic from the Non-Psychotic Personalities" (1957) and "Attacks on Linking" (1959), influenced greatly my understanding and my technique. But I do not think this is directly reflected in my papers. On the other hand, his work on the growth of the mental apparatus, the alpha and beta elements, and his concept of the relation between the container and the contained, I refer to directly. See, for instance, my papers on countertransference and on dreams, chapters 6 and 7. His work made me much more aware of the subtleties of projective identification. This has altered my technique in the direction of much greater awareness of the interplay between transference and countertransference.

The analysis of psychotic parts of the personality faces one with the problem of symbol formation, an area of investigation opened up by Melanie Klein's "The Importance of Symbol Formation in the Development of the Ego" (1930). This paper had a profound influence on my work.

This volume contains some papers on the psychoanalysis of psychotics and some material from child analysis as well as a paper on the technique of child analysis. Though I am sometimes considered a "specialist" in those fields, I do not see myself as such. I have analyzed some psychotics and have some experience in the analysis of children. I have also supervised many analysts of both children and psychotics. This work was extremely rewarding and enriched my understanding of the infantile and psychotic parts of personality, essential for the psychoanalyzing in depth of any analysand.

But my only "specialty" is psychoanalysis. I see myself as a practitioner, a student, and a teacher of psychoanalysis. This is the field in which I hope to acquire a growing knowledge and skill.

References

Bion, W. R. (1957). Differentiation of the psychotic from the non-psychotic personalities. *International Journal of Psycho-Analysis* 38:266-275. In W. R. Bion, *Second Thoughts*. New York: Jason Aronson, 1977.

——— (1959). Attacks on linking. *International Journal of Psycho-Analysis* 40:308-315. In W. R. Bion, *Second Thoughts*. New York: Jason Aronson, 1977.

Klein, M. (1930). The importance of symbol-formation in the development of the ego. *International Journal of Psycho-Analysis* 1:24-39. In M. Klein, *Contributions to Psycho-Analysis 1921-1945*, pp. 236-250. London: Hogarth, 1948.

——— (1946). Notes on some schizoid mechanisms. *International Journal of Psycho-Analysis* 27:99-110.

Rosenfeld, H. (1947). Analysis of schizophrenic state with depersonalisation. *International Journal of Psycho-Analysis* 28:130-139.

Acknowledgments

The papers that appear in this volume have been published as follows:

Some Aspects of the Analysis of a Schizophrenic *(International Journal of Psycho-Analysis*, 1950).

A Psycho-Analytical Approach to Aesthetics *(International Journal of Psycho-Analysis*, 1952).

A Necrophilic Fantasy *(International Journal of Psycho-Analysis*, 1953).

A Note on Schizoid Mechanisms Underlying Phobia Formation *(International Journal of Psycho-Analysis*, 1954).

Depression in the Schizophrenic *(International Journal of Psycho-Analysis*, 1956).

Notes on Symbol Formation *(International Journal of Psycho-Analysis*, 1957).

Fear of Death: Notes on the Analysis of an Old Man *(International Journal of Psycho-Analysis*, 1958).

The Curative Factors in Psycho-Analysis *(International Journal of Psycho-Analysis*, 1962).

Phantasy and Other Mental Processes *(International Journal of Psycho-Analysis*, 1964).

Melanie Klein's Technique (in *Psychoanalytic Techniques*, ed. B. B. Wolman. New York and London: Basic Books Inc., 1967).

Melanie Klein's Technique of Child Analysis (in *Handbook of Child Psychoanalysis*, ed. B. B. Wolman. New York: Von Nostrand Reinhold Co., 1972).

A Note on Internal Objects, "A Propos des Objets Internes," *(Nouvelle Revue de Psychoanalyse*, 1972).

A Psychoanalytic Approach to the Treatment of Schizophrenia (in *Studies of Schizophrenia* ed. M. H. Lader. Ashford, Kent: Headley Brothers Ltd., 1975).

Delusion and Artistic Creativity *(International Review of Psycho-Analysis, 1974).*

Countertransference *(International Journal of Psychoanalytic Psychotherapy, 1977).*

Psychoanalysis and Freedom of Thought (Inaugural Lecture, Freud Memorial Visiting Professor of Psychoanalysis, University College, London 1977-78. Published by H. K. Lewis, London).

PART I

THE KLEINIAN
APPROACH

1

Melanie Klein's Technique

THE RATIONALE

The Kleinian Technique is psychoanalytical and strictly based on Freudian psychoanalytic concepts. The formal setting is the same as in classical Freudian analysis; the patient is offered five or six fifty-minute sessions a week; a couch is provided for him to recline on, with the analyst sitting behind him; he is invited to free-associate, and the analyst interprets his associations. Not only is this formal setting the same as that in classical technique, but in all essentials the psychoanalytic principles as laid down by Freud are adhered to. The role of the analyst is confined to interpreting the patient's material, and all criticism, advice, encouragement, reassurance, and the like, is rigorously avoided. The interpretations are centered on the transference situation, impartially taking up manifestations of positive and negative transference as they appear. By transference I mean here not only the "here-and-now" relation to the analyst, but the relation to the analyst, including reference to past relationships as transferred onto the analyst, and current problems and relationships in their interrelation with the transference. Special attention is paid to the transference onto the analyst of internal figures from the patient's inner world. The level at which the interpretations are given, again as indicated by Freud, is determined by the level of the patient's maximum unconscious anxiety. In these respects,

3

the Kleinian analyst may be considered to be following the classical Freudian technique with the greatest exactitude, more so indeed than most other Freudian analysts, who find that they have had to alter their analytical technique in some of its essential aspects when dealing with prepsychotic, psychotic, or psychopathic patients. Analysts using the Kleinian approach (Rosenfeld 1965, Segal 1950, 1956, Bion 1956, 1957, 1958, 1959) find it both possible and useful to retain the strictly psychoanalytical technique even with these patients.

Could it be said, therefore, that there is no room for the term *Kleinian technique*? It seems to me that it is legitimate to speak of a technique as developed by Melanie Klein in that the nature of the interpretations given to the patient and the changes of emphasis in the analytical process show, in fact, a departure, or, as Melanie Klein saw it, an evolution from the classical technique. She saw aspects of material not seen before, and interpreting those aspects, she revealed further material which might not have been reached otherwise and which, in turn, dictated new interpretations seldom, if ever, used in the classical technique.

To understand the rationale of the Kleinian approach and to appreciate the way in which the technique grew, it is best to place it in its historical setting. When Melanie Klein, in the 1920s, started her work with children, she assumed that Freud's method could be applied to children with only such modifications as would not alter the essence of the psychoanalytical relationship and the interpretative process. Since children do not verbalize easily, and since play is one of their major means of expression, she provided each child patient with a drawer of small, simple toys and play material, and she interpreted their play, behavior, and verbal communications in the way in which she would have interpreted an adult's free associations. She observed that children develop a transference, both positive and negative, very rapidly and often intensely. She found that the children's communications, through various activities in the session, revealed their unconscious conflicts with a clarity identical to or even greater than that of the adult's free associations. The analysis of children fully confirmed Freud's deductions about childhood derived from work with adults, but, as might be expected, certain new facts emerged. The Oedipus complex and the superego seemed both to be in evidence at an earlier age than one would have expected and to have pregenital, as well as genital, forms. Indeed, the roots of the oedipal situation seemed to lie as far back as the second oral phase. The superego of the small child was equally well in evidence, possessed of savage and primitive oral, anal, and urethral characteristics. She was impressed by the prevalence and power of the mechanisms of projection and introjection: the introjections leading to the building of a complex inner world and the projections coloring most of the child's perceptions of reality. Splitting was very active as an early mechanism preceding repression, and the child's development appeared to be a constant struggle toward integration and the overcoming of powerful splitting mechanisms. Once seen in the child, these more primitive levels of experience could be understood and detected in the material of adult patients.

THE CONCEPT OF PHANTASY

Working at the primitive level of the child's world led Melanie Klein to broaden the concept of unconscious phantasy.

> As the work of psychoanalysis, in particular the analysis of young children, has gone on and our knowledge of early mental life has developed, the relationships which we have come to discern between the earliest mental processes and the later more specialized types of mental functioning commonly called "phantasies" have led many of us to extend the connotation of the term "phantasy" in the sense which is now to be developed. (A tendency to widen the significance of the term is already apparent in many of Freud's own writings, including a discussion of unconscious phantasy.) [Isaacs 1952]

"Unconscious phantasy" springs directly from the instincts and their polarity and from the conflicts between them. Susan Isaacs (1948) defined it as "the mental correlate of the instincts" or "the psychic equivalent of the instincts." In the infant's omnipotent world, instincts express themselves as the phantasy of their fulfillment. "To the desire to love and eat corresponds the phantasy of an ideal love-, life- and food-giving breast; to the desire to destroy, equally vivid phantasies of an object shattered, destroyed and attacking" (Segal 1964). Phantasy in the Kleinian view is primitive, dynamic, and constantly active, coloring external reality and constantly interplaying with it.

> Reality experience interacting with unconscious phantasy gradually alters the character of phantasies, and memory traces of reality experiences are incorporated into phantasy life. I have stressed earlier that the original phantasies are of a crude and primitive nature, directly concerned with the satisfaction of instincts, experienced in a somatic as well as a mental way, and, since our instincts are always active, so a primitive layer of primary phantasies are active in all of us. From the core, later phantasies evolve. They become altered by contact with reality, by conflict, by maturational growth. As instincts develop

instinct derivatives, so the early primitive phantasies develop later derivatives and they can be displaced, symbolized and elaborated and can even penetrate into consciousness as daydreams, imagination, etc. [Segal 1964]

This broader concept of phantasy provides a link between the concept of instinct and that of ego mechanisms.

What Freud picturesquely calls here "the language of the oral impulse," he elsewhere called "the mental expression" of an instinct, i.e. the phantasies which are the psychic representatives of a bodily aim. In this actual example,[1] Freud is showing us the phantasy that is the mental equivalent of an *instinct*. But he is at one and the same time formulating the subjective aspect of the *mechanism* of introjection (or projection). Thus *phantasy is the link between the id impulse and the ego mechanism*, the means by which the one is transmuted into the other. "I want to eat that and therefore I have eaten it" is a phantasy which represents the id impulse in the psychic life; it is at the same time the subjective experiencing of the mechanism or function of the introjection. [Isaacs 1948]

This applies to all mental mechanisms, even when they are specifically used as defenses.

We are all familiar with phantasying as a defensive function. It is a flight from reality and a defence against frustration. This seems contradictory to the concept of phantasy as an expression of instinct. The contradiction, however, is more apparent than real; since phantasy aims at fulfilling instinctual striving in the absence of reality satisfaction, that function in itself is a defence against reality. But, as mental life becomes more complicated, phantasy is called upon as a defence in various situations of stress. For instance, manic phantasies act as a defence against the underlying depression. The question arises of the relation between the defensive function of phantasy and mechanisms of defence. It is Isaac's contention that what we call mechanisms of defence is an abstract description from an observer's point of view of what is in fact the functioning of unconscious phantasy. That is, for instance, when we speak of repression, the patient may be having a detailed phantasy, say, of dams built inside his body holding back floods, floods being the way he may represent in phantasy his instincts. When we speak of denial, we may find a phantasy in which the denied objects are actually annihilated, and so on. The mechanisms of introjection and projection, which long precede repression and exist from the beginning of mental life, are related to phantasies of incorporation and ejection; phantasies which are, to begin with, of a very

---

1. The example of introjection is from Freud's "Negation" (1925).

concrete somatic nature. Clinically, if the analysis is to be an alive experience to the patient, we do not interpret to him mechanisms, we interpret and help him to relive the phantasies contained in the mechanisms. [Segal 1964]

The understanding of Melanie Klein's use of the concept of phantasy is necessary for the understanding of her technical approach to resistance, if we take resistance to be synonymous with defenses against insight. The criticism has been advanced that the Kleinian analyst interprets the content of unconscious phantasies and neglects the analysis of defenses. This criticism is, I think, based on a misunderstanding of our way of handling defenses. We attach great importance to analyzing the unconscious anxiety that is defended against in conjunction with the analysis of the defenses against it, so that the emergence of the defended material into consciousness is facilitated not only by the analysis of the defenses but also by the lessening of the unconscious anxiety. This is particularly important when one reaches into the deep psychotic layers of the personality, as otherwise the ego may be flooded by psychotic anxieties. In the early days of psychoanalysis it was considered dangerous to analyze prepsychotics because it was believed that analysis of defenses could expose the weak ego to a psychotic breakdown. This anxiety was fully justified. It is far safer to analyze prepsychotics now, when we do not analyze predominantly resistance or defenses, leaving the ego defenseless, but have some understanding of the psychotic phantasies and anxieties that necessitate these defenses and can modify these anxieties by interpretations, which are directed at the content as well as at the defenses against it. The concept of mental mechanisms as one facet of phantasy life implies also that there is less division between interpretations of defense and those of content, and interpretation can deal more readily with the patient's total experience.

The same applies to the interpretations of structure. Susan Isaacs established the connection between the concepts of instinct, mental mechanism, and phantasy. I have extended it further, connecting phantasy with ego and superego structure, a connection that is implied in Isaacs's paper, but not explicitly stated.

If one views the mechanisms of projection and introjection as being based on primitive phantasies of incorporation and ejection, the connection between phantasy and mental structure becomes immediately apparent. The phantasies of objects which are being introjected into the ego, as well as the loss to the ego by phantasies of projective identification, affect the structure of personality. When Freud described the superego as an internal object in active relationship with the id and the ego, he was accused by academic psychologists of being "anthropomorphic." But what was he in fact describing? This structure within the ego is the end result of complex phantasies. The child in phantasy projects some of his own aggression into a parental figure; he then, in phantasy, incorporates this figure and, again in phantasy, attributes to this figure various attitudes and functions. Melanie Klein has shown that other objects, earlier than the superego described by Freud, are similarly introjected, and a complex internal world is built in phantasy and structuralized. The fact that structure is partly determined by unconscious phantasy is of paramount importance from the therapeutic point of view, since we have access to these phantasies in the analytic situation and, through mobilizing them and helping the patient to relive and remodel them in the process of analytic treatment, we can affect the structure of the patient's personality (Segal 1964).

THE FIRST SESSION

This view of phantasy affects the technique, in that the patient's material is looked at differently than in the classical technique. All the patient's communications in the session are viewed as containing an element of unconscious phantasy, though they may seem concerned with incontrovertible external facts. For instance, a patient may open a session by complaining that it is cold and raining. The analyst will keep an open mind about a possible phantasy content. Is the patient complaining of the analyst's unfriendliness? Is he complaining about the interval between sessions, and if so, did he feel like a baby left crying in the cold or like a baby left with a wet diaper? Did he feel that his omnipotent urination has led to a flood? No interpretation will be given, of course, until further material provides the meaning, but the analyst is alerted to the fact of coldness and wetness as a communication about something in the patient's inner world as well as in the weather.

In the phantasy world of the analysand, the most important figure is the person of the analyst. To say that all communications are seen as communications about the patient's phantasy as well as current external life is equivalent to saying that all communications contain something relevant to the transference situation. In Kleinian technique the interpretation of the transference is often more central than in the classical technique.

Our understanding of the central role played by unconscious phantasy and transference affects the course of the analysis from the very first session. The question is often asked by students, Should transference be interpreted in the first session? If we follow the principle that the interpretation should be given at the level of the greatest unconscious anxiety and that what we want to establish contact with is the patient's unconscious phantasy, then it is obvious that, in the vast majority of cases, a transference interpretation will impose itself. In my own experience I have not had a case in which I did not have to interpret the transference from the start. A patient undertaking a psychoanalysis is bound to come to his first session full of hopes and fears and is sure to have formed phantasies about the analyst as soon as he came in contact with him, or even before—as soon as he knew he was going to meet him. These hopes and fears, and the resistance against them, are often more clearly presented in the first session than in later ones. Interpreting them has the effect of both lessening the unconscious anxiety and, from the start, focusing the patient's attention on the central role of the analyst in his unconscious. These interpretations have, of course, to be formulated in a way that is acceptable and understandable to a patient as yet unfamiliar with the analytic technique. To give a not uncommon example, an obviously frigid and "shut-in" woman patient, in her first session, is first silent, then expresses some anxiety about how to behave, what to say, and so forth. The analyst may interpret her fear of his getting in touch with her mind. Then the patient proceeds to describe her father as a violent man, often drunk, who used to terrify her. The analyst can interpret that she hopes he will get in touch with her and understand her, but that she is also frightened that his interpretations will be violent and terrifying and that he will penetrate her mind and damage it. In this situation the fear of being physically raped, which may already be clear to the analyst, need not be interpreted, but its mental equivalent is near enough to the patient's anxieties to be brought into consciousness. A correct interpretation of this anxiety is necessary to enable the patient to "open out."

Another question, often asked in relation to the first session, concerns the level of interpretation. Should interpretations be deep or superficial? This again is dictated by the principle of interpreting at the level at which anxiety is active. It is by no means true that the patient presents first genital, then anal, and finally oral material. He presents material at the level at which, at that moment, anxiety is centered. For instance, to establish contact with a schizophrenic, it is usually necessary from the start to interpret the most primitive forms of projective identification if one is to get in touch with him at all. Thus, I interpreted, in the first session, to a schizophrenic adolescent, that she felt she had put all her "sickness" (the word she used) into me the moment she entered the room, and, as a result, felt me to be a sick and frightening person. A little later in the session I interpreted that she was afraid that my talking would put the "sickness" back into her. These interpretations, in my view, lessened her immediate paranoid reactions and enabled her to stay in the room and communicate with me.

Even in the relatively healthy individual, however, oral or anal anxieties may be clearly presented in the transference situation in the first session. Thus, a candidate started the session by declaring his determination to be qualified in the minimum time and to get in all the analysis he could in the shortest possible time. Later in the session he spoke of his digestive troubles and, in another context, of cows, presenting a picture of his phantasy about the relation to the analyst so clearly as to enable me to make the interpretation that I was the cow, like the mother who breast-fed him, and that he felt that he was going to empty me greedily, as fast as possible, of all my analysis—milk; this interpretation immediately brought out material about his guilt in relation to exhausting and exploiting his mother.

I have described the approach to the first session in order to emphasize that, from the start, we try to get in touch with the patient's unconscious phantasy, as manifested in the transference. This does not mean, however, that analysis is concerned with the description of phantasies in the void. A full interpretation of an unconscious phantasy involves all its aspects. It has to be traced to its original instinctual source, so that the impulses underlying the phantasy are laid bare. At the same time, the defensive aspects of the phantasy have to be taken into account, and the relation has to be traced between phantasy and external reality in the past and the present.

It is the contention of Melanie Klein and her co-workers that the application of these principles in the analysis of children, adults and, in more recent years, psychotic patients as well, has enabled us to reach deeper layers of the unconscious. These deeper layers must be taken into consideration if we are to understand the analysand's anxieties and the structure of his internal world, the basis of which is laid in early infancy. This accounts for the fact that interpretations at an oral or anal level and of introjective or projective mechanisms play a much larger part than in the classical technique.

THE PARANOID-SCHIZOID POSITION

In the development of psychoanalysis, as in most sciences, there is an interrelation between technical innovations and theoretical concepts, changes in technique revealing new material, leading to new theoretical formulations, and the theoretical concepts in turn leading to new techniques. It is impossible to speak of Melanie Klein's technique without bringing in some aspects of theory. As is probably well known by now,

Melanie Klein describes two stages in the oral phase, corresponding roughly to Abraham's preambivalent and ambivalent stages. She calls them the paranoid-schizoid and the depressive positions and describes two different types of ego and object-relation organization belonging to these two stages. In the paranoid-schizoid position, the infant has no concept of a whole person. He is related to part objects, primarily the breast. He also experiences no ambivalence. His object is split into an ideal and a persecutory one, and the prevalent anxiety at that stage is of a persecutory nature, the fear that the persecutors may invade and destroy the self and the ideal object. The aim of the infant is to acquire, possess, and identify with the ideal object and to project and keep at bay both the bad objects and his own destructive impulses. Splitting, introjection, and projection are very active as mechanisms of defense. The analysis of these persecutory anxieties and of the defenses against them plays an important part in Kleinian technique. For instance, if the analyst is very idealized, he will be particularly watchful for the appearance of bad figures in the patient's extraanalytical life and take every opportunity of interpreting them as split-off bad aspects of himself. He will also be watchful for the projection of the patient's own destructive impulses into these bad figures.

An important mechanism involved in the paranoid-schizoid position is that of projective identification. In projective identification, a part of the patient's ego is in phantasy projected into the object, controlling it, using it, and projecting into it his own characteristics. Projective identification illustrates perhaps most clearly the connection between instincts, phantasy, and mechanisms of defense. It is a phantasy that is usually very elaborate and detailed; it is an expression of instincts in that both libidinal and aggressive desires are felt to be omnipotently satisfied by the phantasy; it is, however, also a mechanism of defense in the same way in which projection is—it rids the self of unwanted parts. It may also be used as a defense, for instance, against separation anxiety. Here is an example of the difference between interpreting only projection and interpreting projective identification. A student reported a case in which his woman patient, preceding a holiday break, was describing how her children bickered and were jealous of one another in relation to her. The student interpreted that the children represented herself, jealous about him in relation to the holiday break, an interpretation that she accepted without being much moved. He did not interpet that she felt that she had put a jealous and angry part of herself into the children, and that that part of her was changing and controlling them. The second interpretation, for which there was plenty of material in preceding and subsequent sessions, was of very great importance, in that it could be shown to the patient how, by subtle manipulations, she was in fact forcing the children to carry those parts of herself. Often a transference situation can only be understood in terms of projective identification, a situation, for instance, in which the patient is silent and withdrawn, inducing in the analyst a feeling of helplessness, rejection, and lack of understanding, because the patient has projected into the analyst the child part of himself with all its feelings.

At the beginning of the analysis of a schizophrenic patient, an analysis that I supervised, the patient would stand with his back to the analyst, a huge table separating them. This patient had been separated from his mother and sent overseas when he was a small child. The analyst interpreted mainly that the table represented the ocean that separated him from his mother and how he used it to "turn the tables on her." In turning his back to her, he was the rejecting mother, and he was putting into the analyst the desperate child part of himself. Following certain indications, such as the patient's change of posture, and using her countertransference feelings, she could interpret in great detail the kind of feelings he felt he was projecting into her. The patient reacted to this interpretation sometimes as a persecution, which would then be interpreted as his feeling that she was forcibly and perhaps vengefully pushing these feelings back into him. Gradually the feelings of persecution lessened, the patient gave up his posture behind the table and felt able to communicate with the analyst by speech. Such a situation can also be seen as reversal, a well-known mechanism described by Freud. It is not, however, sufficient to interpret to the patient that he is reversing the situation of separation. One has to interpret in detail his introjective identification with the rejecting mother and the projective identification of the rejected child part of himself, identifying and describing its feelings and interpreting the detail of the phantasy of how this part is projected. For instance, the feces and the flatus may contain the parts that the patient wishes to project. Hence, turning his back to the analyst could have not only a symbolic meaning but could also relate to phantasies connected with his wish to defecate into the analyst.

States of mind in which projective identification predominates may leave the patient feeling depleted, since part of himself is missing, persecuted by the analyst filled with his projections, and confused with the analyst. This is particularly noticeable in the case of the schizophrenic, who immediately forms a violent psychotic transference, and whose anxiety and confusion can only be relieved by interpretations of identification (Rosenfeld 1965, Segal 1964).

It is to be emphasized, however, that the analysis of the paranoid-schizoid object relationships and defenses is not confined to the analysis of the psychotic and the prepsychotic only; the schizoid defenses, though originating in the earliest stages of development, are repeatedly regressed to and revived as a defense against feelings aroused in the depressive position.

THE DEPRESSIVE POSITION

The depressive position starts when the infant begins to recognize his mother. Throughout the paranoid-schizoid position, normal processes of maturation are helped by, and help in turn, the psychological drive to integration, and eventually, sufficient integration is achieved for the infant to recognize his mother as a whole object. The concept of the whole object contrasts both with that of the part object and that of the object split into good and bad. The infant begins to recognize his mother not as a collection of anatomical parts, breasts that feed him, hands that tend him, eyes that smile or frighten, but as a whole person with an independent existence of her own, who is the source of both his good and his bad experiences. This integration in his perception of his object goes *pari passu* with the integration in his own self. He gradually realizes that it is the same infant, himself, who both loves and hates the same person, his mother. He experiences ambivalence. This change in his object relations brings with it a change in the content of his anxieties. While he was previously afraid that he would be destroyed by his persecutors, now he dreads that his own aggression will destroy his ambivalently loved object. His anxiety has changed from a paranoid to a depressive one. Since at that stage the infant's phantasies are felt as omnipotent, he is exposed to the experience that his aggression has destroyed his mother, leaving in its wake feelings of guilt, irretrievable loss, and mourning. His mother's absence is often experienced as a death. As the depressive position starts in the oral stage of development, where the infant's love and hatred are linked with phantasies of incorporation, this ambivalence is felt also in relation to the mother as an internal object. And in states of depressive anxiety and mourning, the infant feels that he has lost not only his mother in the external world, but that his internal object is destroyed as well. Melanie Klein viewed these depressive anxieties as part of normal development and an unavoidable corollary to the process of integration. They become reawakened up to a point in any subsequent situation of loss. There is a difference here between the Kleinian view and the classical view. In the classical view, melancholic illness involves ambivalence in relation to an internal object and regression to an oral fixation (Freud 1917, Abraham 1912), but normal mourning involves only the loss of an external object. In the Kleinian view, ambivalence toward an internal object and the depressive anxieties associated with it are a normal stage of development and are reawakened in the normal mourning. It is often contended by classical Freudian analysts that when a patient is actually mourning it is usually an unproductive period in his analysis. Kleinian analysts, in contrast, find that analysis of mourning situations and tracing them to their early roots often helps the patient greatly in working through the mourning and coming out of it enriched by the experience.

I should like to describe here the dream of a patient soon after his mother's death. He dreamed that he was crawling on all fours around marshy ground, a kind of bog. He woke up with a sinking feeling, a mixture of depression and nausea. He described the nausea as a feeling as though the marshy ground were bubbling up inside his stomach. He associated first to crawling on all fours and connected it with an incident, too long to report in detail, referring to his mother's pregnancy when he was a toddler, and the acute feelings of rage and loss he experienced in relation to his mother about the time of his sister's birth. Then he tried to describe the marshy ground, but found it very difficult, until he suddenly realized that it looked exactly like a microscope slide of a cancerous breast. His mother did not die of cancer of the breast, but he always thought this was the disease she would die of. He remembered hitting her in the breast and being terrified she would develop cancer. A further analysis of his dream led to a great deal of material about his early phantasies of attacking his mother's breast orally and anally, and incorporating a destroyed breast, a focal point of his depression and the psychosomatic ailments in his childhood, reproduced in his nausea on the morning following his dream. The death of his mother reawakened all his earlier experiences of losing her, as at the birth of his sister and at weaning, and made him experience the loss as one of his internal mother as well, now experienced as the marshy bog in his internal world. This bog also represented the analytic breast identified with the original breast of his mother, and he expressed anxiety that his analysis might be "bogged down." Thus, his mourning situation could be analyzed both in relation to its early genetic roots and in the transference.

THE MANIC DEFENSES

The intensity of pain and anxiety in the depressive position mobilizes new and powerful defenses, namely the system of manic defenses. The manic defenses involve a regression to splitting, denial, idealization, and projection, basically schizoid mechanisms, but organized into a system to protect the ego from the experience of depressive anxiety. The depressive anxiety arises out of the infant's recognition of the mother as a whole object on whom he depends and in relation to whom he experiences ambivalence and the subsequent guilt and fear of loss. Because of this, the whole relation has to be denied. Denial of the importance of his object and triumph over it, control, contempt, and devaluation take the place of depressive feelings.

A patient, following recognition of his oral attachment to the analyst, his greed for analysis, and his angry urinary attacks against her, had the following two dreams. In the first dream, he saw a house on fire and collapsing, but he drove past it, thinking it had little importance. In the second dream, he stole two buns from a bread shop, but he thought it did not matter very much, as they were such little buns. He defended himself against his depressive feelings about phantasies of stealing the analyst's breasts and destroying her body with his urine by denial and contempt. The anxiety and guilt about the fire is dealt with by denial—"it had little importance"—and the guilt about stealing by contempt, the analysis being represented by "such little buns." The fire associated among other things with the burning in his stomach (he had a gastric ulcer), and the collapsing house reminded him of his recurring anxieties about a depressive collapse, so that it could be clearly shown to him how those attacks were directed at the analyst and analysis in his internal world. He frequently dealt with his anxieties about his mental and physical health in the typically manic ways illustrated by this dream.

The manic defenses lead to a vicious circle. The depression results from the original attack on the object; the manic defenses keep the experience of depression from the ego, but they also preclude a working through of the depressive position and necessitate a further attack on the object by denial, triumph, and contempt, thereby increasing the underlying depression. It is well known that where manic phenomena are encountered one has to look for the underlying depression. It is less well known that where there is a presenting depressive illness one has to look for unconscious manic defense systems, impeding the working through of the depressive feelings. In the Kleinian view, the triumph over the internal object, which Freud describes as a feature of melancholic illness, is a part of manic defenses, perpetuating a situation of depression.

The working through of the depressive position in normal development depends on the capacity to make reparation. When the infant feels that in his hatred he has destroyed his good external and internal object, he experiences not only an intense feeling of guilt and loss but also pining and a longing to restore the lost loved object externally and internally, and to re-create the lost harmony and well-being. He mobilizes all his love and creativity to that end. It is this reparative drive that, in the Kleinian view, is the most important source of mental growth and creativity. The dream of a patient illustrates this. She dreamed that she was putting together a jigsaw puzzle representing a house in a landscape. The associations led to many past situations, particularly in her parental home. The putting together of the jigsaw puzzle was the analytical process, felt as a restoration and re-creation inside her of what she felt to be a very shattered internal world; but it also represented a book she was currently writing—her wish to write being stimulated by this need to produce a whole picture out of shattered fragments.

With the repeated experiences of loss and recovery of his object, a recovery that is felt by him to be also a re-creation, the infant acquires an increasing confidence in the strength of his good object and in his own love and creativity. It is in the depressive position also that reality sense gradually develops. The depressive anxiety about the object leads the infant to withdraw his projections and to allow his object a more independent and separate existence. In recognizing his own ambivalence and his phantasies, he becomes aware of his inner reality and begins to differentiate it from the external reality of his object. A successful working through of the depressive position is fundamental to mental health. In the process of working through, the ego becomes integrated, capable of reality testing and sublimation, and it is enriched from the introjection and assimilation of good objects. This, in turn, lessens the child's omnipotence and therefore his guilt and fear of loss.

It will be clear from the foregoing that technically we attach the greatest importance to the analysis of the manic and schizoid defenses; this enables the patient to experience depressive anxiety and to work it through by way of restoration of the internal objects and the self. The paranoid-schizoid and depressive positions are not only stages of development. They are two types of ego integration and organization, and the ego has a constant struggle to maintain a state of integration.

Throughout his lifetime an individual oscillates between a paranoid-schizoid and a depressive internal organization. These oscillations vary in force with each individual psychopathology. At one end of the spectrum there is the schizophrenic or autistic patient who may rarely reach a depressive integration. At the other end is the fully mature individual with a well-integrated inner world. This is a person who has largely overcome depressive anxiety, who has a trust in a well-established good internal object and his own creative potential, and who has the capacity to deal in realistic and creative ways, with such depressive anxiety as is unavoidably stirred. The analysis of the Oedipus complex in the Kleinian technique, as in the Freudian, remains a central task, but the technique is affected by the considerations stated above, and the paranoid-schizoid and depressive components in the oedipal situation are carefully taken up.

OEDIPUS COMPLEX

A patient presented the following dream. He dreamed that he was in a strange place where the washroom was out in the open, and he had to undress and wash naked. There were other naked people present. He suddenly noticed on a kind of platform a couple facing one another, each pointing at the other an identical lethal weapon. It was like a camera but more bottle-shaped, and it was covered by something like a camera hood made out of tinfoil. If the tinfoil were lifted, a lethal ray or radiation would be released. He was absolutely sick with anxiety, knowing beforehand what would happen. One of them, probably the woman, lifted the hood, and he hoped for a moment that the other one would not retaliate, since it was so senseless; but of course he retaliated immediately, and the dreamer felt a sense of hopelessness, doom, and despair at the senselessness of the destruction. He also felt some anxiety about himself because he thought that he might have been in the field of the rays and that they might have got into him. His associations started with the fear of nuclear warfare, but then turned to memories of his sexual curiosity in childhood. The camera with the lethal ray associated in his mind with his fear of his mother's eyes, who, he felt, could control and attack his father and himself by her looking. Sometimes he felt that her looks could kill. The association he found most upsetting was to the tinfoil. He knew precisely what it reminded him of. He had purchased two bottles of brandy as Christmas presents: one for his analyst (a woman) and one for his wife's analyst (a man). He was shocked at the thought that his gifts to this couple of analysts appeared in his dream as lethal weapons, with which they were supposed to annihilate one another. This dream is clearly concerned with the patient's oedipal feelings, his sexual curiosity about his parents, and his hostility, which changed their intercourse into a lethal combat.

In this dream, the patient's curiosity about the parents' sexual intercourse and his jealous feelings about it, both in the transference and in terms of his memories emerging from the repression were all analyzed. In addition, the following elements were taken up: (1) the projective elements in his voyeurism; (2) its effect on his perception of his parents in relation to himself (his fear of his mother's controlling eyes) and to one another (their intercourse becoming a mutual lethal attack); (3) the introjection of the situation, expressed in the dream by the patient's feeling that he is "in the field of the rays," that they "may have got into him," and the effect of this introjection on the patient's internal world, particularly his hypochondria-cal anxiety, always fairly active in this patient and referred to by him in connection with anxiety about himself in the dream; (4) the depressive element, which is evidenced by his tremendous feeling of pity and loss (though the hostility is projected into the parents and they become dan-gerous to one another and to him, they are felt in the dream to be victims as much as persecutors, and obviously love and concern for them are in large measure retained).[2]

I have stated before that Melanie Klein found in the analysis of very small children that the Oedipus complex has very early roots in the oral phase. When she later developed the concept of the depressive position, it became clear that the Oedipus complex begins at the same time. This indeed is implicit in the definition of the depressive position. If the infant becomes aware of his mother as a whole person, a whole separate person leading a life of her own, having other relationships of her own, he is immediately exposed to the experience of sexual jealousy. The fact that his world is still colored by his omnipotent projections increases his jealousy, for when he senses the emotional tie between his parents, he phantasies them as giving one another precisely those satisfactions he desires for himself. Thus he will experience his jealousy first of all in oral terms, but the triangular situation will have the configuration and the intensity of the Oedipus complex described by Freud.

The child's experience of the oedipal situation will be dictated by the stage of his own libidinal development and expresses itself, to begin with, in oral terms. Also, the earlier the stage of the Oedipus complex, the more it will be dominated by the infant's omnipotent projections. This is very important technically because, in analyzing the early roots of the oedipal conflict, one liberates it from the dominance of omnipotent mechanisms and phantasies. Tracing the Oedipus complex to its early roots enables one also to analyze the complex interplay between the early relationship to the breast and the Oedipus complex; for instance, how anxieties experienced in relation to the breast make the infant turn to the penis or, conversely, how the oedipal jealousy may affect the feeding relationship to the breast.

Here is an example of how oedipal jealousy interferes with the introjec-

---

2. The appearance of the phallic woman (she has the same weapon as the man) is related to the patient's projection into her of his own dangerous penis—the brandy bottle.

tion of a good breast. The patient had been for months, off and on, preoccupied with a situation in his office. There was a young couple, Mr. and Mrs. L, of whom he was constantly complaining. They were interfering with his work and his relationships and were in a collusive relationship with their boss, Mr. R, who was thoroughly hated by the patient. In the session preceding the one I am going to describe in more detail, he told me that he had heard that Mrs. L was on the point of a breakdown and might be leaving the office. He felt suddenly terribly sorry for the L's. He realized that for months he had been complaining what a nuisance they were to him and had never given a thought to their predicament and the pressure they were under from Mr. R, whose paranoia, intrigues, and incessant demands were preying upon them and poisoning them. He was near tears speaking about them. He said that Mr. R was behaving mentally just the way he was physically. The patient had often referred in the past to Mr. R's tendency to diarrhea—"just shitting all over the place." Often in the analysis, Mr. R played the role of the bad sexual father, who dirtied the mother, but also that of the patient's split-off "dirtying" self as projected into the father. The next day the patient started the session by complaining of headache and diarrhea. He then said that he had had three short dreams. In the first dream he had spent twenty-four hours speaking to Mrs. M (the wife of a psychoanalyst). In the second, he saw some beautiful mountains, round and white, like a woman's breast, with a most beautiful lake, but he knew that the lake was full of some infection or poison, so that he could neither drink nor bathe in it, and he had to go away. In the third dream, he was in a holiday resort. The mistress of the hotel was a kind of courtesan and he wanted to kiss her, but had some anxiety about her as a dirty prostitute. The first associations were to Mrs. M. A few days previously he had seen Dr. M giving me a ride in a Rolls-Royce and felt very jealous. The mountain landscape made him think of the forthcoming analytic holiday. The poison in the water associated in his mind with a typhoid epidemic in Switzerland, which in turn reminded him of his own diarrhea. He had also the previous day read in a newspaper about an infection in tinned food, so that a couple of tins could poison a whole family. He was particularly impressed by the thought of secret poison or infection because the lake looked so beautiful and unspoiled.

The interpretation dealt in essence with the situation in which the patient's oedipal jealousy, stirred by the holiday and by the sight of the rich Dr. M driving his analyst off in a car, interrupted the idealized feeding situation represented in the first dream, and led to a secret anal attack by diarrhea against the analyst as the feeding mother. Thus the lake connected with the beautiful white mountains (the breast) became poisonous to him, like a couple of tins of poisoned food. The interpretation also emphasized how secret these attacks were, since on the face of it his relation to the analyst was so good. This interpretation mobilized an admission of many hostile thoughts about the analysis, and the analyst personally, and suspicions that the analytic treatment would make him worse. His thoughts then returned to the couple at the office. He showed tremendous concern and anxiety about them, particularly Mrs. L, repeating "This poor woman, will she ever recover?" He knew that his concern was for the analyst and the analysis—would it ever recover from his secret dirtying? As he went on speaking of the couple, it sounded more and more as if he were speaking about himself, because the expressions he applied to them were increasingly reminiscent of things he said about himself when he was depressed—"How will they ever get out of this mess? They will never recover from it, they won't be able to cope"—and one got an increasingly clear picture of his introjection of, and his identification with, a parental couple irrecoverably ruined and destroyed by the Mr. R part of himself. In this patient's experience, one could also see a move from a paranoid to a more depressive experience of his Oedipus complex. He started by being completely persecuted by the L's as a parental couple. In his dreams and the associations to it there was also a paranoid suspicion of the feeding breast, represented by the infected lake, and, in the transference, his suspicions of the analyst. Toward the end of the session, his feeling in relation to mother—"this poor woman"—and the parental couple was full of guilt and concern. He was particularly concerned with this destroyed couple in his internal world and with his identification with them.

WORKING THROUGH

These oscillations between the paranoid-schizoid and the depressive feelings underlie, in my opinion, the process of working through. In the analytic situation, the patient relives his relation to his original objects. His attachment to them has to be lived through again and given up again. In Freud's view, no object can be given up without being introjected into the ego. In the Kleinian view, this introjection is part of the depressive process. No object can be given up successfully without a complete process of mourning, as in the depressive position, ending in the introjection of a good internal object, strengthening the ego. Any new insight of any importance necessitates this process. The pain of the mourning situation mobilizes new manic and schizoid defenses, but with each repeated experience the ego is strengthened, the good object is more securely established, and the need to have recourse to new defenses is lessened. The process of working through is completed when some aspect of the object has been given up in this way.

It is impossible to speak of the Kleinian technique of today without mentioning the special attention paid to the factor of envy. Since the publication of *Envy and Gratitude* (Klein 1957), the analysis of envy has played an increasingly important role. The analysis of early oral anxieties led Melanie Klein to believe that envy has very early roots and plays a large part in the infant's relation to the breast. She distinguished between it and greed and jealousy and considered it more primitive than jealousy. Jealousy is based on love and aims at the possession of the loved object and the removal of the rival. It pertains to a triangular relationship and therefore to a time of life when objects are clearly recognized and differentiated from one another. Envy, on the other hand, is a two-part relation in which the subject envies the object for some possession or quality; no other live object need enter into it. Jealousy is necessarily a whole-object relationship, while envy is essentially experienced in terms of part-objects, though it persists into whole-object relationships.

> Greed aims at the possession of all the goodness that can be extracted from the object, regardless of consequences; this may result in the destruction of the object and the spoiling of its goodness, but the destruction is incidental to the ruthless acquirement. Envy aims at being as good as the object, but, when this is felt as impossible, it aims at spoiling the goodness of the object, to remove the source of envious feelings. It is this spoiling aspect of envy that is so destructive to development, since the very source of goodness that the infant depends on is turned bad, and good introjections, therefore, cannot be achieved. Envy, though arising from primitive love and admiration, has a less strong libidinal component than greed and is suffused with the death instinct. As it attacks the source of life, it may be considered to be the earliest direct externalization of the death instinct. Envy stirs as soon as the infant becomes aware of the breast as a source of life and good experience; the real gratification which he experiences at the breast, reinforced by idealization, so powerful in early infancy, makes him feel that the breast is the source of food and warmth, love, understanding and wisdom. The blissful experience of satisfaction which this wonderful object can give will increase his love and his desire to possess, preserve and protect it, but the same experience stirs in him also the wish to be himself the source of such perfection. He experiences painful feelings of envy which carry with them the desire to spoil the qualities of the object which can give him such painful feelings. [Segal 1964]

The importance of envy lies in the fact that it interferes with the normal operation of the schizoid mechanisms. Splitting into an ideal and a bad object cannot be established since it is the ideal object that is the object of envy, and therefore hostility. Thus, the introjection of an ideal object, which could become the core of the ego, is disturbed at its very roots. Defenses against envy may be equally detrimental to growth. The devaluation of the object and the projection of envy into it give rise to persecutory anxiety and lead to the formation of an envious superego, which interferes with the development of the ego. The analysis of patients suffering from an excessively severe superego often reveals that it is the envious aspect of the superego that is felt as most damaging, since it is directed not only against the aggressive wishes of the ego, but also, and often predominantly, against any positive or creative strivings of the ego. In the analytic situation, envy manifests itself often by negative therapeutic reactions. As soon as the analysis is felt as good, and the analyst is felt as the source of the good analysis, it has to be attacked and destroyed. Envy brings in its wake feelings of hopelessness. Bad experiences are bad, but good experiences also become bad, since they stir envy; therefore there seems to be no hope for a good experience. Since a good object cannot be introjected, the ego does not feel that it can grow and eventually bridge the gap between the self and the original object by introjection and assimilation. This in turn increases envy, leading again to hopelessness. The analysis of envy, which has been split off, denied, and projected, is extremely painful and disturbing, but it reintroduces hope through the establishment of a good and enviable object. Latent appreciation can be mobilized and the battle can be fought again between love and gratitude and envy.

It is difficult to give a brief example here, since envy is usually heavily defended against and has to be tracked in painful detail, but I would like to describe the dream of one patient, showing some emergence of hope, when, for the first time, he could admit some envy in relation to the analyst. This patient, a borderline case, came to the first session carrying two bags of food, a thermos bottle of coffee and one of tea, and throughout the session fed himself a number of drugs, such as dexedrine. He made it clear from the start who had possession and control of the feeding breast. In the early stages of his analysis, he developed the following pattern. He would frequently miss a session or come very late, but after the session he would spend hours in the lavatory, doing his "post analysis," that is, writing notes on his session, categorizing them, drawing conclusions, and so forth. He often said that this "post analysis" was of far more value to him than the analysis. Since the patient had a large number of anal perversions it was not difficult to show him, with the help of his dreams, that in his phantasy, he was feeding himself on his own feces which he considered far superior to the mother's food. His feeling of superiority was so absolute that an interpretation of envy would have been quite laughable to him, though the enormity of his envy of both men and women, particularly women, was blatantly obvious. One could, however, get at it by interpreting his projective identification. There was no doubt in his mind about the analyst's inferiortiy and her feelings of dependence on him, rejection by him, envy of his riches, and so forth. The analyst, in his mind, had the same characteristics as his extremely envious superego, by which he was controlled to such a degree that he was not allowed, for instance, to read a book or listen to the radio, because it wasted time. He felt equally controlled and nagged by his analyst. Accompanying this was a state of despair of such absoluteness that it had become painless. When he finally began to be aware of his own envy in relation to the analyst, primarily as a feeding breast, he had the following dream. He dreamed that under an enormous pile of dead leaves he found a single snowdrop, white as a drop of milk. His waking association was that at last, under a pile of feces, he had found a single drop of milk as a sign of hope.

The discovery of early envy and the way in which it operates has given great impetus to new work, particularly with psychotics (Bion 1959) and other intractable cases, for instance, severe acting out and drug addiction (Rosenfeld 1965). It is, however, impossible in this chapter to discuss it at length.

TERMINATION OF ANALYSIS

Has the Kleinian outlook on analysis altered the criteria for the termination of an analysis and the therapeutic aim? In certain basic ways the criteria remain the same—the lifting of repression, insight, freeing the patient from early fixations and inhibitions, and enabling him to form full and satisfactory personal relationships.

The Kleinian analyst will be guided in his evaluation of the therapeutic progress mainly by his assessment of the patient's internal world; he will try to evaluate the state of integration in the patient's ego and his internal objects, and his capacity to maintain the state of integration in situations of stress.

Melanie Klein (1950) wrote:

My criterion for the termination of an analysis is, therefore, as follows: have persecutory and depressive anxieties been sufficiently reduced in the course of the analysis, and has the patient's relation to the external world been sufficiently strengthened to enable him to deal satisfactorily with the situation of mourning arising at this point? By analysing as fully as possible both the negative and the positive transference, persecutory and depressive anxieties are diminished and the patient becomes increasingly able to synthesise the contrasting aspects of the primary objects, and the feelings towards them, thus establishing a more realistic and secure attitude to the internal and the external world. If these processes have been sufficiently experienced in the transference situation both the idealisation of the analyst and the feelings of being persecuted by him are diminshed; the patient can then cope more successfully with the feelings of loss caused by the termination of the analysis and with that part of the work of mourning which he has to carry out by himself after the end of the analysis.

References

Abraham, K. (1912). Notes on the psycho-analytical investigation and treatment of manic-depressive insanity and allied conditions. In K. Abraham, *Selected Papers on Psycho-Analysis*. London: Hogarth, 1927.

Bion, W. R. (1956). Development of schizophrenic thought. *International Journal of Psycho-Analysis* 37:344-346. In W. R. Bion, *Second Thoughts*. New York: Jason Aronson, 1977.

——— (1957). Differentiation of the psychotic from the non-psychotic personalities. *International Journal of Psycho-Analysis* 38:266-275. In W. R. Bion, *Second Thoughts*. New York: Jason Aronson, 1977.

——— (1958). On hallucination. *International Journal of Psycho-Analysis* 39:341-349.

——— (1959). Attacks on linking. *International Journal of Psycho-Analysis* 40:308-315. In W. R. Bion, *Second Thoughts*. New York: Jason Aronson, 1977.

Freud, S. (1917). Mourning and melancholia. *Standard Edition* 19:233-239.

Isaacs, S. (1948). The nature and function of phantasy. *International Journal of Psycho-Analysis* 29:73-97.

Klein, M. (1932). *The Psycho-Analysis of Children*. London: Hogarth.

——— (1950). On the criteria for the termination of an analysis. *International Journal of Psycho-Analysis* 31:78-80, 204.

——— (1957). *Envy and Gratitude*. New York: Basic Books.

Rosenfeld, H. (1965). *Psychotic States: A Psychoanalytical Approach*. London: Hogarth.

Segal, H. (1964). *Introduction to the Work of Melanie Klein*. New York: Basic Books.

2

Melanie Klein's Technique
of Child Analysis

THE CONTROVERSY which arose between Anna Freud and Melanie Klein in the early days of child analysis is probably well known, and by now many issues have become less controversial. Therefore, there would be no point in restating the arguments here. Nevertheless, in order to present the Kleinian technique of child analysis one has to go back to the papers she wrote at that time and to the introduction to *The Psycho-Analysis of Children* (1932). In those papers she describes most clearly the basic principles of her technique, and those principles remain unaltered in their essentials in our procedure today. I want to take up three basic points that Melanie Klein makes in those papers: transference, the analytic situation, and the play technique.

TRANSFERENCE

According to her observations, children, like adults, develop a real transference on the analyst. It had been argued that children could not develop a proper transference because they were still, in reality, attached to and dependent on their real parents. Nevertheless, the transference occurred, and it could be seen that it developed on the basis of the child's projection onto the analyst of internal parental figures. Since the child's object relation already had a long history in which parental figures were both internalized and distorted, it is those figures, pertaining to the internal world and to the past, which form the basis of the transference. Just as in adult analysis, it is not the current parental figures but the internal ones which are projected onto the analyst. Furthermore, since splitting is an important mechanism, particularly in small children, the child would readily transfer onto the analyst split-off aspects of his parents.

THE ANALYTIC SITUATION

Melanie Klein aimed at establishing with children an analytic situation as strictly as it could be done. Unlike other workers in the field at the time, she found that such an analytic situation could be established and maintained with children, however small, if one relied on the interpretative work and kept an analytic attitude uncontaminated by moral, educative, or reassuring attitudes. These two aspects of the situation were, according to her, interdependent: one could not observe the transference if one did not establish a proper analytic situation, and a proper analytic situation could not be established if one did not analyze the transference. Reassurance is derived by the child in the course of the analysis, but it results from the analytic situation itself: the child derives a basic and more lasting reassurance from the analyst's uncritical understanding, from his reliability and his capacity to relieve anxiety, than he would from any reassuring attitudes or maneuvers. As with adults, reassurance coming from the analytic process itself proceeds in depth, through real changes in the child's inner world and in the nature of his internal objects. The educative process as well is affected by the analysis, by relieving the vicious circle between anxiety and aggression and by increasing the child's tendency toward introjection and identification with the analyst and the parental objects in their good aspects; the analytical work lessens destructive processes in the mind which interfere with education and learning.

THE PLAY TECHNIQUE

The specific technique that Melanie Klein introduced for the analysis of children is the play technique. She understood the child's play as a symbolic expression of his conflicts and anxieties and used it as an analytical tool. Since small, or even older, children cannot be asked to free associate, and since their more natural mode of expression is play, Melanie Klein treated the child's play, as well as his verbal communications, as free associations, and used the symbolic content of both for purposes of interpretation.

The play technique setting. Since the time she introduced the play technique, the use of toys for child analysis, psychotherapy, treatment in child guidance clinics, etc., has become commonplace. The setting and the toys used, however, vary enormously. It may therefore be worthwhile to describe the kind of room and equipment recommended by Melanie Klein, as this is an essential part of the technique. It is important that every child have his own individual drawer, if there is a chest of drawers in the room, or his own individual box. The toys he uses become very much his own. (This is often not followed in child guidance practice, where the toys are often shared.) In the individual drawer or box the child gets the following kinds of toys: small bricks, fences, a few small cars or trains, one or two balls, a few animals of various sizes, a few human figures, preferably in two sizes, to be used easily as adult and child figures, and small containers. All these toys are small, to make them easy for the child to handle, and as far as possible non-descript so that they do not suggest games. Nonrepresentational materials are also provided, such as paper, pencils, possibly glue and clay; if the child is not too small, scissors, and string. The aim of this material is to provide the child with toys which leave maximum scope for his imagination. Apart from the individual toys, it is better if running water is available and some equipment common to all the children, such as rags for cleaning up and soap.

The room should not contain anything easily breakable; electric fires, lights, and the like should be well out of the child's reach. Life is also made easier if the walls are washable and if there is a good floor covering. The room should be so organized that the child is free to express aggression without danger to himself or actual damage to the surroundings. There should be a table and at least a couple of chairs. A couch is desirable. This can be used for play or the children may gradually start lying down when they feel like free associating. The analyst himself is an important part of the setting. As I have suggested, the analyst should maintain the proper analytic role in his therapeutic relation to the child; nevertheless, as long as the child is in the consulting room, the analyst, unlike his position vis-a-vis the adult patient, is also an adult in charge of the child, that is, he must take the ordinary adult responsibility in relation to the child's safety. He must be able to stop an action of the child that is dangerous to the child himself as well as put a brake on any physical aggression against the analyst. He may also have to restrain the child from destructive behavior in the room which would lead to lasting damage and prevent the room's being used by other patients.

Children are very quick to grasp the difference between the toys in their

individual drawer, which are for their use only, and the room itself and such
equipment as belongs to the room, an attack on which is an interference
with the analytic setting and the analyst's other child patients. While they
are free to do what they please with their own equipment, and what they do
with it is an object of interpretation, what they do to the room has quite a
different character and sometimes has to be restrained as well as interpreted.

This setting naturally has to be altered somewhat according to the age
and the degree of illness in the child. With psychotic children or ag-
gressively psychopathic latency or puberty children, one may, for instance,
have to remove sharp or hard toys when they are used primarily as weapons.

The interpretative technique. Basically, with the use of the play material
and the child's other communications, the analyst aims from the start at
establishing contact with the child's unconscious. There is no attempt at
"taming" the child or "getting him used to the situation," or at appealing
to his good behavior. There is no particular catering to his wishes or
interests, such as providing him with the kind of toys he might be interested
in. From the first contact, the analyst tries to understand the child's
communication and relies on the fact that his interpretation relieves unconscious anxiety to maintain the child's interest and cooperation.

I can give as an example a first session with a child of two and three-
quarters. When I came to collect her from the waiting room she was
clinging to her mother, obviously anxious, and refused to follow me into
the playroom, the door of which was open so that she could see it from the
waiting room. I started interpreting to her in a very general way, suggesting
that she was afraid of me because she did not know me; knowing that she
suffered from nightmares, I went on to say, after a little while, that she was
afraid of this unknown room and unknown person rather in the same way
as she might be afraid of the dark and the unknown things happening in the
dark. When I said that, she looked at me with evident interest. After a little
while she started throwing covert, curious glances at the playroom. I then
said that she was also very curious about the unknown things in the room
and that maybe during the night she was not only frightened but also
curious about what was going on in the dark. At that point she let go of her
mother and shyly advanced into the playroom. The mother stayed just
outside the door so that the child could still see her. She inspected the room
and looked into the drawer with the toys, while I explained to her briefly
and simply that, as her mother had probably told her before, she would now
come to play with me every day except on the weekend; and I indicated that

the toys in the drawer were for her to use. She inspected her toys quite contentedly until she discovered a little toy lion among the animals; she immediately showed signs of anxiety and stopped playing. I interpreted to her that she seemed to be afraid of the little lion, as at the beginning she was afraid of me and the room; and maybe she was afraid that I was like a lion and would eat her up. Soon after, she ran out to her mother, showing some signs of anxiety, but mostly becoming very possessive and demanding in relation to her mother (this being one of the things the parents had complained of in her behavior). She insisted on opening her mother's bag, demanded sweets, etc. and her mother was obviously annoyed and irritated.

I interpreted to her that she felt she was now, like the greedy lion, making demands on her mother, and that this made her afraid of her mother being angry and of me being like an angry mother who would be punishing her, which I thought explained why she was afraid I would be like a lion. She came back to the playroom and started sorting out the animals into families. When the end of the hour came she was reluctant to leave.

Between the first and the second session the mother called me to tell me that several times during the day the child asked to be brought back to the playroom. When the time for her session came, however, she clung to her mother, with her back firmly turned toward me. I interpreted to her the resentment at not being allowed to come when she wanted to come and her punishing me now by not wanting to play with me and turning her back on me. After a time she laughed and followed me into the room. She took out a cow, which she said was a "nice milky cow," and a little pig, which she called "nasty piggy." I interpreted to her that after I kept her waiting she was not sure if I was going to be like the nice milky cow or like a nasty piggy, because she had been so angry with me. She looked at me for a long time, then said: "You talk very funny, but go on talking." And a little later, while still playing with the animals, when I was silent, she turned to me and repeated, "Go on talking . . . tell me." I think from that moment the analytic relation was established. She perceived my "funny talk" as a kind of communication different from what she was used to—an analytic language that we were beginning to develop, she and I, and she obviously appreciated it as such.

I think those sessions can also be used to illustrate what I meant by saying that children transfer onto the analyst split-off aspects of parents, internal figures from the past, already a part of the child's internal world. The little girl had a clinging, loving relationship to her actual external mother: she saw in me the lion-mother; that lion-mother was split off from the external idealized mother (probably seen as the nice milky cow). It was also a figure introjected at an earlier stage of the child's development, when the relation to mother, or to the breast as a part-object, was predominantly oral. One could also begin to see how this lion-mother contained the projection of the child's own biting impulses.

There are of course as many beginnings as there are children. Sometimes the first contact will be made with hope and expectation rather than anxiety. For instance, a latency boy (not a case of mine) in his first session drew toys which he liked, and the analyst was able to interpret the child's hopes and expectations of the wonderful things his treatment would give him—in his case it was primarily potency. Only later in the session did anxiety supervene, linked with the thought of the rivalry and jealousy of the other children at the wonderful gifts he would be getting in his session.

Those are the easy beginnings. With more withdrawn children, or with latency children well armed with their latency defenses, one may for a long time have to interpret rigid and defensive attitudes, while always looking for clues to the underlying unconscious anxiety.

With adolescents one has to be particularly careful to be able to establish contact with their infantile anxieties, without offending the susceptibilities of their young-man or young-woman image of themselves, so touchy in adolescence.

Here is an example of a session which I thought was handled well by a candidate in training. The patient was a foreign boy of fifteen who had had some psychotherapy in his own country. He was brought to his first session by his mother. She started explaining to the analyst that as the boy had a partial organic deafness he might not hear the buzzer opening the door. (This was in spite of the fact that in the original consultation with the analyst his deafness had, of course, been discussed.) She went on to say that he had a cold and would the analyst phone for a taxi to collect him at the end of the session. Then, as if afraid that she was making her son appear less clever than he was, she added that on other days it would not be necessary, as he was most expert in finding his way about. The analyst made a noncommittal answer, saying that all this no doubt would be discussed with the boy in his sessions.

When they went into the room the boy said, rather defensively, that in fact he heard the buzzer very well, but did not push the door because he was interested in watching some cars in the street. He then started inspecting the analyst's room, comparing it with the room of his psychotherapist in his own country, and saying with some relief that he could not see any toys like the ones he had had during his childhood psychotherapy.

At that point, the analyst interpreted that he was wondering how she would compare with his previous psychotherapist, and particularly whether she would try to make him feel small and childish, the way he felt maybe his mother made him feel small when she was so protective of him at the beginning of the session. The boy relaxed visibly, sat down, and said that he thought maybe it would be best if he told her about his interests. He went on talking for a time about his interest in football, how good he was at table tennis, etc. He was interested in which team his analyst would support in a forthcoming football match between his country and Great Britain. Throughout this, the analyst made only a few comments, including one about his anxiety—"Whose side would she be on?" Then the boy gradually started talking about his country, its warmth and beauty compared with England, his family left behind, and his friends. The analyst was able to interpret to him his longing for his own home and country and his anxieties about separation, relating it also to separations in the past. (Since the boy's father was a diplomat, he had been subjected to a great many changes of country and environment.)

He moved on to talk about his sister, who was left behind, being pregnant, and how much he looked forward to having a nephew. When the analyst asked him why he was so sure it would be a nephew, not a niece, he said he was sure of it, and only a nephew would do, as he could teach him things like football. As he went on talking about his nephew, it became clear that he was shifting between seeing himself as the father of the child and identifying with him: "only a nephew would do" because the new baby was to be himself. After a time he started drawing a star, saying he wanted to make a beautiful star—a five-pointed star (he was to have five sessions a week), but he was afraid that from her side it looked messy and absolutely terrible. As this followed on the material about the very idealized baby nephew, the analyst interpreted that he wanted to be her star baby, like the little baby still inside mother—his nephew—and how afraid he was that she could see him quite differently, as quite terrible and messy. He then started looking around the room and asking her if she had many other children patients, and were they older or younger. She interpreted to him his curiosity about her other babies and his jealousy of them. He then resumed his talk about football. The candidate interpreted to him how that part of him that wanted to be the baby star inside her was felt by him as a great threat to the part of him that wanted to be the big boy, playing football and very masculine.

I thought this was a well-handled session; the analyst was able to see the conflict in the adolescent between his masculine genital position and his infantile self longing to be "star baby," and the anxieties ("it will look terrible to you") belonging to this infantile position.

The problem of communication with children of various ages presents, of course, difficulties slightly different from problems in the psychoanalysis of adults. The small child communicates primarily by movement and play. The latency child can alternate between communication through speech, and sometimes true free association, and communication through play and behavior. The adolescent is capable of free association, but more prone than the average adult to express himself by behavior, acting in and acting out. It is the task of the analyst to accept all these modes of communication, and, whenever possible, to communicate back to the child by his interpretations.

Unlike the analyst of adults, however, the analyst of the child, particularly of a small child, must up to a point also cooperate in the child's play. He must occasionally perform services which the child cannot do himself, such as sharpening a broken pencil or tying a knot, and must, up to a point, participate in the child's game when the game requires two players. This is particularly important when the child wants to express something by personification, and expects the analyst to take on a role. To what extent the analyst should participate in the child's play is an extremely knotty technical problem and one requiring a lot of experience to gauge accurately. The main principle should be that the analyst should participate as little as possible in action and cooperate only to the extent to which his cooperation is necessary for the child to express himself or herself fully. From the viewpoint of the analyst, the child's play is a communication that has to be understood and interpreted, and all his actions should be directed only at furthering this communication. To give a typical example, a little girl of six wants to play at being a teacher and wants the analyst to be the child. As the child, the analyst is to be stupid and ignorant, and the little patient playing the teacher is relentlessly mocking and attacking, humiliating her and punishing her. The analyst accepts this role, though being very careful not to introduce anything of her own into the play, and acting only on the child's instructions. Once a game is in progress, the analyst starts interpreting how the little girl got rid of the unbearable feeling of being an ignorant and stupid child into the analyst, and how she identified with adults experienced as cruel and mocking. (It is interesting to note that that particular girl went to a liberal and progressive school and that she was never punished at home. The cruel punishments seemed to be of her own invention.) As is frequent in this kind of situation, the child resisted the interpretation, screaming and shouting the analyst down. It could be interpreted to her how she needed to put herself in the role of the teacher because she felt it so unbearable to be little and not to know, but also how in doing that she stopped herself from learning (this being one of her important symptoms). After a time, the child changed the game, making the analyst be the teacher, while she as a child secretly mocked her and attacked her, the second game coming closer to her real feelings of inferiority and anger. In this game the analyst's interpretations did effectively deal with the child's projective identification and the game changed, with the child giving up the reversal.

Often, however, particularly with latency children, the child will insist on going on with the game because of the gratification derived from the position of control and from sadistic attacks. The game becomes not a communication but a repetitive "acting in." In such situations the analyst may have to stop acting the role that the child demands and confine himself to interpretations—often directed at the child's rage and distress when he finds out that he cannot control his object. Repetition compulsion is what the patient aims at: this may express itself in the repetitive play. The analyst's task is to modify the repetition compulsion by understanding. In this respect the situation is similar to analysis with adults, but since the analyst of adults uses only verbal interpretation, he is less likely to be a partner in the repetition compulsion. Here, the task of the child's analyst is technically more difficult because he must participate in the child's game to understand what the child's pattern is but by doing so risks becoming a partner and colluding in the repetition compulsion. We always have to watch the patient's response, not only to our interpretations but also to our behavior. A cough, a squeaking of the chair—all actions are experienced by the patient as communications. The analyst of the child has to be active to a far greater extent and must therefore watch the child's response very carefully. The apparently most innocent actions become imbued with meaning. For instance, a small child breaks a pencil in drawing and asks the analyst to sharpen it. Soon it happens again. And again. A look of sly triumph begins to appear on the child's face. What has started as a reality-situation, that is, the pencil must be sharpened if the child is to draw, becomes a situation of gratification in terms of getting control over the analyst, getting an endless supply of goods, castration of the analyst, etc. Any situation in which the analyst participates can be easily used for purposes of repetition compulsion and/or direct gratification of instincts.

Often the question is raised: how well can little children really follow and understand verbal interpretations, particularly complex ones? It has invariably been my experience, both in analyses and in supervisions, that, provided the interpretations are put in simple language, and provided they are correct and close to the child's experience, the child can follow the interpretations, on the whole more easily than a sophisticated adult, who tends to mobilize intellectual defenses much more readily.

As an illustration, I remember particularly well a session with the little girl whose first session I reported above. She was just under four. I was then having supervision on this child with Melanie Klein and, being in a hurry to present some rather difficult sessions at the end of the week, I wanted to summarize for her very briefly the sessions at the beginning of the week. I said that on Monday it seemed the little girl was preoccupied with a phantasy of my pregnancy over the weekend, and then, taking a deep breath, I said "And I interpreted to her that an introjection done under a preponderance of envious greed leads to the fragmentation of the internal object, fragmentation of self, internal persecution, confusion, a loss of identity, particularly sexual identity." I saw then that Melanie Klein looked at me with a really shocked expression, and she said, very quietly, "I think I would rather like to see this session: I do not quite see how you interpreted all that to a child under four." I then told her the session in detail and she agreed with the line of interpretation.

The little girl had come into the room. She looked at my abdomen and said, "You've got fatter over the weekend." She then showed me a little purse, of which she was obviously very proud. She then went to a drawer and pulled out a brown paper bag, which the previous week she had filled up with her toys. She looked at the bag and said, with real fury, "Your purses are always bigger than my purses." I interpreted then that she thought my tummy was always bigger than her tummy and she thought mine was full of babies, like the paper bag, and that was why it was so fat. She then filled the basin with water, tore the paper bag into shreds, and put the torn bag and all the animals into the basin. She also put her own purse there, saying, "Anyway, they're not *your* toys—they're *my* toys." She started swirling the water around angrily and putting in bits of soap, making the water cloudy. As in the past, putting things into this water basin often represented introjection, and, since she accompanied it by saying "They're my toys," I interpreted to her that she wanted to take my tummy and my babies inside her tummy to make it into her babies—but she was so angry that it was mine to begin with, that in taking it in she tore it all into pieces. Then she looked at me less angrily and said that on Sunday she had had a nasty tummyache. I related the nasty tummyache to her having phantasied that she had torn off bits of my tummy and babies inside her, and the bits were angry and making her hurt. Then she looked at the basin and said, "Oh, what a muddle" (feeling muddled is something she occasionally insightfully complained of). I interpreted to her that she put the bits of soap in to make the water cloudy because she did not want to know which bits inside her were hers and which she thought she had stolen from me; that she then felt muddled inside about what was her and what was me; and that she felt this muddle both as a tummyache in her tummy and as a muddle in her thoughts. She did not know which thoughts were hers and which came from me. She then started looking for her purse in the water and became very anxious and angry when she could not readily find it "in the muddle." I then interpreted that when she so much wanted to have my insides inside her and all muddled up with her, and was also so angrily tearing them into bits, then she became very frightened that she could not properly feel her own body. She went on feeling in the basin with one hand and with the other searching between her legs for her genital. I said that this feeling of not being able to find her own things made her feel sometimes that she could not find her own "baby-hole" because in her mind she felt it was so muddled up with mine. After this interpretation she readily found the purse, took it out of the water, and showed great relief.

At no time in the session did I have the feeling that my interpretations were too complicated for her or that she could not follow them. And though she verbalized little in this session, in the next she spoke quite freely of her anxieties that either I or her mother would go on producing new babies, and of her envy and wish to be a "mummy full of babies" herself.

One can well see, however, that in summarizing one's interpretation one may sound as though one were talking a language which would be complete gibberish to the child.

The problem of language can sometimes present difficulties with adolescents who are using an "in" language. The problem arises, how far should the analyst use the patient's language and how far should he respond in his own "common usage" language. One has to steer between the Scylla of using the adolescent's language with an unconscious implication of "I-am-one-of-you" and a collusion against the adult world, and the Charybdis of rejecting the adolescent's mode of communication and being experienced as a rigid and un-understanding superego figure. I have always used the patient's own language—"groovy" or "high" or whatever the current "in" word is—when referring to what the patient has said himself. When interpreting, however, I use the current ordinary English. The patient's language itself should also become an object of analysis. Often those slang words, consciously meant to describe vague and un-defined feelings, such as "groovy," when analyzed yield rich unconscious phantasy content. If one can analyze the patient's language itself, one can make him experience that one does indeed understand his language and does not reject it, but that one is not oneself involved and identified with the patient's unconscious processes as expressed by his language.

A particular problem present in child analysis is the relation to the parents. When we analyze the adult, as changes occur in his internal world the patient himself can materially affect his external circumstances. Not so with the child: the child's external environment is largely determined by his parents. Sometimes, as the child's treatment progresses, vicious circles in the interaction between child and parent are resolved, and the parents may respond to the child's improvement by a better relationship to him. Often, however, the environment whose pressure contributed to the child's illness continues exercising some pressure and, as is well known, sometimes the parents even react adversely to the child's improvement if the child's illness was necessary to the family. We can enable the child to deal better with his environment by strengthening his good internal figures and his ego, but we cannot alter the environment itself. It is always a great temptation for the analyst to try to influence or educate the parents. It has, however, been an almost invariable experience that this does not lead to favorable results and is liable to interfere with the psychoanalytic relation between the patient and the analyst. If the parents seek help and advice, it is always best to find suitable help for them from a person other than the child's analyst.

Whether, and how often, one has contact with parents, I have found, varies with the individuality of the analyst and the needs of the parents. I do not think that in all my experience of analysis and supervision there have been two situations in which I would deal with the parents in the same way.

Often the question is raised, What is the aim of child analysis, and in what way does it differ from the analysis of an adult? Nowadays, when psychoanalytic findings have become the basis of many psychotherapeutic techniques, one has to be particularly clear about the nature of the psychoanalytic process and the aim of psychoanalysis in the treatment of a child. I think that essentially the aim of psychoanalysis is the same whatever the age of the patient: it is always to get the patient in touch with his psychic realities. The analysis of defenses and of object relations, in phantasy and reality, should help him to differentiate between external and internal realities, and to foster the process of psychic growth.

References

Klein, M. (1926). Infant analysis. *International Journal of Psycho-Analysis* 7:31-63. In M. Klein, *Contributions to Psycho-Analysis 1921-1945*, pp. 87-116. London: Hogarth, 1948.

——— (1929). Personification in the play of children. *International Journal of Psycho-Analysis* 10:193-204. In M. Klein, *Contributions to Psycho-Analysis 1921-1945*, pp. 215-226. London: Hogarth, 1948.

——— (1930). The importance of symbol-formation in the development of the ego. *International Journal of Psycho-Analysis* 11:24-39. In M. Klein, *Contributions to Psycho-Analysis 1921-1945*, pp. 236-250. London: Hogarth, 1948.

——— (1932). *The Psycho-Analysis of Children*. London: Hogarth.

——— (1961). *Narrative of a Child Analysis: The Conduct of Psycho-Analysis of Children as Seen in the Treatment of a Ten-Year-Old Boy*. London: Hogarth.

Meltzer, D. (1967). *The Psychoanalytic Process*. London: Heinemann Medical Books.

PART II

MENTAL PROCESSES

3

Phantasy and Other Mental Processes

MY PRESENTATION WILL, of necessity, be rather abstract and schematic, as I wish, in the space allowed, to cover some well-known material and some that I hope is new. I shall be concerned with the relation between the function of phantasy and other mental phenomena, namely instincts, mental mechanism, structure and higher mental processes like thinking. In her paper "The Nature and Function of Phantasy," Isaacs (1948) elaborated the relation between unconscious phantasy and instincts and mental mechanisms. She stated the phantasy may be considered the psychic representative or the mental correlate, the mental expression of instinct. Strachey (1957), in his editorial notes to Freud's paper "Instincts and their Vicissitudes," drew attention to the fact that Freud wavered between two definitions of instincts. In some papers he described the instinct as "a concept on the frontier between the mental and the somatic. . . . the psychical representative of the stimuli originating within the organism and reaching the mind," in another paper "the concept on the frontier between the somatic and the mental. . . . the psychical representative of organic forces." Strachey said, "These accounts seem to make it plain that Freud was drawing no distinction between the instinct and its 'psychical representative.' He was apparently regarding the instinct itself as the psychical representative of somatic forces. If now, however, we turn to later papers in the series we seem

41

to find him drawing a very sharp distinction between the instinct and its psychical representative." And Strachey went on to give several references, for instance quoting from the paper on "The Unconscious," "An instinct can never become an object of consciousness—only the idea that represents the instinct can. Even in the unconscious, moreover, an instinct cannot be represented otherwise than by an idea."

It seems to me that Isaacs's way of using the concept of phantasy (1948), bridges the gap between the two ways in which Freud viewed instinct. The ideas representing the instinct would be the original primitive phantasies. The operation of an instinct in this view is expressed and represented in mental life by the phantasy of the satisfaction of that instinct by an appropriate object. Since instincts operate from birth, some crude phantasy life can be assumed to exist from birth. The first hunger and the instinctual striving to satisfy that hunger are accompanied by the phantasy of an object capable of satisfying that hunger. As phantasies derive directly from instincts on the borderline between the somatic and psychical activity, these original phantasies are experienced as somatic as well as mental phenomena. So long as the pleasure-pain principle is in the ascendant, phantasies are omnipotent and no differentiation between phantasy and reality experience exists. The phantasied objects and the satisfaction derived from them are experienced as physical happenings. Freud assumes that, to begin with, the infant responds to situations of deprivation by hallucinatory wish fulfillment. Those early hallucinations are expressions of phantasy life, if the concept is used in the way suggested by Isaacs (1948) and Klein.

Freud's formulations about hallucinatory wish fulfillment preceded his discovery of the death instinct; therefore, his statements about hallucinatory wish fulfillment must be read as pertaining only to libidinal wishes. We have reason to assume, however, that the death instinct and the destructive impulses into which it is deflected also give rise to phantasied hallucinatory fulfillment. To the desire to love and eat corresponds the phantasy of an ideal love-, life- and food-giving breast. To the desire to destroy correspond equally vivid phantasies of an object shattered, destroyed and attacking. If the infant contentedly sucking his thumb is hallucinating a good experience, the infant who wakes up screaming, kicking and even sometimes turning away from his mother and her breast is probably hallucinating bad and persecuting objects.

The omnipotence of phantasy, however, is never complete. From the beginning there is interaction between phantasy and reality. The phantasy of the ideal breast breaks down if the frustration is too prolonged or intense. Equally, the persecutory phantasies can be alleviated or overcome by the reality of a good experience. At the same time, however, the infant perceives reality in terms of his omnipotent phantasy, good experiences merging with ideal phantasies, and frustration and deprivation being experienced as a persecution by bad objects.

Reality experience, in interaction with unconscious phantasy, gradually alters the character of phantasies, and memory traces of reality experiences are incorporated into phantasy life. I have stressed earlier that the original phantasies are of a crude and primitive nature, directly concerned with the satisfaction of instincts. These phantasies are experienced in a somatic as well as a mental way, and, since our instincts are always active, a primitive layer of primary phantasies is active in all of us. From this core later phantasies evolve. They become altered by contact with reality, by conflict, by maturational growth. As instincts develop instinct derivatives, so the early primitive phantasies develop later derivatives. These can be displaced, symbolized and elaborated upon and even penetrate into consciousness as daydreams, imagination, etc.

The concept of unconscious phantasy is implicit in many of Freud's formulations, though he rarely used it explicitly. He spoke of unconscious omnipotent ideas or unconscious theories which could be seen as manifestations of unconscious phantasying. Children's sexual theories, as described by Freud, can be seen as conscious derivatives of unconscious sexual phantasies.

I have so far concerned myself with the relation between phantasy and instinct. In her paper, Isaacs (1948) established another equally important connection, correlating the concept of phantasy with that of mental mechanisms. We are all familiar with phantasying as a defensive function. It is a flight from reality and a defense against frustration. This seems contradictory to the concept of phantasy as an expression of instinct. The contradiction, however, is more apparent than real: since phantasy aims at fulfilling instinctual striving in the absence of reality satisfaction, that function in itself is a defense against reality. But, as mental life becomes more complicated, phantasy is called upon as a defense in various situations of stress. For instance, manic phantasies act as a defense against the underlying depression. The question arises of the relation between the defensive function of phantasy and mechanisms of defense. It is Isaacs's contention that what we call mechanisms of defense are abstract descriptions from an observer's point of view of what is in fact the functioning of unconscious phantasy. That is, when we speak of repression, for instance, the patient may be having a detailed phantasy, say, of dams built inside his body holding back floods, floods being the way he may represent in phantasy his instincts.

When we speak of denial, we may find a phantasy in which the denied objects are actually annihilated, and so on. The mechanisms of introjection and projection, which long precede repression and exist from the beginning of mental life, are related to phantasies of incorporation and ejection— phantasies which are, to begin with, of a very concrete somatic nature. Clinically, if the analysis is to be an alive experience to the patient, we do not interpret to him mechanisms, we interpret and help him to relive the phantasies contained in the mechanisms.

Isaacs was concerned with discussing the derivation of phantasies from the matrix of the id and with the relation phantasies bore to mental mechanisms. I shall attempt to establish two further links, the connection between phantasy and personality structure and that between phantasy and higher mental functions like thinking.

If one views the mechanisms of projection and introjection as being based on primitive phantasies of incorporation and ejection, the connection between phantasy and mental structure becomes immediately apparent. The phantasies of objects which are being introjected into the ego, as well as the loss to the ego by phantasies of projective identification, affect the structure of personality. When Freud described the superego as an internal object in active relationship with the id and the ego, he was accused by academic psychologists of being anthropomorphic. But what was he in fact describing? This structure within the ego is the end result of complex phantasies. The child in phantasy projects some of his own aggressions into a parental figure; in phantasy, he then incorporates this figure and, again, in phantasy, attributes to this figure various attitudes and functions. Melanie Klein has shown that other objects, earlier than the superego described by Freud, are similarly introjected, and a complex internal world is built in phantasy and structuralized. The fact that structure is partly determined by unconscious phantasy is of paramount importance from the therapeutic point of view, since we have access to these phantasies in the analytic situation, and through mobilizing them and helping the patient to relive and remodel them in the process of analytic treatment, we can affect the structure of the patient's personality.

I should like now to consider the relation between phantasy and what appears to be the opposite, namely thinking. Phantasy belongs originally to functioning in terms of the pleasure-pain principle. In "The Two Principles of Mental Functioning," Freud (1911) says "With the introduction of the reality principle, one mode of thought-activity was split off; it was kept free from reality-testing and remained subordinated to the pleasure principle alone. This activity is *phantasying*." Thought, on the other hand, was developed in the service of reality-testing, primarily as a means of sustaining tension and delaying satisfaction. Quoting from the same paper: "Thinking was endowed with characteristics which made it possible for the mental apparatus to tolerate an increased tension of stimulus while the process of discharge was postponed." Nevertheless, these two mental activities have one important thing in common. They *both* enable the ego to sustain tension without immediate motor discharge. The infant capable of sustaining a phantasy is not driven to discharge to, in Freud's words, "relieve the psyche of an accretion of stimuli." He can sustain his desire with the help of phantasy for some time, until satisfaction in reality is available. If the frustration is severe, or the infant has little capacity for maintaining his phantasy, the motor discharge takes place, often accompanied by the disintegration of the immature ego. So until reality testing and thought processes are well established, phantasy fulfills in the early mental life some of the functions later taken over by thinking.

In a footnote to his paper "Formulations on the Two Principles of Mental Functioning," Freud said, "It will rightly be objected that an organization which was a slave to the pleasure principle and neglected the reality of the external world . . . could not have come into existence at all. The employment of a fiction like this is, however, justified when one considers that the infant—provided one includes with it the care it receives from its mother—does *almost* realize a psychical system of this kind." I emphasize the word "almost" here, because, from very early on, the healthy infant has some awareness of his needs and the capacity to communicate them to his mother. From the moment the infant starts interacting with the outer world, he is engaged in testing his phantasies in a reality setting. I want to suggest that the origin of thought lies in this process of testing phantasy against reality; that is, that thought is not only contrasted with phantasy, but based on it and derived from it.

I would like to use a simile here. The naive picture of a scientist is that he observes facts without any preconceptions and draws his conclusions from observation. In fact, we know that the scientist who proceeded like that could draw no conclusions. The scientist has a well-defined hypothesis, or maybe a series of alternative hypotheses, not to mention his preconscious, and even unconscious, expectations. Armed with these, he observes facts with certain definite questions in his mind. He can then test his hypotheses against the facts and confirm them, or correct them or even refute them and formulate new ones suggested to him by the facts. Similarly, it would be naive to think that the infant learns reality thinking by discarding his phantasies. On the contrary, the infant approaches reality armed, as it were, with expectations formed by his unconscious phantasy. By testing them in reality, he gradually learns which are applicable and which modes of his own functioning enable him to deal with reality.

In *"A Theory of Thinking"* (1962, pp. 112-113), Bion described the origin of thought in what he calls "a matching of preconception with realization." He compares this preconception to Kant's concept of empty thought. I would suggest that this preconception is the infant's phantasy, the first of which is that of the good and the bad breast. Bion has made the point that the outcome of this matching of preconception with realization is largely determined by the infant's capacity to bear frustration, as well as the environment's capacity to keep this frustration within bearable limits. If the infant can bear the frustration and his phantasies meet a reality different from expectation, the differentiation is established between his expectation, which is the thought, and the reality of the perception. In Bion's words the infant may conclude "no breast, therefore a thought." If the circumstances are such that the infant cannot bear the disillusionment of reality, the omnipotence of the phantasy is increased and the reality perception is denied and annihilated. The infant has to continue functioning in terms of omnipotent phantasy and thought does not develop. Furthermore, since this omnipotent phantasy cannot in fact rid him of the painful stimuli, he will be driven more and more to the phantasy of projective identification and to attacks on his own ego, particularly his organs of perception, in an attempt to rid himself to these stimuli. The most severe psychotic disturbances of thought occur in this way.

We know that the reality principle is but a modification of the pleasure principle, a modification brought about by reality-testing. I would suggest that thinking is a modification of unconscious phantasy, a modification similarly brought about by reality testing. The richness, depth, and accuracy of a person's thinking will depend on the quality and malleability of the unconscious phantasy life and the capacity to subject it to reality testing.

I have, in this paper, followed Isaacs's use of the concept of phantasy as the psychic representation of instinct and I have tried to show some further implications of using the concept in that way. The value of this use of the concept of unconscious phantasy is that it integrates in a dynamic way the various aspects of the mental apparatus, welding together the concepts of instincts, mental mechanism and mental structure, and providing a bridge between the primary and secondary processes.

Postscript 1979: On Phantasy Notes to the Paper on Phantasy

I must have written this paper under pressure and did not sufficiently check my references. I imply in this paper that Susan Isaacs made no link between phantasy and higher mental functions. This is not correct. She described the link between unconscious phantasy and higher mental functioning by means of symbolism. My view, that higher mental functioning arises out of phantasy by reality testing is complementary to Isaac's view. Both symbolism and reality testing are developments of the depressive position, in which gradually the external and internal worlds get differentiated.

The paper was part of a symposium at the Twenty-third Psychoanalytic Congress and is therefore severely limited in length. I give a longer and more fully elaborated account of the subject in my *Introduction to the Work of Melanie Klein* (1964).

References

Bion, W. R. (1962). A theory of thinking. *International Journal of Psycho-Analysis* 43:306-310. In W. R. Bion, *Second Thoughts*. New York: Jason Aronson, 1977.

Freud, S. (1908). Creative writers and day-dreaming. *Standard Edition* 9:141-153.

——— (1911). Formulations on the two principles of mental functioning. *Standard Edition* 12:218-226.

Isaacs, S. (1948). The nature and function of phantasy. *International Journal of Psycho-Analysis* 29:73-97.

Segal, H. (1964). *Introduction to the Work of Melanie Klein*. London: Hogarth.

Strachey, J. (1957). Editor's note to "Instincts and their vicissitudes." *Standard Edition* 14:111-116.

4

Notes on Symbol Formation

THE UNDERSTANDING and interpretation of unconscious symbolism is one of the main tools of the psychoanalyst. Often he is faced with the task of understanding and recognizing the meaning not only of a particular symbol but also of the whole process of symbol formation. This applies particularly to work with patients who show a disturbance or inhibition in the formation or free use of symbols, as for instance, psychotic or schizoid patients.

Two very elementary examples follow. Patient A was a schizophrenic in a mental hospital. He was once asked by his doctor why he had stopped playing the violin since his illness. He replied with some violence, "Why? do you expect me to masturbate in public?"

Another patient, B, dreamed one night that he and a young girl were playing a violin duet. He had associations to fiddling, masturbating, etc., from which it emerged clearly that the violin represented his genital and playing the violin represented a masturbation phantasy of a relation with the girl.

Here then are two patients who apparently use the same symbols in the same situation: a violin representing the male genital, and playing the violin representing masturbation. The way in which the symbols function, however, is very different. For A, the violin had become so completely equated with his genital that to touch it in public became impossible. For B, playing the violin in his waking life was an important sublimation. We might say that the main difference between them is that for A the symbolic meaning of the violin was conscious, for B unconscious. I do not think, however, that this was the most important difference between the two patients. In the case of B, the fact that the meaning of the dream became completely conscious had in no way prevented him from using his violin. In A, on the other hand, there were many symbols operating in his unconscious in the same way in which the violin was used on the conscious level.

Another example comes from a schizophrenic patient in an analytical situation. In the first weeks of his analysis, he came into a session blushing and giggling, and throughout the session would not talk to me. Subsequently we found that before this hour he had been attending an occupational therapy class where he made a canvas stool, which he brought with him. The reason for his silence, blushing and giggling was that he could not bring himself to talk to me about it. For him, the stool on which he had been working, the word "stool" which he would have to use in connection with it, and the stool he passed in the lavatory were so completely felt as one and the same thing that he was unable to talk to me about it. His subsequent analysis revealed that this equation of the three "stools," the word, the chair, and the feces, was at the time completely unconscious. All he was consciously aware of was that he was embarrassed and could not talk to me. (This patient is described in detail in chapter 8.)

The main difference between the way that the first and second patients used the violin as the symbol for the male genital was not that in the one case the symbol was conscious and in the other unconscious, but that in the first case it was felt to *be* the genital, and in the second to *represent* it.

According to Ernest Jones's definition (1916), the violin of A, the schizophrenic, would be considered a symbol, as it is in the dream of B. But it would not be a symbol in B's waking life when it was used in sublimation.

In his paper, Jones (1916) differentiated unconscious symbolism from other forms of "indirect representation," and made the following statements about true unconscious symbolism:

   (i) A symbol represents what has been repressed from consciousness, and the whole process of symbolism is carried on unconsciously.
  (ii) All symbols represent ideas of "the self and of immediate blood relations and of the phenomena of birth, life and death."
 (iii) A symbol has a constant meaning. Many symbols can be used to represent the same repressed idea, but a given symbol has a constant meaning which is universal.

(iv) Symbolism arises as the result of intrapsychic conflict between the "repressing tendencies and the repressed." Further: "Only what is repressed is symbolized; only what is repressed needs to be symbolized."

Jones further distinguished between sublimation and symbolization. "Symbols," he said, "arise when the affect investing the symbolized idea has not, as far as the symbol is concerned, proved capable of that modification in quality which is denoted by the term sublimation."

Summarizing Jones's points, one might say that when a desire has to be given up because of conflict and is repressed, it may express itself in a symbolic way, and the object of the desire which had to be given up can be replaced by a symbol.

Further analytic work, and particularly play analysis with young children, has fully confirmed some main points of Jones's formulation. The child's first interests and impulses are directed to his parents' bodies and to his own; and it is those objects and impulses existing in the unconscious which give rise to all further interests by way of symbolization. Jones's statement, however, that symbols are formed where there is no sublimation soon gave rise to disagreement. In fact, Jones, as well as Freud, wrote many interesting papers analyzing the content of works of art. In her 1923 paper on infant analysis, Melanie Klein did not agree with this view of the relation between symbolization and sublimation. She tried to show that children's play—a sublimated activity—is a symbolic expression of anxieties and wishes.

We might consider it a question of terminology and accept Jones's view that we should call symbols only those substitutes which replace the object without any change of affect. On the other hand, there are very great advantages in extending the definition to cover symbols used in sublimation. In the first place the wider definition corresponds better to common linguistic usage. Jones's concept excludes most of that which is called "symbol" in other sciences and in everyday language. Second, and I shall elaborate this point later, there seems to be a continuous development from the primitive symbols described by Jones to the symbols used in self-expression, communication, discovery and creation. Third, it is difficult to establish a connection between the early primitive desires and processes in the mind and the later development of the individual, unless the wider concept of symbolism is admitted. In the analytic view, the child's interest in the external world is determined by a series of displacements of affect and interest from the earliest to ever new objects. And, indeed, how could such a displacement be achieved otherwise than by way of symbolization?

In 1930, Melanie Klein raised the problem of inhibition in symbol formation. She described an autistic little boy of four, Dick, who could not talk or play; he showed no affection or anxiety and took no interest in his surroundings apart from doorknobs, stations, and trains, which seemed to fascinate him. Analysis revealed that the child was terrified of his aggression toward his mother's body, and of her body itself, because he felt it had turned bad through his attacks on it. Because of the strength of his anxieties, he had erected powerful defenses against his phantasies about her. There resulted a paralysis of his phantasy life and of symbol formation. He had not endowed the world around him with any symbolic meaning and therefore took no interest in it. Melanie Klein came to the conclusion that if symbolization does not occur, the whole development of the ego is arrested.

If we accept this view, it follows that the processes of symbolization require a new and more careful study. To begin with, I find it helpful, following Morris (1938), to consider symbolizing as a *three*-term relation, i.e. a relation between the thing symbolized, the thing functioning as a symbol, and a *person* for whom the one represents the other. In psychological terms, symbolism would be a relation between the ego, the object, and the symbol.

Symbol formation is an activity of the ego attempting to deal with the anxieties stirred by its relation to the object and is generated primarily by the fear of bad objects and the fear of the loss or inaccessibility of good objects. Disturbances in the ego's relation to objects are reflected in disturbances of symbol formation. In particular, disturbances in differentiation between ego and object lead to disturbances in differentiation between the symbol and the object symbolized and therefore to the concrete thinking characteristic of psychoses.

Symbol formation starts very early, probably as early as object relations, but changes its character and functions with the changes in the character of the ego and object relations. Not only the actual content of the symbol but the very way in which symbols are formed and used seems to reflect precisely the ego's state of development and its way of dealing with its objects. If symbolism is seen as a three-term relation, problems of symbol formation must always be examined in the context of the ego's relation with its objects.

I shall try to describe briefly some basic attitudes of the ego to its objects, and the way in which I think the objects influence the processes of symbol formation and the functioning of symbolism. My description is based here on Melanie Klein's concepts of the paranoid-schizoid position and of the depressive position. According to her, the oral stage of development falls into two phases, the earlier being the point of fixation of the schizophrenic group of illnesses, the later that of the manic-depressive. In my description, which of necessity will be very schematic, I shall select only those points which are directly relevant to the problem of symbol formation.

The chief characteristics of the infant's first object relations are the following. The object is seen as split into an ideally good and a wholly bad one. The aim of the ego is total union with the ideal object and total annihilation of the bad one, as well as of the bad parts of the self. Omnipotent thinking is paramount and reality sense intermittent and precarious. The concept of absence hardly exists. Whenever the state of union with the ideal object is not fulfilled, what is experienced is not absence; the ego feels assailed by the counterpart of the good object—the bad object, or objects. It is the time of the hallucinatory wish-fulfillment, described by Freud, when the mind creates objects which are then felt to be available. According to Melanie Klein, it is also the time of the bad hallucinosis when, if the ideal conditions are not fulfilled, the bad object is equally hallucinated and felt as real.

A leading defense mechanism in this phase is projective identification. In projective identification, the subject in phantasy projects large parts of himself into the object, and the object becomes identified with the parts of the self that it is felt to contain. Similarly, internal objects are projected outside and identified with parts of the external world which come to represent them. These first projections and identifications are the beginning of the process of symbol formation.

The early symbols, however, are not felt by the ego to be symbols or substitutes but to be the original object itself. They are so different from symbols formed later that I think they deserve a name of their own. In chapter 8, I suggest the term *equation*. This word, however, differentiates them too much from the word *symbol* and I would like to alter it here to *symbolic equation*, a term used by Klein (1930) in a somewhat different sense.

The symbolic equation between the original object and the symbol in the internal and the external world is, I think, the basis of the schizophrenic's concrete thinking; substitutes for the original objects, or parts of the self, can be used quite freely, but, as in the two examples of schizophrenic patients which I quoted, they are hardly different from the original object. These substitutes are felt and treated as though they were *identical* with it. This nondifferentiation between the thing symbolized and the symbol is part of a disturbance in the relation between the ego and the object. Parts of the ego and internal objects are projected into an object and identified with it. The differentiation between the self and the object is obscured. Then, since a part of the ego is confused with the object, the symbol—which is a creation and a function of the ego—becomes, in turn, confused with the object which is symbolized.

Where such symbolic equations are formed in relation to bad objects, an attempt is made to deal with them as with the original object, that is by total annihilation and scotomization. In Melanie Klein's (1930) discussion, it seemed as if Dick had formed no symbolic relations to the external world. The paper was written very early on in Dick's analysis, and I wonder, on the basis of my own experience with schizophrenics, whether it did not, perhaps, subsequently transpire that Dick had formed numerous symbolic equations in the external world. If so, these would have carried the full anxiety experienced in relation to the original persecutory or guilt-producing object: his mother's body, so that he had to deal with them by annihilation, that is by total withdrawal of interest. As his analysis progressed, and he started to show an interest in certain objects in the consulting room, Dick seemed to have formed such symbolic equations. For instance, when he saw some pencil shavings he said, "Poor Mrs. Klein." To him the shavings were Mrs. Klein cut into bits.

This was the case in the analysis of my patient Edward (see chapter 8). At one stage in the analysis a certain degree of symbol formation on a symbolic equation basis had occurred so that some anxiety was displaced from the person of his analyst, felt as a bad internal object, onto substitutes in the external world. Then the numerous persecutors in the external world were dealt with by scotomization. That phase of his analysis, which lasted several months, was characterized by an extreme narrowing of his interests in the external world. At that point also his vocabulary became very poor. He forbade himself and me the use of many words which he felt had the power to produce hallucinations and therefore had to be abolished. This is strikingly similar to the behavior of a Paraguayan tribe, the Abipones, who cannot tolerate words which remind them of the dead. When a member of the tribe dies, all words having any affinity with the names of the deceased are immediately dropped from the vocabulary. In consequence, their language is most difficult to learn, as it is full of blocks and neologisms replacing forbidden words (Fraser 1922).

The development of the ego and the changes in the ego's relation to its objects are gradual. Also gradual is the change from the early symbols, which I called symbolic equations, to the fully formed symbols during the depressive position. It is only for the sake of clarity that I make here a very sharp distinction between the ego's relations in the paranoid-schizoid position and in the depressive position respectively, and an equally sharp distinction between the symbolic equations and the symbols which are formed during and after the depressive position.

When the depressive position has been reached, the main characteristic of object relations is that the object is felt as a whole object. In connection with this there is a greater degree of awareness of differentiation and of the separateness between the ego and the object. At the same time, since the object is recognized as a whole, ambivalence is more fully experienced. The ego in this phase is struggling with its ambivalence. Its relation to the object is characterized by guilt, fear of loss or actual experience of loss and mourning, and a striving to re-create the object. At the same time, processes of introjection become more pronounced than those of projection, in keeping with the striving to retain the object inside as well as to repair, restore and re-create it.

In normal development, after repeated experiences of loss, recovery, and re-creation, a good object is securely established in the ego. As the ego develops and integrates, these changes in relation to the object affect fundamentally the ego's reality sense. With an increased awareness of ambivalence, the lessening of the intensity of projection, and the growing differentiation between the self and the object, there is a growing sense of reality both internal and external. The internal world becomes differentiated from the external world. Omnipotent thinking, characteristic of the earlier phase, gradually gives way to more realistic thinking. Simultaneously, and as part of the same process, there is a certain modification of the primary instinctual aims. Earlier on, the aim was to possess the object totally if it was felt as good or to annihilate it totally if it was felt as bad. With the recognition that the good and the bad objects are one, both these instinctual aims are gradually modified. The ego is increasingly concerned with saving the object from its aggression and possessiveness. And this implies a certain degree of inhibition of the direct instinctual aims, both aggressive and libidinal.

This situation is a powerful stimulus for the creation of symbols, and symbols acquire new functions which change their character. The symbol is needed to displace aggression from the original object and, in that way, to lessen the guilt and the fear of loss. The aim of the displacement is to save the object, and the guilt experienced in relation to it is far less than that due to an attack on the original object. Thus, the symbol here is not equivalent to the original object. The symbols are also created in the *internal* world as a means of restoring, re-creating, recapturing and owning again the original object. But in keeping with the increased reality sense, they are now felt as created by the ego and therefore never completely equated with the original object.

Freud (1923) postulates that a modification of instinctual aims is the basic condition of sublimation. In my view, the formation of symbols in the depressive position necessitates some inhibition of direct instinctual aims in relation to the original object and therefore the symbols become available for sublimation. The symbols, created internally, can then be reprojected into the external world, endowing it with symbolic meaning.

The capacity to experience loss and the wish to re-create the object within oneself gives the individual the unconscious freedom in the use of symbols. And as the symbol is acknowledged as a creation of the subject, unlike the symbolic equation, it can be freely used by the subject.

When a substitute in the external world is used as a symbol it may be used more freely than the original object, since it is not fully identified with it. But inasmuch as it is distinguished from the original object, the symbol is also recognized as an object in itself. Its own properties are recognized, respected, and used because no confusion with the original object blurs the characteristics of the new object used as a symbol.

In an analysis, we can sometimes follow very clearly the changes in the symbolic relations in the patient's attitude to his feces. On the schizoid level, the patient expects his feces to be the ideal breast. If he cannot maintain this idealization, his feces become persecutory; they are ejected as a bitten-up, destroyed and persecuting breast. If the patient tries to symbolize his feces in the external world, the symbols in the external world are felt to be feces— persecutors. No sublimation of anal activities can occur under these conditions.

On the depressive level, the feeling is that the introjected breast has been destroyed by the ego and can be re-created by the ego. The feces may then be felt as something created by the ego out of the object and can be valued as a symbol of the breast and at the same time as a good product of the ego's own creativity.

When this symbolic relation to feces and other body products has been established, a projection can occur on to substances in the external world such as paint, clay, etc., which then can be used for sublimation.

When this stage of development has been achieved, it is, of course, not irreversible. If the anxieties are too strong, a regression to the paranoid-schizoid position can occur at any stage of the individual's development and projective identification may be resorted to as a defense against anxiety. Then symbols which have been developed and have been functioning as symbols in sublimation, revert to concrete symbolic equations. This is mainly due to the fact that in massive projective identification, the ego again becomes confused with the object; the symbol becomes confused with the thing symbolized and therefore turns into an equation.

In the example of the schizophrenic patient A quoted at the beginning of this paper, there was a breakdown of an already established sublimation. Prior to his schizophrenic breakdown, the violin had been functioning as a symbol and used for purposes of sublimation. It had only become concretely equated to the penis at the time of his illness. Words which had developed at the time when the ego was relatively mature become equated with the objects that they should represent and are experienced as concrete objects when projective identification occurs. Confusion results between the symbols created by the ego, the word, or even the thought, and the object that they were to symbolize.

I should like at this point to summarize what I mean by the terms "symbolic equation" and "symbol" respectively, and the conditions under which they arise. In the symbolic equation, the symbol-substitute is felt to *be* the original object. The substitute's own properties are not recognized or admitted. The symbolic equation is used to deny the absence of the ideal object or to control a persecuting one. It belongs to the earliest stages of development.

The symbol proper, available for sublimation and furthering the development of the ego, is felt to *represent* the object; its own characteristics are recognized, respected, and used. It arises when depressive feelings predominate over the paranoid-schizoid ones, when separation from the object, ambivalence, guilt, and loss can be experienced and tolerated. The symbol is used not to deny but to overcome loss. When the mechanism of projective identification is used as a defense against depressive anxieties, symbols already formed and functioning as symbols may revert to symbolic equations.

Symbol formation governs the capacity to communicate, since all communication is made by means of symbols. When schizoid disturbances in object relations occur, the capacity to communicate is similarly disturbed: first because the differentiation between the subject and the object is blurred, second, because the *means* of communication are lacking since symbols are felt in a concrete fashion and are therefore unavailable for purposes of communication. One of the ever-recurring difficulties in the analysis of psychotic patients is this difficulty of communication. Words, for instance, whether the analyst's or the patient's, are felt to be objects or actions, and cannot be easily used for purposes of communication.

Symbols are needed not only in communication with the external world, but also in internal communication. Indeed, it could be asked what is meant when we speak of people being in touch with their unconscious. It is not that they have consciously primitive phantasies, like those which become evident in their analyses, but merely that they have some awareness of their own impulses and feelings. However, I think that we mean more than this; we mean that they have actual *communication* with their unconscious phantasies. And this, like any other form of communication can be done only with the help of symbols. So that in people who are "in touch with themselves" there is a constant free symbol formation, whereby they can be consciously aware and in control of *symbolic expressions* of the underlying primitive phantasies. The difficulty of dealing with schizophrenic and schizoid patients lies not only in their failure to communicate with us but even more in their failure to communicate with themselves. Any part of their ego may be split off from any other part with no communication available between the parts.

The capacity to communicate with oneself by using symbols is, I think, the basis of verbal thinking. This is the capacity to communicate with oneself by means of words. Not all internal communication is verbal thinking, but all verbal thinking is an internal communication by means of symbols—words.

An important aspect of internal communication is the integration of earlier desires, anxieties, and phantasies into the later stages of development by symbolization. For instance, in the fully developed genital function, all the earlier aims—anal, urethral, oral—may be symbolically expressed and fulfilled, a point beautifully described in Ferenczi's *Thalassa* (1923).

And this takes me to the last point of my paper. I think that one of the important tasks performed by the ego in the depressive position is that of dealing not only with depressive anxieties, but also with unresolved earlier conflicts. A new achievement belonging to the depressive position is the capacity to symbolize and in that way to lessen anxiety and resolve conflict. This is used in order to deal with *earlier* unresolved conflicts by symbolizing them. Anxieties which could not be dealt with earlier on because of the extreme concreteness of the experience with the object and the object-substitutes in symbolic equations, can gradually be dealt with by the more integrated ego by symbolization. In that way they can be integrated. In the depressive position and later, symbols are formed not only of the whole destroyed and recreated object characteristic of the depressive position but also of the split object (extremely good and extremely bad) and not only of the whole object but also of part objects. Some of the paranoid and ideal object relations and anxieties may be symbolized as part of the integrative process in the depressive position.

The fairy tale is an example in point. It deals basically with the witch and the fairy godmother, Prince Charming, the ogre, etc., and has in it a great deal of schizophrenic content. It is, however, a highly integrated product, an artistic creation which very fully symbolizes the child's early anxieties and wishes. I should like to illustrate the function of the fairy tale by some material from the analysis of an adolescent schizophrenic. This girl had been subject to hallucinations and openly schizophrenic since the age of four. She had, however, a great many depressive features and there were in her life phases of relatively greater integration. In these phases, when she felt less persecuted, and, as she told me, could experience some longing for her parents, she used to write fairy tales. In the bad phases, the bad figures of her fairy tales came to life and persecuted her. One day, after many weeks of silence, when she was obviously hallucinated in a very persecutory way she suddenly turned to me and asked with great fear, "What are the Lancashire witches?" I had never heard of the Lancashire witches, she had never mentioned them before, but I knew that she herself came from Lancashire. After some interpretations she told me that when she was about 11, a time when she was free of hallucinations, she had written a fairy tale about Lancashire witches. The phase of her analysis following this session has been very revealing. It turned out that the Lancashire witches represented both herself and her mother. The anxiety situation went right back to early childhood, when she saw herself and her mother as devouring one another or devouring her father. When a greater degree of integration was achieved and she established a more realistic relation to her parents, the earlier situation was dealt with by symbol formation: by writing the fairy tale about the Lancashire witches. In the subsequent deterioration of her health, the early persecutory situation recurred with concrete intensity but in a new form. The fairy tale came to life: the Lancashire witches—the fairy tale figures which she had created, had become a concrete external reality. In the consulting room it was quite clear how this concretization of the fairy tale depended on projective identification. She turned to me and asked me about the Lancashire witches. She expected me to know who they were. In fact, she thought that I was a Lancashire witch. She had unconsciously phantasied that she had put into me the part of herself which had invented the Lancashire witches, and she had lost contact with this part. She lost all sense of reality in this projection and all memory that she had created this symbol, the "Lancashire Witches." Her symbol became confused with me, an actual external object, and so became for her a concrete external reality—I had turned into a Lancashire witch.

The way in which the maturing ego, in the process of working through the depressive position, deals with the early object relations, is of paramount importance. Some integration and whole object relations can be achieved in the depressive position, accompanied by the splitting off of earlier ego experiences. In this situation, something like a pocket of schizophrenia exists isolated in the ego and is a constant threat to stability. At worst, a mental breakdown occurs and earlier anxieties and split-off symbolic equations invade the ego. At best, a relatively mature but restricted ego can develop and function.

However, if the ego in the depressive position is strong enough and capable of dealing with anxieties, much more of the earlier situations can be integrated into the ego and dealt with by way of symbolization, enriching the ego with the whole wealth of the earlier experiences.

The word "symbol" comes from the Greek term for throwing together, bringing together, integrating. The process of symbol formation is, I think, a continuous process of bringing together and integrating the internal with the external, the subject with the object, and the earlier experiences with the later ones.

POSTSCRIPT 1979:
NOTES ON SYMBOL FORMATION

Since writing this paper, and largely under the influence of Bion's work on the relationship between the container and the contained, I have come to think that it is not projective identification per se that leads to concretization. One has to take into account the particular relationship between the projected part and the object projected into: the container and the contained. For a more detailed explanation, I refer the reader to chapter 7. In relation to symbol formation, this relationship is of great importance. I want to give two examples.

In the first one, the environmental factor plays an important role. A neurotic young man was able much of the time to function on a depressive level. He could communicate in a symbolic way and had numerous sublimations. These achievements were, however, insecure and at moments of stress, he tended to use massive projective identification accompanied by regression to concrete levels of functioning. Sometimes, for instance, he had near hallucinatory states of mind.

He came to one session very perturbed because on waking up he had a hallucinatory experience. It differed from hallucination only insofar as he clung desparately to the belief that it must be the product of his own mind. When he woke up, he felt that his head was solid and he saw a motorcycle riding into his head. The rider had a kind of mask on, which made his head look like a finger. He felt terrified and thought his head would explode. Then he looked at his own index finger, and got frightened because his finger looked like a gorilla. He emerged from a state of acute anxiety only when he made himself remember the previous session, in which he was disturbed by a very intrusive noise of motorcycles outside the consulting room windows. He thought the motorcycles were connected with my son. He associated the gorilla to a psychotic boy who was described in a paper as looking like a gorilla. The finger he associated to anal masturbation, about which he had spoken a few days earlier. His anal masturbation was always associated with violent projective identification into the anus of the analyst/mother, as described by Meltzer (1966). We could analyze that the motorcycles outside the window represented his own intrusive self identified with his finger and penis, projected into an external object—the motorcycle—and intruding into him. It is important in this connection that there was in the external world an actual intrusive object into which this projection fitted. It repeated a childhood situation in which there was, in fact, a very instrusive older sibling interfering with his relation to the mother even when he was a tiny baby. Thus, his projections were concretized for him in the external world.

My second example was a much more disturbed young woman. In her case, the disturbance seemed to spring from excessive envy and narcissism projected into an overly narcissistic mother. This patient was not psychotic but she may well have been the most difficult patient I have ever had to understand. Her verbal communications were very difficult to follow. I often had difficulty in grasping the conscious meaning. She tended to misuse words, mix languages. There were non sequiturs and contradictions in what she said. Often there was little connection between what she said, what she meant to say and what she actually thought. The unconscious meaning was even more confused. In other patients, when verbal communications are so difficult, one may get important nonverbal clues. With her, the nonverbal clues were often lacking or misleading. The tone of her voice or her facial expression often bore no relation to her state of mind. Typically, she would greet me with a friendly, relaxed smile, giving no indication that she was in fact in a turmoil of anxiety, confusion and hostility. Her symbolism was at times very concrete. She had states of bodily excitement, bizarre bodily sensations, psychosomatic, hypochrondriacal, hysterical symptoms and often complained that she had no feelings, only physical sensations. She often responded to interpretations by physical sensation. Words were experienced as concrete things, felt as a lump inside her. This was often accompanied by fears of cancer. In those situations, one could often see that she felt she has invaded my speech and made it into a physical possession of hers. But there was an opposite phenomenon. Her speech could be called completely abstract. She spoke most of the time in metaphors, cliches, technical terms. She often generalized in a way which left no meaning. Sometimes she spoke for a long time, and I realized she had said nothing concrete or real that I could get hold of. At the same time, I could observe how she emptied my words of all meaning as if she listened to an interpretation and immediately translated it into some philosophical or psychoanalytic abstract term, often distorting its meaning completely. The underlying phantasy was that she entered me and emptied me of all contents and she felt equally emptied by me. Stealing was an ever-recurring theme. At other times, she might communicate dissociated fragments of bits of her experience that seemed to function as Bion's "bizarre objects" (Bion 1957).

In those modes of functioning, one can see a disturbance between the container and the contained. When she was overly concrete, the projected part was totally identified with the container. When her communication was empty of meaning, the container and the contained had a relation of mutually emptying one another. When she was fragmented and produced "bizarre objects" type of associations, her projections had split the container into fragments.

In her case, this mutually destructive relation between the part she projected and the container seems to be related to envy and to narcissism. Nothing was allowed to exist outside herself which could give rise to envy. I would like to give some material to illustrate this.

She had several dreams characteristic of her, depicting her narcissism. For instance, she dreamed she was in bed with a young man, glued and fused to him, but the young man was herself. Following several such dreams, she brought a different one: "She was in a house, the roof of which was disintegrating. She did not want to take any notice because she lived in the middle floor between the ground and the top floor." She had a number of useful, and surprisingly comprehensible, associations to the dream. She owned one of three apartments in a house. The owner of the house wanted her to participate in the costs of repairing the attic. She was furious about it because she felt it wasn't fair. It was true she signed a contract that she would, but she had been foolish to agree to it. Her own apartment was not in danger from the leaking roof, being in the middle, but she felt bad about it because of her friends who lived in the top apartment. Then she said that the middle must be her tummy and started complaining of her physical symptoms and the state of her mind. The attic must be her head, which she thought was in a terribly disintegrated state. She couldn't think; she couldn't work. She thought her head should be entirely my concern. I had interpreted to this patient her repudiation of the analytic contract that we should both be concerned with her head and related the friends who live in the top flat to internal objects, thoughts and feelings that she did not want to concern herself with. But somewhat later in the session I noticed that, despite her lamentations about her head, there was something very superior in her attitude. I particulary noted that though she complained later in the session of how empty she felt and unable to communicate, she seemed to take quite some pride in her metaphors, which were getting more and more flowery as her session progressed. When I drew her attention to this, she rather reluctantly said that while she was speaking of the middle floor, she was in fact thinking of the "first floor," which in her native language is a colloquial expression for belonging to superior, upper classes. Thus, it was her narcissism which prevented her from relating to and taking care of internal objects. That, in turn, seemed to prevent her symbolizing and communicating. The pain in her tummy—her middle floor—is where she kept me, totally controlled by and identified with her gut. If she integrated me into her head, she would be aware of her own feeling of dependence, felt by her as great inferiority. Also, the middle floor, which is also the first floor, represented both her superiority and her illness.

Verbalization can be looked at from the angle of the relation between the container and the contained. Unlike the unconscious forms of symbolism, speech has to be learned. Though the baby begins by producing sounds, those sounds have to be taken up by the environment to be converted into speech, and words or phrases have to be learned from the environment. The infant has had an experience and the mother provides the word or phrase which binds this experience. It contains, encompasses and expresses the meaning. It provides a container for it. The infant can then internalize this word or phrase containing the meaning. My patient had the greatest difficulty in experiencing any interpretation, any phrase of mine as containing and giving expression to *her* meaning. Strange things happened to my interpretations. They could become a pain in her belly or sexual excitement. They could be learned by heart and applied to others. They were frequently fed back to me as her own product but usually a bit distorted, often deprived of emotional meaning, sometimes completely reversed. She had a dream, associations to which illustrated this difficulty. To understand them, I refer you to a beautiful passage in Helen Keller's autobiography (1954) where she described how she first rediscovered speech. For a long time her teacher had tried to communicate with her by writing on her hand. Helen did not respond. After a long period of breaking and smashing things without concern, she broke a doll and for the first time cried about it. That afternoon when the teacher tried again to communicate with her and wrote a word on her palm, Helen Keller understood and responded. Thus, a capacity to understand symbolic communication followed immediately and directly from her first experience of depressive feelings, an experience very familiar to those who analyze autistic children. This sequence was first described by Emilio Rodrigue (1955) in "The Analysis of a Three-year-old Mute Schizophrenic." To return to my patient's dream. She dreamed of a little girl with long nails and ferocious teeth greedily attacking a table, scratching and biting. Her first associations were to my having given her my vacation date; this probably stirred up her greed. She produced a kind of lament, without any genuine feeling, of how primitive she was, how the little girl in the dream represented her, etc. But then she added another association. She recently read a book by, or about, a little girl who lost her sight and hearing and was like a little wild animal until the day she *invented* a sign language and taught it to her teacher. (The book was obviously Helen Keller's, read by my patient.) I think Helen Keller's description and my patient's version of it exemplify different kinds of symbol formation. With all her handicaps, Helen Keller had achieved a complete communication with her audience; but my poor patient was not yet able to speak in a way easily understandable to others. She still had not accepted that she learned to speak from her mother.

References

Bion, W. R. (1957). Differentiation of the psychotic from the non-psychotic person-
    alities. *International Journal of Psycho-Analysis* 38:266-275. In W. R. Bion,
    Second Thoughts. New York: Jason Aronson, 1977.
Ferenczi, S. (1923). *Thalassa: A Theory of Genitality.* New York: W. W. Norton,
    1968.
Fraser, J. G. (1922). *The Golden Bough,* abridged edition, London: MacMillan.
Freud, S. (1923). The ego and the id. *Standard Edition* 19:1-66.
Jones, E. (1916). The theory of symbolism. In E. Jones, *Papers on Psycho-Analysis.*
    2nd ed. London: Ballière, Tindall and Cox, 1918.
Keller, H. (1954). *Story of My Life.* New York: Doubleday.
Klein, M. (1930). The importance of symbol-formation in the development of the
    ego. *International Journal of Psycho-Analysis* 11:24-39. In M. Klein, *Contribu-
    tions to Psycho-Analysis 1921-1945,* pp. 236-250. London: Hogarth, 1948.
Meltzer, D. (1966). The relation of anal masturbation to projective identification.
    International Journal of Psycho-Analysis 47:335-342.
Morris, C. (1938). Foundations of the theory of signs. *International Encyclopedia of
    Unified Science.* Chicago: University of Chicago Press.

Rodrigue, E. (1955). The analysis of a three-year-old mute schizophrenic. In *New Directions in Psychoanalysis*, ed. M. Klein, P. Heimann, and R. Money-Kyrle, pp. 140-179. New York: Basic Books.

PART III

PSYCHOANALYTIC TECHNIQUE

5

The Curative Factors in Psychoanalysis

THE PSYCHOANALYTIC TECHNIQUE is a method both of research and of therapy. The practitioner of psychoanalysis who undertakes to treat patients must never lose sight of the fact that his contractual relationship to his patients is therapeutic. We cannot and do not promise improvement or cure; but our acceptance of the patient and his fees implies our considered opinion that psychoanalysis is the treatment of choice for him. On the other hand, Freud repeatedly stated that nothing interferes as much with the proper conduct of a psychoanalysis as "therapeutic zeal." He stated that the primary aim of the psycho-analyst is to know and that he should not be preoccupied with the therapeutic goal. He condemned, at least theoretically, all intervention other than interpretation, all active participation in the relationship with the patient, since such interventions are apt to blur the patient's transference and therefore interfere with the clarity of the analyst's vision and understanding.

Is there an inherent contradiction in these two attitudes—(1) that our contractual relationship with the patient is therapeutic, and (2) that the aim of the analyst is only to acquire and impart knowledge? To my mind, there is no contradiction between these attitudes, if we accept that insight is the central factor in the therapeutic process. It is with Freud's discovery of resistance, with his technique of lifting repression to render the uncon-

scious conflicts conscious, that psychoanalytic technique historically started. It has, of course, always been a basic tenet of psychoanalytic theory that
insight is therapeutic. In recent years, however, much stress has been laid on
other therapeutic factors, such as the importance of the recovery of a good
object in the analyst and therefore the importance of the analyst's actual
personality, the role played by the setting, and many others.

The thesis of my paper is that insight is a pre-condition of any lasting
personality change achieved in the analysis and that all other factors are
related to it. I mean here specifically psychoanalytic insight, that is: the
acquiring of knowledge about one's unconscious through experiencing
consciously and, in most cases, being able to acknowledge explicitly and
verbally, previously unconscious processes. To be of therapeutic value, it
must be correct and it must be deep enough. It must reach to the deep layers
of the unconscious and illuminate those early processes in which the
pattern of internal and external relationships is laid down and in which the
ego is structured. The deeper the layers of the unconscious reached, the
richer and the more stable will be the therapeutic result.

Such insight, as we know, can only be experienced in the transference
relationship, in which the patient can relive his past and present experiences, real and phantasied. Melanie Klein has enriched and expanded our
concept of transference. By paying minute attention to processes of projection and introjection, she showed how, in the transference relationship,
internal object relations are mobilized by projection onto the analyst and
modified through interpretation and experience as they are reintrojected.
Similarly, parts of the ego projected onto the analyst undergo modification
in this new relationship. Thus, what had been structured is again experienced as a dynamic process. The role of the analyst is to understand this
process and to interpret it to the patient. A full transference interpretation—
and though we cannot always make a full interpretation, we aim eventually
at completing it—a full interpretation will involve interpreting the patient's feelings, anxieties, and defenses, taking into account the stimulus in
the present and the reliving of the past. It will include the role played by his
internal objects and the interplay of phantasy and reality.

The transference relationship can develop only in the psychoanalytic
setting. Therefore, whatever the meaning of the setting to the patient, which
we have to understand and interpret to him, this setting is part of our
contractual relationship. When we offer a patient analysis, we undertake to
provide the conditions in which it can be conducted. The analytic setting
has been often described. I want to mention here, however, that the analyst's
attitude is an essential part of this setting. If we accept that insight is by itself

the main curative factor, we must provide that the analyst shall do nothing to blur the development of the transference; he should be there as a person whose sole function is to understand sympathetically and to communicate to the patient such relevant knowledge as he has acquired, at the moment when the analysand is most ready to understand it. This is a part of the setting.

Of course, the statement that insight is at the root of all lasting therapeutic change begs the whole question. How do therapeutic changes result from insight? What is the answer to those who say, "I understand it all, but it doesn't help"? I shall put forward for your consideration two points which I hope to substantiate later and which are interdependent. First, insight is therapeutic because it leads to the regaining and reintegration of lost parts of the ego, allowing therefore a normal growth of personality. The reintegration of the ego is inevitably accompanied by a more correct perception of reality. Second, insight is therapeutic because knowledge replaces omnipotence and therefore enables a person to deal with his own feelings and the external world in more realistic terms.

Having a better knowledge of oneself and the world is no guarantee of happiness and success, but it leads to a fuller use of potentialities external and internal. I think that what I said implies a definition of what I understand by "cure." Cure does not mean conformity with any stereotyped pattern of normality prejudged by the analyst. It means restoring to the patient access to the resources of his own personality, including the capacity to assess correctly internal and external reality. These conditions are necessary, and, I think, also sufficient, for another aspect of cure, namely, better object relationships.

I should like at this stage to illustrate with clinical material some of the changes occurring in ego structure and object relationships following the experience of insight.

The patient, a young lawyer, started the session by complaining about his weakness when faced with demands; he found it difficult to be on time, but when he was late it was never his own fault, it was always because some other person made a last minute demand which he could not resist. This reminded him of a dream he had had that night. "His whole apartment was invaded by crowds and crowds of smokers. They smoked and drank all over the place. They made his place dirty and untidy, they wanted his company and made constant demands on him. Suddenly he became aware that in his waiting room there was a client to whom he had given an appointment and he was going to be late. He started shooing the smokers away, trying to put his place in order and to see his client. Then his wife appeared and told him that she had been to his analytic session instead of him, since it was clear that he could not get rid of the smokers in time both to see his client and his analyst. He then felt very depressed.

The patient had rich associations to the dream, but with one glaring omission. He made no reference to the fact that his analyst is a heavy smoker. In the dream the analyst is split into an external ideal object out of his reach, and the internal greedy, dirty smokers, who invade and weaken his ego, represented by his apartment. Most of his associations dealt with his feeling that the smokers and drinkers represented a greedy, destructive, dirty part of himself. This part was first projected into the analyst, who mostly represented his mother, always felt by the patient as dirty, and then, since the persecution in the transference was felt as unbearable, further transferred and dispersed into many objects in the external world. As a result, the patient felt prey to constant minor persecutions in his environment. He could not establish a fruitful relationship with the analyst, since he had to split off and deny the persecution, and his ego was weakened by projection and dispersal. The analysis of this dream and many similar situations enabled the patient gradually to own more and more of the greedy and destructive part of himself. This led to his establishing a more real relationship with his analyst, a lessening of the persecution and a strengthening and development of his ego. He realized, for instance, how important it was to own again his greed and aggression, since in projecting them he also deprived himself of his appetite for good things and his capacity to fight for them.

The same patient felt puzzled at times as to why he felt so much better after long and painful stretches of his analysis, which showed both his parents and himself in a very bad light and often induced a feeling of total hopelessness, when he felt that both his constitution and his environment were bad and inadequate. He came to the conclusion that the relief was due to two things. (1) He felt himself more whole. He found that he had a continuity from the past to the present, instead of feeling that he lived from moment to moment, in his own words "all disjointed." (2) He felt that he was less anxious. There seemed to be less danger lurking in his past and in his unconscious, now that he knew more and felt that he could tolerate more. He realized that integration of lost experiences, whatever they were, brought about strengthening of his ego.

At this point I would like to mention the importance of integrating split-off early envy. Melanie Klein drew attention to the particularly devastating effects of envy in relation to the original object. Since envy through attacking the good object spoils the very source of gratification, it interferes from the start with the introjection of a gratifying object. This object would otherwise become part of the ego, and the benevolent and helpful part of the superego. The violent defenses against envy are equally damaging. For instance, devaluation, which both defends against envy and expresses it, spoils all good experiences. Since envy is rooted in admiration and received gratification, the analysis of these defenses and the conscious experience of envy may again establish the object as enviable and, therefore admirable, and again mobilize feelings of gratification which have been denied. Conflict between love and gratitude and envy can be experienced anew in a more favorable setting.

Another defense of great importance is excessive idealization leading to a vicious circle. To defend against an experience of envy, the patient may idealize his object excessively. This, however, leads to an increase of unconscious envy and therefore to an increased need for idealization. The patient's feeling of inferiority and his unconscious envy become more intense. Analysis of these defenses lessens the idealization and therefore the envy, and when the tremendous gap between the ego and the object is reduced, envy becomes more tolerable and may give rise to more normal feelings of admiration, emulation, and rivalry. Also, when envy is diminished, a good object can be introjected, increasing the feeling of value in the ego and establishing a more benevolent circle.

We often observe, when we pay careful attention to the fluctuations in the patient's phantasies and the transference, that what is lost in the course of development is not only bad experiences but also good ones. Good objects may be denied and repressed as a defense against feelings of guilt and loss. Good parts of the self may be projected for a variety of reasons, such as the need to repair damage done by projection, which has to be followed by an equally projective and self-destroying reparation; or good parts of the self may be projected to safeguard them against conflict with bad parts which are felt to be stronger. The recovery of these parts is, of course, essential to the restoration of the damaged ego of the patient. This, I think, is particularly important in the case of the borderline psychotic and the psychopath. I should like to illustrate this point.

The patient in question suffered from severe feelings of inferiority, weakness, and depletion, alternating with manic omnipotence and self-aggrandizement. He was almost always a prey to suspicion, bordering on delusion; for several weeks he had been particularly suspicious that his wife was poisoning his food and damaging their baby son. These persecutions were brought into the transference. Upon analysis in one session the patient clearly felt that it was he himself who was dangerous and poisonous to his wife and child and to the analyst and to her food and baby as represented by the analysis. In the next session he came in a very different mood. He stated that his baby was not well at night and cried, but he did not get up. It was always his wife who got up at night and gave the child love and care. He extolled the virtues of his wife and of the analyst, who gave him so much care and patience. Then he added in a very derisive voice, "Whenever I say bad things about my wife or you, it is interpreted that they represent bad parts of myself, so I suppose all the good things I say about you and her are good parts of myself, which I can only see in others." He was extremely resistant when it was shown to him that it was indeed so. The reason for the projection was that, having admitted his own murderous impulses, he could not then admit the good parts of himself, since this would lead to what he was particularly avoiding: conflict, guilt, and the necessity for work. Thus, he generally left all the work to his wife and his analyst, establishing them as ideal objects and leaving himself wholly bad and depleted. This, however, immediately led to a vicious circle. Later in the session, he thought with fury that he had given his wife a present of some of his shares, which turned out to be the best of the lot. He felt himself robbed by her. He also accused the analyst of robbing him of his self-confidence. The excessive idealization led to a feeling of being persecuted by his ideal objects. It led to an increase of hatred and fury and further attacks which turned his ideal objects again into persecutors. It needed a very prolonged analysis to enable this patient to regain and tolerate in himself some of his own good feelings and qualities. When this was achieved a more benign circle could be formed, in which, feeling less valueless himself, he was also less envious and could better tolerate the good qualities of his objects and introject them. He thereby gained increasingly the feeling of value in himself.

I have given two very simple examples of loss through projection of parts of the ego that are felt to be bad or good. In a more psychotic patient, the damage is more extensive. The patient succeeds in disintegrating his ego, including his perceptual apparatus, in the way described by Bion.

In the measure in which the patient's splitting and projections can be analyzed and the patient recovers lost parts of his personality, he is increasingly exposed to reliving in the transference his original conflicts. As he approaches the re-experiencing of real depressive anxiety, all his omnipotence will be mobilized to prevent this experience. Insofar as he is able with the help of the analyst to live through this experience and allow it to become conscious, far-reaching changes will happen in the structure of his ego and his orientation toward objects. I shall illustrate these changes by giving in greater detail some material which was crucial in the analysis of a little girl of four and a half, and which I think illustrates vividly various steps in development that happen interdependently and simultaneously when insight can be acquired and tolerated. The changes which I shall illustrate are: the replacing of denial by acceptance of phychic reality; acceptance of conflict, ambivalence, and guilt; the replacing of omnipotence by a realistic attitude to the task at hand (particularly being able to use the analyst's help realistically); the lessening of persecutory anxiety and aggression, and the increase of love and confidence in the self and in others, acting out giving way to symbolization and symptom to sublimation; the acceptance and use of verbal thinking and communication.

Preceding my vacation which represented to the child the parental intercourse and the mother's pregnancy, Anne became very aggressive. In her play, the box of paints came to represent primarily the mother's breast, and the drawer with the toys the mother's body full of babies. She would make a mess of the paints and "drown" all the toys in the drawer. The gist of her activity represented a destruction of her mother's breast, changing the milk into poisonous urine, tearing the breast and changing it into bad feces, which she would then use to attack the inside of her mother's body. This was not a game but a furious uncontrollable acting in. There was no pleasure in her activity, and toys were smashed and destroyed. It was accompanied by a relentless attack on my words, which would be drowned in shrieking or torn to bits by her dividing them into syllables which she would then chant and turn into nonsense. After about a week of this activity and the analysis of it, she calmed down and produced a drawing which showed clearly that she was treating my words as mother's food, changing them into feces which were then used as weapons. She also confirmed it verbally.

Following her acceptance of this interpretation and a further verbal confirmation on her part of interpretations relating to her attacks on her mother's body, her mood changed, and the next session was devoted to a manic omnipotent attempt to repair the paint-box by magic. She wanted it to be "mended very quickly and made exactly as it was before." There was a complete lack of any realistic or constructive approach to this task. She was chanting, "eezy, beezy, let's get busy," which she called her "magic," and she was violently pushing my hands around to do the mending. She used my hands as a part-object (primarily the father's penis), controlling me and shouting at me. Occasionally she would shut her eyes, pretending to go to sleep, and open them suddenly, hoping to see the paint-box repaired. Her excitement was rising all the time, and behind the excitement, desperate anxiety. She was obviously hating and dreading the paint-box which remained damaged, and me, whom she could not effectively control to repair it the way she wanted it repaired.

This reparation had to be magic, omnipotent, and immediate, because it was a defense against insight. The box had to be made immediately exactly as it had been before, so that at no time should she experience anxiety, loss, and guilt about what she had done. Her attacks on my interpretation became still more furious. The interpretations, since they brought insight, were felt as a persecution and an interference with her reparation, for reparation was aimed at avoiding insight. It was only toward the end of the session that she could tolerate a complete interpretation relating her reparative activities to her attacks in the previous sessions and to my holidays, and an interpretation about her hatred of verbal communications as bringing awareness of the experience. She then calmed down and left the session quietly.

The next session, which I shall report in some detail, was a turning point in her analysis, and I believe it illustrates some of the therapeutic changes achieved through the analysis of her manic defenses. As soon as she came into the room, she opened the paint-box and said with a little sigh, "Isn't it a pity it is so spoiled—let's try and mend it together." She did not insist on either the speed or the completeness of reparation. With a little white powder and water, and some paint that was still left over, we managed to restore the box sufficiently to use if for another day. She then moved to the table to do some painting, and took some crayons to make up for the inadequacy of the paints. She asked for my help in the drawing, and painted a house with a pointed roof inside a bigger house. She said it was Daddy inside Mummy. When I interpreted that it represented Daddy restoring Mummy and giving her new babies, she turned the paper over, showed that it was covered with a brown mess of paint, and said with a mock sigh, "It's all a mess again." She spent a good part of the session representing in various ways the parental couple and her fecal attacks on their intercourse, and symbolically attacking me by dropping wood shavings on my lap and then cleaning me carefully. Several times she said, "Oh dear, I've done it again. We have got to do the cleaning again and again." In contrast to the prior sessions there was no real destruction of toys or attack on me. In this session the child did not act out. She played.

After a time, she painted a pattern and asked me to help her name the colors which she was trying to memorize. This pattern represented her internal world, and in her associations she, herself, linked it to the vacation and her wish to know what was going on inside her when I was away. She made clear in her associations that the colors represented her feelings and various internal objects. There was a full acknowledgment that the help she derived from the analysis was the "naming"—the verbalization which helped her to know, to differentiate, and therefore to feel more able to control her feelings and her internal objects.

I think that the following changes are shown in this session. Denial was replaced by insight. Her saying, "We have to do it again and again" is an acknowledgment not only of the aggression in the past or present, but also of her recognition of the psychic reality that, whenever the parents came together in intercourse, jealous and aggressive feelings would be aroused, and that, therefore, reparation was a difficult task. There was an acknowledgment that her aggression would be ever present, and that the battle against it cannot be won magically once and for all. At the same time she acknowledged that the recognition of psychic reality is a help and asked me to do the "naming." Instead of attacking verbal thought, which brings the pain of the recognition of psychic reality, she now wanted to use verbal thought to help her understand and control this reality. With this recognition of psychic reality and the abandoning of magic as a means of doing away with it, she could orient herself realistically to the actual mending of the box, accept the limitations of her ability to do reparation and use the analyst's help realistically, both in the mending of the box and in the analytic process. At the same time, the analyst and the parents became whole objects toward whom she could feel increasing love instead of being treated as part-objects whom she tried magically to control or to destroy.

The session concerned with magic reparation shows, I think, a point of fixation for what could have become an obsessional neurosis based on unresolved ambivalence and on magic obsessive reparation without insight. In the next session, though she said it had to be done "again and again," this referred to an acknowledgment of psychic reality. In fact, however, with the changes brought about by this insight, she could approach her reparation realistically; once the box was repaired, she had no need to go on repairing it and could use it for further activities like painting.

Freed of her obsessional need to restore magically her mother's body, she could also, for the first time in her analysis, move forward, in the next session, to a positive, instead of an inverted Oedipus complex. I do not wish to imply, of course, that the therapeutic result was brought about by the work done in this session. It was the result of work of many months. The structural changes achieved in her analysis allowed, after its termination, a normal growth of her personality.

The few examples I have given are meant to illustrate my thesis that insight experienced in the process of analysis leads to therapeutic changes. It enables the individual to regain parts of the self lost by projection, to correct distortions of external and internal reality, to face his conflicts and to use realistically his own resources and objects capable of helping him, in short, to work through his conflicts, instead of denying and endlessly repeating them. Insight brings about a restructuring and strengthening of the ego.

I am following here Melanie Klein's theory that infantile neurosis is a working through of infantile psychosis. In my view, all neurotic defenses are rooted in psychotic omnipotence, particularly the omnipotent denial of psychic reality, that is, conflict, ambivalence, and the attendant depressive anxiety. These defenses disturb both the growth of the ego and object relationships.

I have left to the last the problem of lifting repressions, which I mentioned at the beginning. I have done so because, in view of later discoveries, it seems to me that repression is a complex phenomenon, and its detailed consideration is beyond the scope of this paper. We say that a neurotic is ill because he represses too much; a psychotic, however, is ill because he is incapable of repression. What about the vast majority of our patients, the borderline cases? Do they repress too much or too little? I think that this quantitative approach could be usefully replaced by a qualitative one, distinguishing more precisely between normal and pathological repression.

Freud has described repression as a mechanism of defense that appears late in development and is related to the genital phase. I want to suggest here that repression used by a healthy ego, well-integrated after the working through of the depressive position, is not a pathological process and is not conducive to symptom formation. Indeed, under such normal conditions, the repressive barrier becomes a dynamic layer between the unconscious and the conscious, in which symbol formation occurs. Thus, the unconscious part is not cut off from the conscious but in a state of constant communication and symbolic working through. This gives richness to our conscious life and leads to sublimation. Pathological repression, responsible for symptom formation, is qualitatively different. It is based on an earlier split, in which parts of the self have been split off and never integrated with the rest. "The return of the repressed," described by Freud, is the return of the pathologically repressed. It is a breakthrough of the split-off parts of the ego, objects and impulses, still under the sway of psychotic mechanisms, using psychotic concrete thinking and related to reality in a psychotic, magic, omnipotent way. The lifting of the pathological repression involves, therefore, the analysis of psychotic processes, even in the neurotic patient.

The psychoanalytic insight which initiates therapeutic changes is different from insight in any other situation. It is different, for instance, from the insight possessed by the artist or the ordinary well-integrated, intuitive person. It involves conscious knowledge of archaic processes, normally inaccessible to the most intuitive person, through reliving in the transference the very processes that structured one's internal world and conditioned one's perceptions. The insight itself is a constant new factor in the process, and it is always dynamically altering. For instance, the moment the patient realizes how he has split himself, he is already integrating. When sufficiently worked through and integrated, the structural changes remain stable.

After the completion of an analysis, the patient does not usually retain insight in the way in which it is experienced in the analysis. It can undergo normal repression. In that sense, one could speak of unconscious insight, though it sounds self-contradictory. Such unconscious insight remains under repression but is accessible to the ego like other experiences under normal repression.

The patient, after the completion of his analysis, is usually insightful only in the non-analytic sense. He has a good knowledge of himself, good relations to others; and the unconscious parts of his personality, including his unconscious insight, remain in constant and free communication with the conscious through the dynamic and fluctuating layer in which repression and symbol formation operate.

Postscript 1979:
The Curative Factors in Psychoanalysis

This paper is somewhat one-sided, concentrating as it does on the importance of insight. It was part of a symposium in which the two other contributors put an emphasis on "corrective experience," the analyst's love of the patient, and "therapeutic alliance." Do I think that analysis is a corrective experience? Of course it is. Projecting parts of one's self or one's internal objects into the analyst, who does not identify with those projections and does not react to them, is a corrective experience. However, the term "corrective experience" has become attached to a particular technique in which the analyst tries to be a good object to the patient rather than to make the patient aware as to why he is experienced in a particular way. And this is a technique which, to my mind, interferes with the psychoanalytic process and the acquiring of insight. Similarly, with love, I think that the analyst must have a deep positive relation to the patient, but that there are appropriate ways of expressing love. It is inappropriate for a parent to express sexual love. It is inappropriate for the analyst to manifest sexual or parental love. The appropriate expression of love by the analyst is understanding.

The same is true of the concept of the "therapeutic alliance." Of course there must be a therapeutic alliance between the analyst and that part of the patient's ego which is capable of cooperating. It used to be called simply cooperation. But again, the term "therapeutic alliance" came to be associated with a particular technique in which the patient's cooperation is obtained by means of reinforcing the positive transference and excluding, to begin with, the interpretation of negative transferences. In Psycho-Analysis of Children, Melanie Klein (1932) describes very vividly how the child's cooperation immediately increases when an interpretation relieves anxiety. I think that the therapeutic alliance is gradually forged between patient and analyst as a function of the diminishing anxiety and of the insight obtained.

Had time been available, I would have expanded the one original part of this paper, that concerning the difference between well-functioning repression and pathological repression. Normal repression is an outcome of the working through of the depressive position and is linked with creative symbolism, as I suggested in Chapter 4. Pathological repression denotes the failure of that process. I would also have liked to expand the point on insight after analysis. I think my view that pathological repression is replaced by normal repression and that the ex-patient is insightful mostly in a nonpsychoanalytic sense was correct. But I would add that, when needed, he should be able to regain psychoanalytic insight and subject himself to psychoanalytic scrutiny.

The psychoanalyst's insight, after the end of his own analysis, is different. He has to retain as much as possible of true psychoanalytic insight and keep himself constantly under psychoanalytic scrutiny.

Reference

Klein, M. (1932). *The Psycho-Analysis of Children*. London: Hogarth.

6

Countertransference

As ANALYSIS DEVELOPED, transference, at first considered a major obstacle in treatment, came to be seen as the fulcrum on which the psychoanalytic situation rests. Similarly, countertransference, first seen as a neurotic disturbance in the psychoanalyst, preventing him from getting a clear and objective view of the patient, is now increasingly recognized as a most important source of information about the patient as well as a major element of the interaction between patient and analyst. In her pioneering paper on the subject, Paula Heimann (1950) drew attention to the fact that, though not recognized as such, countertransference had always been a guide in psychoanalytical work. She suggested that Freud's discovery of resistance was based on his countertransference, his feeling that he was meeting a resistant force in the patient. Once our attention is drawn to it, this view of countertransference seems almost obvious.

To take a single example, I had a patient who evoked in me a whole gamut of unpleasant feelings. It would have been very foolish of me to ignore these feelings or consider them my own neurotic reactions, since this patient's principal complaint was her terrible unpopularity. Obviously, the way she affected me was a function of her psychopathology—a function of utmost importance to her, and one which it is crucial for us to understand.

This view of countertransference as a function of the patient's personality is not universally accepted. It is still often contended that ideally countertransference should be eliminated, though it is recognized that in practice this might not be possible. On the other hand, the view of countertransference as an important part of the psychoanalytic process is widely recognized. The literature on the subject is far too vast to discuss in this short paper, but, to mention only a few, there are papers on the subject by Winnicott (1949), Money-Kyrle (1956), Leon Grinberg (1962), and a book by Heinrich Racker (1968). Many authors simply take countertransference for granted and describe the uses to which they put it as Bion (1967) does in his account of his work with psychotics.

Our changing views on countertransference are, in part, related to changes in our views on transference. Originally, the analyst was seen as a mirror *onto* which the patient projects his internal figures and to whom he then reacts. As Enid Balint put it succinctly in a paper read in the British Society, "We now have a more three-dimensional view of the transference." We do not think of the patient projecting *onto*, but rather *into* the analyst. This view assumes that transference is rooted in primitive preverbal infantile experience, and is consistent with the Kleinian concept of projective identification. We see the patient not only as perceiving the analyst in a distorted way, reacting to this distorted view, and communicating these reactions to the analyst, but also as doing things to the analyst's mind, projecting *into* the analyst in a way which affects the analyst.

We are all familiar with the concepts of acting in, which can happen in quite a gross way; I speak here, however, not of gross acting but of something constantly present—a nonverbal constant interaction in which the patient acts on the analyst's mind. This nonverbal activity takes many forms. It may be underlying and integrated with other forms of communication and give them depth and emotional resonance. It may be the predominant form of communication, coming from preverbal experiences which can only be communicated in that way. Or it may be meant as an attack on communication; though when understood, even this can be converted into communication. Of course, all communication contains elements of desire for action. We communicate in order to produce some effect on the other person's mind; but the degree to which action occurs, whether nonverbal or apparently verbal (using words to act rather than to communicate), varies enormously from situation to situation and patient to patient. As a general rule, the nearer we are to the psychotic processes, the more this kind of acting takes precedence over symbolic or verbal communication. If we look at transference in this way, it then becomes quite clear that what Freud describes as free-floating attention refers not only to intellectual openness of mind, but also to a particular openness of feelings—allowing our feelings, our mind to be affected by the patient to a far greater degree than we allow ourselves to be affected in normal social intercourse, a point stressed by Paula Heimann (1950).

By speaking of these free-floating feelings in the analyst am I saying that there is no difference between transference and countertransference? I hope I am not saying anything of the kind, because at the same time as the analyst is opening his mind freely to his impressions, he has to maintain distance from his own feelings and reactions to the patient. He has to observe his own reactions, to conclude from them, to use his own state of mind for the understanding of his patient but at no point be swayed by his own emotions. The analyst's capacity to contain the feelings aroused in him by the patient can be seen as an equivalent to the function of a mother containing the infant's projections, to use Bion's model (1967). Where the parents react instinctively, however, the analyst subjects his state of mind to an examination—a reflection, albeit, much of the time preconscious.

In the past we have thought of an ideal analyst as cold, objective, having no feelings, etc. Am I presenting here in the analyst's perfect containment, a similarly unattainable ideal? I think so. This would be an idealization of the analyst's capacity. In fact, this capacity for containment can be breached in many ways. There is a whole area of the patient's pathology (I am ignoring for the moment the analyst's pathology) which specifically aims at disrupting this situation of containment, such as: invasion of the analyst's mind in a seductive or aggressive way, creating confusion and anxiety, and attacking links in the analyst's mind. We have to try to turn this situation to good account and learn about the interaction between the patient and ourselves from the very fact that our containment has been disturbed. It is from such disturbances in the analyst's capacity to function that one first gets an inkling of such psychotic processes as, for instance, attacks on links, again a subject with vast literature.

There is a particular countertransference difficulty (described also by Grinberg [1962] as projective counter-identification) produced by some patients who, as infants, have been themselves subjected to heavy parental projections. I shall give an example here from the second session with a patient—a mild example of the kind of thing I have in mind. In the first session the patient had spoken about the various ways in which she felt she had been a great disappointment to her parents and to herself. In the next session, she seemed extremely depressed, spoke in a hardly audible voice and went on at fairly great length describing how terrible she felt. She was depressed, she felt dead, terribly weak, she had an awful headache, perhaps it was due to her period which was about to start. The session went on for a time and I felt unduly affected by it. I wondered if I had done something wrong in the previous session. I felt helpless and very eager to understand her. In answer to a question the patient said that, no, she did not usually have headaches with her periods, but her mother had that symptom. I knew that the patient at that point was identifying with her mother, but somehow this knowledge did not help, and I felt that there would not be much point in interpreting it to her. I was more puzzled by my own overreaction and slowly came to realize that now I felt that I was a disappointment both to her and to myself. I was in the position of a helpless and rather bewildered child, weighed down by projections coming from a depressed mother, and it was an interpretation emphasizing that aspect which produced a change in the situation.

Later on the patient related that she had perfect pitch, but that though she was trained and encouraged and apparently gifted enough to become a soloist, she could never do it and so had specialized as an accompanist. When she was a child, her mother sang and she used to accompany her on the piano. It seemed to me that this patient had developed perfect pitch for her mother's depression and found a way of getting on with her some of the time, but only as an accompanist. I also understood that my quite unwarranted concern in the second session that I did not understand my patient perfectly arose because, somehow, she managed to make me feel, right at the start, that I must now be the child with perfect pitch. I shall return to the problem of the perfect pitch. This situation can be compared and contrasted with a much more violent though similar one.

The patient mentioned earlier, who complained of unpopularity, was particularly able to disrupt my capacity to function. The experience of closeness with her has been an experience of almost unceasing discomfort or pain. She has evoked anxiety, confusion, guilt, anger, irritation; occasions on which I felt more relaxed were dangerous. I was immediately and unexpectedly assaulted in some way or other. Her stream of accusations was almost incessant. This patient is the child of parents who had hated one another at the time of her birth. So far as I can reconstruct, from infancy she was flooded with extreme anxiety by her mother (an anxiety neurotic) and with the hatred derivative of her mother's hatred for her father. The father, on the other hand, a near psychotic, flooded her with either aggressive accusations or gross sexuality. She described how after she was older and her parents divorced, her father would pour accusations and complaints about her mother at her and how, when she was with her mother, the mother on a few occasions pinned her to the armchair and made her listen to violent attacks on the father. This later situation probably reproduced what was originally a nonverbal but violent experience of projection from both parents. In the countertransference, it may be this experience that she tried to inflict on me, often with success. I frequently felt with her that I was pinned into my armchair and forced to listen to violent outpourings of accusation against some third person. I felt attacked; I did not want to hear them and could not defend myself against them. The experience is not that of a parent bombarded by infantile projections, but of an infant bombarded by overpowering projections, often beyond its understanding. This lends to the countertransference feelings of a particular kind of helplessness, and there is always a danger of reacting by withdrawal, omnipotence, hatred of the patient, etc.—in other words, of mobilizing our own infantile defenses against helplessness. We are all familiar of course with patients reversing roles and putting us in the position of a helpless child. But here I think is an infrequent added dimension. This patient is a borderline case, and her method of projecting infantile experiences into the analyst may be what protects her from psychosis.

The cases of these two patients may be compared and contrasted. From the "unpopular" patient it is exceedingly difficult to obtain any kind of nondestructive communication. In defending herself against projections, she projects violence and in turn experiences her objects as projecting it back in a vicious circle of increasing distress and violence. The first patient, the one with perfect pitch, had obviously developed some kind of satisfactory communication with her mother, albeit, one based on a split and at great cost to her own personality (becoming an accompanist).

But I knew her perfect pitch would cause other big problems. One was her expectation, projected into me, that I, too, should have perfect pitch (hence my discomfort in the second session). Another was the early indication of her perfect pitch in relation to me. In the third session she spotted some minor change in my expression—one unnoticed by other patients. If we think of the transference/countertransference situation as an interaction, we must take into account that the patient's perceptions of us are not all projections. Patients do, indeed, react to aspects of our personalities, changes of mood, etc., whether these are a direct response to their material or come from some other source, and patients with perfect pitch present a particular problem in that way. I think this perfect pitch is a function of the patient's dependence. It is the extremely dependent patient who develops an unusual sensitivity to the slightest change in the analyst's attitude. Usually, the pitch is only selectively perfect. We are all familiar with the misleading perfect pitch of the paranoid patient, who most correctly perceives anything negative and is totally blind to any evidence of positive attitudes, or with that of the depressive patient, who is most sensitive to any sign of weakness or illness. Be that as it may, one must be aware of the patient's pitch, or responsiveness to what comes from us, and not deny it in ourselves. I am not advocating here breast beating or confessions of countertransference, just awareness of the nature of the interaction and recognition of it in the interpretation.

Of course, all this is easier said than done. I have noticed that when people speak of transference they recognize that the major part of the transference is unconscious, while, when speaking of countertransference, they apparently speak as though countertransference referred only to the analyst's conscious feelings. Of course the major part of the countertransference, like the transference, is always unconscious. What we do become aware of are conscious derivatives. The way I visualize it is that at depth, when our countertransference is, say, in a good functional state, we have a double relation to the patient. One is receptive, containing and understanding the patient's communication; the other active, producing or giving understanding, knowledge, or structure to the patient in the interpretation. It might be analogous to the breast as containing and the nipple as feeding, or to the maternal/paternal functions. This does not exclude our own infantile experience, since our capacity to perceive and contain infantile parts of the patient depends on our capacity to contain the infant part of ourselves. We must not, however, equate that analytic function with the parental function. We give over part of our mind to this experience with the patient, but we also remain detached from it as professional analysts, using professional skills to assess the interaction between the patient and the parental parts of ourselves. In other words, we are deeply affected and involved but, paradoxically, uninvolved in a way unimaginable between an actual good parent and a child. When our countertransference works that way, it gives rise to a phenomenon called empathy or psychoanalytic intuition or feeling in touch. It is a guide to understanding. When breaches in this attitude occur, we become aware of disruption in our analytic functioning, and we must, in turn, try to understand the nature of the disruption and the information it gives us about our interaction with the patient. When such disruptions occur, there is always an internal pressure to identify with our countertransference, and it is very important to be aware that countertransference is the best of servants but the worst of masters, and that the pressure to identify with it and act it out in ways either obvious or very subtle and hidden is always powerful.

Countertransference has become a very abused concept and many analytic sins have been committed in its name. In particular, rationalizations are found for acting under the pressure of countertransference, rather than using it as a guide to understanding. I often find myself telling supervisees that countertransference is no excuse; saying that the patient "projected it into me," or "he made me angry" or "he put me under such seductive pressure" must be clearly recognized as statements of failure to understand and use the countertransference constructively. I do not contend here that we must, or indeed, can be perfect, merely that we will not learn from our failures unless we clearly recognize them as such.

References

Bion, W. R. (1967). *Second Thoughts.* London: Heinemann; New York: Jason Aronson, 1977.

Grinberg, L. (1962). On a specific aspect of countertransference due to the patient's projective identification. *International Journal of Psycho-Analysis* 43:436-440.

Heimann, P. (1950). On countertransference. *International Journal of Psycho-Analysis* 31:81-84.

Money-Kyrle, R. (1956). Normal countertransference and some of its deviations. *International Journal of Psycho-Analysis* 37:360-366.

Racker, H. (1968). *Transference and Countertransference.* London: Hogarth.

Winnicott, D. (1949). Hate in the countertransference. *International Journal of Psycho-Analysis* 30:69-74. In *Collected Papers*, pp. 194-203. New York: Basic Books, 1958.

7

The Function of Dreams

ERNEST JONES tells us that until the end of his life Freud considered *The Interpretation of Dreams* his most important work. This is not surprising. While his studies on hysteria revealed the meaning of symptoms, it was his work on dreams that opened up for him and us the understanding of the universal dream world and dream language. For the structure of the dream reflects the structure of personality. What follows is a brief review of the classical theory of dreams.

Repressed wishes find their fulfillment in the dream by means of indirect representation, displacement and condensation, and by the use of symbols. Freud put these symbols in a slightly different category from other means of indirect presentation. Dreamwork is the psychic work put into this process. By means of dreamwork a compromise is achieved between the repressing forces and the repressed, and the forbidden wish can find fulfillment without disturbing the repressing agencies. Freud did not revise the theory of dreams in the light of his further work. For instance, he did not tell us how his views on dreams were affected by his formulation of the duality of instincts and the conflict between libidinal and destructive phantasies. He also, at the time of his basic formulations about the dream, did not yet have available to him the concept of working through. I feel rather uneasy about the dream being conceived of as nothing but a compromise: the dream is not just an equivalent of a neurotic symptom. Dream-work is also part of the psychic work of working through. This accounts for the analyst's satisfaction when, in the course of analysis, "good" dreams appear.

The classical theory of dream function takes for granted an ego capable of adequate repression and of performing the psychic work of dreaming. To my mind this implies that the ego is capable of a certain amount of working through of internal problems. It also takes for granted the capacity for symbolization. Now, when we extend our psychoanalytical research we come across patients in whom these functions, on which dreaming depends, are disturbed or inadequate.

To begin with I shall say a few words about symbolization. Freud took the existence of symbols as given, universal, and, I think, unchangeable. This, of course, was particularly so before he broke with Jung and the Swiss school of analysts. In his paper on symbolism, Jones (1916) referred to the main break with the Swiss school. He implied, though he did not explicitly state, that symbolization involves psychic work connected with repression: "Only the repressed is symbolized—only the repressed needs to be sym-bolized." Melanie Klein (1930) made the next big step forward. In her paper on symbol formation she gave an account of the analysis of an autistic little boy who was incapable of forming or using symbols. In her view, symbol-ization occurs by a repression and displacement of interest in the mother's body so that objects in the external world are endowed with symbolic meaning. In the case of Dick, a phantasied, sadistic, and projective attack on his mother's body gave rise to a paralyzing degree of anxiety so that the process of symbolization came to a standstill and no symbol formation occurred. The child did not speak or play or form relationships. I investig-ated further those phenomena and described the psychic dynamics of the formation of what I call the symbolic equation or the concrete thinking characteristic of psychoses. I also described the symbol proper, which is suitable for purposes of sublimation and communication. Briefly stated, the theory is that when projective identification is in ascendance and the ego is identified and confused with the object, then the symbol, a creation of the ego, becomes identified and confused with the thing symbolized. The symbol and the object symbolized become the same, giving rise to concrete thinking. Only when separation and separateness are accepted and worked through does the symbol become a representation of the object, rather than being equated with the object. This, in my view, implies a full depressive elaboration, the symbol becoming a precipitate of a process of mourning. The disturbance of the relationship between the self and the object is reflected in a disturbance in the relationship between the self, the object symbolized, and the symbol. The terms *symbolic equation* and *symbol* are discussed more fully in chapter 8.

To Jones's "only what is repressed needs to be symbolized," I add "only what can be adequately mourned can be adequately symbolized." Thus, the capacity for nonconcrete symbol formation is in itself an achievement of the ego—an achievement necessary for the formation of the kind of dreams covered by Freud's theory.

We know that in the psychotic, the borderline, the psychopathic, dreams do not function in this way. In the acute psychotic there is often no distinction between hallucination and dream. Indeed, there is no clear distinction between states of being asleep or awake. Delusion, hallucination, nighttime events, which could go by the name of dreams, often have the same psychic value. In non-acute states, but when psychotic processes are in ascendance, dreams may be experienced as real and concrete events. Bion (1958) has reported a patient who was terrified by the appearance of his analyst in his dream, as he took it as evidence of having actually devoured the analyst. Dreams may be equated with feces and used for purposes of evacuation; or, when minute internal fragmentation occurs, they may be experienced as a stream of urine and the patient may react to having dreams as to incidents of incontinence (Bion 1957). A patient can use dreams for getting rid of, rather than working through, unwanted parts of the self and objects and he can use them in analysis for projective identification. We are all familiar with patients who come and flood us, fill us with dreams in a way disruptive to the relationship and to the analysis.

I had the opportunity of observing this type of functioning of dreams in two borderline psychotic patients, both of whom dreamed profusely, but in whom it was the function rather than the content of the dreams to which attention had to be paid. In these patients, dreams were often experienced as concrete happenings. This was particularly clear with my woman patient. This woman, who was very quarrelsome in a paranoid way, would bring a dream in which she was attacked by X or Y, or sometimes by myself. If I attempted to understand some aspect of the dream, she would say indignantly, "But it is X or Y or you who have attacked me," treating the event in the dream as a completely real event. There was apparently no awareness that *she dreamed* the dream. Similarly, an erotic dream in which, say, a man pursued her, was felt as virtual proof of his love. In fact, her dreams, although she called them dreams, were not dreams to her but realities. In this they paralleled another mental phenomenon in her life, in which she used a similarly misleading word. She experienced weird and bizarre sexual phantasies and freely spoke of them as "phantasies," but if one enquired into them more closely, it became apparent that these were not phantasies but hallucinations. They were felt as real experiences. For instance, she walked very awkwardly because she felt she had a penis stuck in her vagina. When she imagined having a relationship with someone, she used the word *phantasy* but in fact believed and behaved as if it were a reality. For example, she accused me of being jealous of her sexual life, of ruining her relationships, when in fact she had no sexual life or relationships. So what she called "phantasy" and what she called "a dream" were in fact experienced as a reality, though she weakly denied it. These so-called dreams constantly invaded the external reality situation. For instance, she would complain about the smell of gas in my room and it would transpire later that she dreamed of bursting a balloon or exploding a bomb. The evacuation that occurred in the dream seemed to invade the perception of the reality.

These concretized dreams lend themselves particularly to purposes of expulsion. This was especially clear in my male patient who used to write his dreams, in extenso, in a little notebook. He had volumes and volumes of them. For instance: following his mother's death he had dreams of triumph over her, aggression, guilt, and loss, but in his conscious life the mourning for his mother was conspicuous by its absence. Such interpretations as "You have got rid of your feelings for your mother in your dream" were more effective in bringing about some conscious experience of his affect than was any detailed analysis of the dream. He was using the dream to get rid of that part of his mind which was giving him pain; he discharged it into his notebook. He dealt similarly with insight. An insightful session was often followed by a dream which seemed closely related to it. In other patients this kind of dream is usually a step in the working through. In his case, however, such a dream more often than not meant that he got rid of all feelings about the previous session by making it into a dream and ridding his mind of it.

Similarly, in the woman patient the dream was part of an expulsive process. For instance, when she complained about the smell of gas in my room, she expelled the gas into the room.

The dreams of both patients were characterized by very poor and crude symbolization. I was struck both by the concreteness of the experience and the invasion of reality, as though there was no difference between their mind and the outside world. They had no internal mental sphere in which the dream could be contained. Elaborating on Winnicott's concept of transitional space, Khan (1972) described it in terms of dream space. In this regard, I found most helpful Bion's model (1963) of mental functioning, particularly, his concept of the alpha and beta elements and of a mother capable of containing projective identification.

Bion has distinguished between alpha and beta elements of mental functioning. Beta elements are raw perceptions and emotions suitable only for projective identification. These raw elements of experience are to be gotten rid of. Beta elements are transformed by the alpha function into alpha elements. Those are elements which can be stored in memory, which can be repressed and worked through. They are suitable for symbolization and formation of dream thoughts. It is the beta elements which can become bizarre objects or concrete symbols in my sense of the word. I think they are elements of the psychotic-type dream; alpha elements are the material of the neurotic and normal dream. Alpha function is also linked with mental space. In Bion's model, the infant's first mode of functioning is by projective identification. This is an elaboration on Freud's idea of the original deflection of the death instinct and Klein's concept of projective identification. The infant deals with discomfort and anxiety by projecting it into the mother. This is not only a phantasy operation. A good mother responds to the infant's anxiety. A mother capable of containing projective identifications can transform the projections in her own unconscious and respond appropriately, thereby lessening the anxiety and giving meaning to it. In this situation, the infant introjects the maternal object as a container capable of containing anxiety, conflict, etc. and elaborating it meaningfully. This internalized container provides a mental space and in this space alpha function can be performed. Another way of looking at it would be that it is in this container, in which alpha functioning can occur, that primary processes begin to be elaborated into secondary ones. The failure of the container and alpha functioning results in the inability to perform the dreamwork and, therefore, the appearance of psychotic, including concrete, dreams.

I would like to give an example which shows vividly, I think, the function of dreaming and its failure, resulting in concretisation. The material comes from an unusually gifted and able man who has a constant struggle with psychotic parts of his personality. We ended a Friday session with the patient expressing enormous relief and telling me that everything in that session had a good resonance in him. On Monday, he came to his session very disturbed. He said he had a very good afternoon's work on Friday and Saturday morning, but he had a dream on Saturday which had disturbed him very much. In the first part of the dream, he was with Mrs. Small. She was in bed and he was either teaching or treating her. There was also a little girl (here he became rather evasive)—well, maybe a young girl. She was very pleasant with him, maybe a little sexy. And then quite suddenly someone removed a food trolley and a big cello from the room. He woke up frightened. He said it was not the first part of the dream that frightened him but the second. He felt it had something to do with a loss of internal structure. On Sunday he could still work, but he felt his work lacked depth and resonance and he felt something was going very wrong. In the middle of Sunday night, he woke up with a dream, but he could not hold on to it and instead became aware of a backache low in his back—maybe the small of his back.

He said the Mrs. Small part of the dream did not disturb him because he could quickly see through it. In the past, Mrs. Small, whom he does not think much of, represented a belittling of Mrs. Klein(klein=small). He understood that and supposed she represented me changed into a patient and also into a sexy little girl. He supposed it was an envious attack, because on Friday he felt so helped by me. He then had some associations to the cello—his niece had one, his admiration for Casals and a few others—which led me to suggest tentatively that it seemed to be a very bisexual instrument. That interpretation fell rather flat. What struck him more, he said, was that it is one of the biggest musical instruments around. He then said that I had a very deep voice, and that another thing that frightened him was that when he woke up from the dream he could not remember what we were talking about in the session.

It seems to me that the whole situation, which in the first night was represented by the dream, in the second night happened concretely. By changing me into Mrs. Small, he had lost me as the internalized organ with deep resonance. The cello represented the mother with deep resonance, the mother who could contain the patient's projections and give a good resonance; with the loss of this organ, there was an immediate concretiza- tion of the situation. In his dream on Saturday night, he belittled me by changing me into Mrs. Small. This led to the loss of the cello: "one of the biggest musical instruments around." He woke up anxious. The function of the dream to contain and elaborate anxiety began to fail. The next night, instead of a dream, he had a pain in the small of his back. Hypochondriasis, much lessened now, had at one time been a leading psychotic-flavored symptom. The attack on the containing functions of the analyst, repre- sented as the organ with the resonance, resulted in the patient's losing his own resonance (his depth of understanding) and his memory (he could not remember the session.) When this happened, he could only experience concrete physical symptoms. The belittled analyst, who in the dream was represented by Mrs. Small, became a concrete pain in the small of his back.

My attention has been drawn recently to a borderline phenomenon exhibited markedly by the two borderline patients mentioned earlier. They both frequently presented what I have come to think of as predictive dreams. That is, their dreams predicted their action, and what had been dreamed had to be acted out. Of course, up to a point, all dreams are acted out, as the dream expresses problems and solutions carried out also by similar means in life, but in these patients the acting out of the dream was extraordinarily literal and carried out in complete detail. For instance, my male patient was often late and, not surprisingly, often dreamed of being late. What drew my attention to the predictive character of his dreams was the extraordinary precision with which a dream predicted his lateness to the minute. He would come two, six, or forty-five minutes late and give me a reason plausible to him, but later in the session he would report a dream in which he was late for a meal or a meeting for exactly the number of minutes which he actually was late on that day. I do not think it was a post hoc interpretation he put on his dreams since he wrote them down carefully first thing in the morning. I also became aware that a Thursday or Friday dream containing plans for acting out over the weekend was by no means a dream substituting for acting out, but often was carried out in precise detail. This, of course, could have been a failure of my analysis of the dream preceding the weekend. Other patients sometimes bring a similar plan for acting out in order to warn the analyst and get help; effective analysis then obviates the need to act out. But I have a feeling that there was something so powerfully automatic in this patient's compulsion to act out the dream that analysis seldom moved it. Often he would not report the dream until after the weekend.

In the woman patient, these predictive dreams relate particularly to paranoid dramas. There was a kind of row with which I had become familiar, that was characterized by an extraordinary automatic progression, apparently totally unaffected by my response. The session could go something like this: She would say in an accusing voice, "You frowned at me." There were any number of responses that I tried at different times. For instance, I could interpret, "You are afraid that I am frowning at you because you slammed the door yesterday." Or I could ask, "What do you think I am frowning about?" Here she might answer, "You frowned at me because I slammed the door." Or I could be silent and wait for develop-ments, but my silence would be taken as a confirmation that I was terribly angry with her. Then it would be, "Not only do you frown, but now you are silent, which is worse." I never said "I did not frown," but I did try pointing out to her that it did not occur to her that she might have been mistaken in her perception. This could only make it worse, because now not only did I frown, but I accused her of being mad. In either case, I had a feeling that my response was completely irrelevant and the quarrel, in which certain roles were assigned me, would continue in a completely automatic fashion. At some point, however, usually when an interpretation touched on some fundamental anxiety, she would tell me a dream. Then it would appear that the row we were supposed to be having in the session was an almost word-for-word repetition of the row she actually had in the dream, either with me or her mother or father or some thinly veiled transference figure, such as a teacher. This response to an interpretation—telling me a dream— only happened, however, when the row had run its course, at least for a time. The other similar interpretation, given earlier in the session, would be ignored or woven into the row. Now, I have come to recognize the particular feeling in the countertransference. It is like being a puppet caught in someone else's nightmare and totally unable to do anything but play the allotted role, usually that of the persecutor. So later, when the row would begin in this particular way, I would sometimes simply say, "You have had a quarrel with me or someone like me in the dream" and sometimes this would obviate her need to act out in the session. It is as if in the predictive dreams of both patients, functioned as what Bion (1963) called a "definatory hypoth-esis." They defined in detail how the session was to unfold.

I was wondering in what ways the predictive dreams differed from the evacuative dreams, whether of the kind I described in my male patient, or the kind that the woman patient experienced, which then spilled over, as it were, into reality. I think they are somewhat different. I think that the evacuating dream actually evacutes something successfully from the pa-tient's inner perception. Thus, after my patient dreamed of mourning his mother, he did not need to mourn her. The predictive dreams, however, seem to be dreams which do not entirely succeed in the evacuation, and they seem to remain in the patient's psyche like a bad object, which the patient then has to dispose of by acting the dream out. The evacuation does not seem to be completed until the dream has been both dreamed *and* acted out. This was very marked with the woman patient. Going through the row, telling me the dream, getting the interpretation gave her enormous relief, but I was seldom convinced that the relief was actually due to an acquired insight. It seemed rather to be due to a feeling of completed evacuation.

In conclusion: We can say that we are far from having exhausted the possibilities of understanding the world of dreams opened up by Freud, but our attention is increasingly drawn to the form and function of dreaming rather than to the dream content. It is the form and the function which reflects and helps illuminate the disturbances in the functioning of the ego.

References

Bion, W. R. (1957). Differentiation of the psychotic from the non-psychotic personalities. *International Journal of Psycho-Analysis* 38:266-275. In W. R. Bion, *Second Thoughts.* New York: Jason Aronson, 1977.

——— (1958). On hallucination. *International Journal of Psycho-Analysis* 39:341-349. In W. R. Bion, *Second Thoughts.* New York: Jason Aronson, 1977.

——— (1963). *Elements of Psycho-Analysis.* London: Heinemann Medical Books. In W. R. Bion, *Seven Servants.* New York: Jason Aronson, 1977.

Jones, E. (1916). The theory of symbolism. In E. Jones, *Papers on Psycho-Analysis.* 2nd ed. London: Ballière, Tindall and Cox. 1918.

Khan, M. (1972). The use and abuse of dreams. *International Journal of Psychotherapy 1.*

Klein, M. (1930). The importance of symbol-formation in the development of the ego. *International Journal of Psycho-Analysis* 11:24-39. In M. Klein, *Contributions to Psycho-Analysis 1921-1945*, pp. 236-250. London: Hogarth, 1948.

PART IV

SCHIZOPHRENIA AND SCHIZOID MECHANISMS

8

Some Aspects of the Analysis of a Schizophrenic

IN RECENT YEARS[1] an increasing number of psychoanalysts have begun to treat schizophrenic patients psychoanalytically, using various modifications of technique. I think that the case I describe will be of interest since I have attempted to analyze a typical schizophrenic—with no doubt about his diagnosis—with only minor deviations from strict analytic technique. I took special care not to step out of the role of the analyst who interprets into that of an ally or an educator.

Edward was a diffident, over-sensitive child and adolescent. Very intellectual and over-ambitious, he was superficially well adapted to his surroundings but, in fact, completely withdrawn and secretive to the point of obsession. As a child, he was already interested in biology and centered on it all his infantile sexual curiosity and his intellectual interests. He found another outlet for his emotions in daydreams, usually about idealized girls, the princesses whom he was going to win over from a terrible father or rival. At school he got along quite well. Somehow his personality seemed to fit the requirements of the old-fashioned public school. His difficulties went unnoticed by himself as well as by his teachers and schoolfellows. Within the limited field of his interests he was quite brilliant and won a scholarship to a famous college, first among hundreds.

---

1. This paper was published in 1950.

When at the age of eighteen and a half he was called up, things became much more difficult. He was sent to India and went to an Engineers' OCTU but could not cope with the training. He said he was very good at blowing mines, but no good at all at building bridges. He failed to get his commission and was referred for six months. Then he started to worry obsessionally about whether he should remain at the OCTU or resign in the hope of getting released sooner and being able to resume his studies. He became anxious, brooding, and showed signs of an approaching breakdown. Eventually, he resigned impulsively when an officer called him a fool. But he could not bear being a private. He felt that he had lost control and was imprisoned. He admitted to an overt sexual jealousy of officers; he felt that a private did not stand a chance with girls. He became hypochondriacal and suspicious.

After a few months he was asked to work in a photographic laboratory, in a darkroom, and that seems to have precipitated a complete breakdown. The breakdown began with worry about his eyes going wrong. Then ever-growing delusions appeared. These concerned Chinese plots to take power in India, a biologist wanting to destroy the whole world and so on. He had his first aural hallucinations. At last he wrote a letter to his Colonel denouncing the biologist who wanted to destroy the world, and this led to his being put in a mental hospital.

There he seems to have gone to pieces completely. In his memories, the six months he spent in the various military hospitals were a horrifying jumble of delusions, nightmares, hallucinations, complete loss of feeling of identity, sense of time and place or any continuity in himself or in the world.

In the hospital notes, I found little beyond brief descriptions of his being hallucinated, deluded, irrelevant, impulsive, etc. I know that he had two series of phrenosol injections which brought no improvement and that he had been diagnosed at different stages as either a hebephrenic or paranoid schizophrenic. When he returned to England he had been examined by an eminent psychoanalytic psychiatrist who diagnosed a rapidly deteriorating schizophrenia. All psychiatric reports noted a poor prognosis.

Since my emphasis is not on the differential diagnosis I should like to stress that no diagnosis other than that of schizophrenia was ever suggested. Further, my account of this analysis may be misleading. It is most important, especially when dealing with a schizophrenic, to link up phantasies with real events present and past, but I have had to avoid many references which might have revealed too much of the patient's background. Also, as a result of the necessary compression of material, it may seem that the patient was very talkative, when, in fact, he was generally silent, except early in the treatment when he would occasionally become over-excited.

I saw Edward for the first time at a short interview in the military hospital. He was completely withdrawn, apathetic, with retarded movements and a half-placating, half-foolish smile that was out of keeping with what he spoke about. He was kept in bed because of aimless wandering and impulsiveness while in the ward. His only spontaneous contribution to the conversation was to ask me if London was all right, because India had become completely altered. I did not answer the question, but suggested that he felt that he himself had changed and the world was changing with him. "Yes," he said, adding with emphasis, "I have been changed."

These two sentences gave me the first intimation of some of his problems. (1) He was afraid that the world was being destroyed. (2) He put a persecutory interpretation on what had befallen him (he had not changed, he had been changed). (3) He seemed unable to distinguish between himself and the world; his own destruction was felt to be equivalent to the destruction of the whole world. The lack of distinction between himself and "everybody" or "everything," together with the emphasis on change, remained characteristic of his attitude throughout the acute stage of his illness. Edward would say to me one day, "Everything is being changed around. The hospital is quite changed," and I would find out from his medical officer that some small alteration had been made in his room. Or he would come into the room coughing and say, "Everybody is coughing today," on a day when another patient was taken to the sanatorium with T.B. When he had hallucinations, he felt that the voices he heard were ubiquitous. He would say, "All prisoners hear voices," or, speaking of shock treatment, "The doctors were so maddened by voices that they tried to stop them by killing the poor patients." Obviously, Edward felt that his own hallucinations were in everybody's mind. At times the boundary between the internal and external world seemed completely obliterated.

After a few days in the military hospital Edward's parents obtained his transfer to a private nursing home where I started a regular analysis of five hours a week. In the first session Edward showed no surprise at seeing me. He was excited, elated and showed flight of ideas. He told me, in a disconnected way, about the terrifying things done to him in the hospitals by the mad doctors and about the necessity of his being allowed out of this prison immediately. He hoped I would help him to get out. There was no question, at this point, of asking him to lie down on the couch or of explaining to him the nature of the treatment.

I did not interpret any of his delusions or hallucinations then but pointed out how cut off and misunderstood he felt. I selected this interpretation because it was obvious that, though Edward was talking to me, I meant no more to him than a piece of furniture; his isolation was complete. Then he looked at me in a different way and said that all the prisoners felt like that and that prisoners in Germany sent him voices. On my suggesting that being in the hospital was like being a prisoner, and being like a prisoner meant to him being actually imprisoned, he seemed relieved and said it was so, but would I please keep it a secret.

The significant point which emerged in this session was Edward's equating the notion of "being like something" and "being something." There was no distinction between the symbol and the thing symbolized. At a later session, he blushed, stammered, giggled and apologized after bringing a canvas stool. He behaved as if he had offered me an actual fecal stool. It was not merely a symbolic expression of his wish to bring me his stool. He felt that he had actually offered it to me. His inability to use symbols, which I interpreted to him repeatedly, was probably the greatest single difficulty throughout his analysis.

Melanie Klein (1930) has described the failure of symbol formation in schizophrenia; but her patient's difficulty was not exactly the same as Edward's. Dick, a boy of four, failed to form symbols and therefore could not use speech, and generally failed to develop. Edward did form symbols but he could not use them as mere symbols. Unlike Dick, he could transfer his interest from the object to the substitute symbol, for instance, from feces to the canvas stool. Once formed, however, the symbol did not function as a symbol but became in all respects equivalent to the object itself. Thus, the canvas stool was to him an object of shame and embarrassment since he thought it really was a fecal stool. In this he resembled another schizophrenic who, when I asked him why he did not want to play the violin any more, answered with a shrug, "Fancy masturbating in public."

The difficulty of forming or using symbols is, I think, one of the basic elements in schizophrenic thinking. This certainly is at the root of the concrete thinking described in schizophrenics. It accounts, probably, for much of the difficulty in understanding schizophrenic speech. When one says, "I don't understand what he is talking about," this may be literally true. The schizophrenic holds in his hand a violin but his speech refers to the penis with which the violin is equated in his mind.

Another frequent symptom, which is largely dependent on the failure of symbol formation, is the poverty of thought so often displayed by the schizophrenic. As I see it the mechanism here can be twofold: either symbols are not formed, as in the case of Melanie Klein's patient, and therefore interests do not develop; or, having been formed, symbols become equivalents instead. Then endowed with all the anxiety belonging to the original object, these symbols have to be repressed or denied. The result is the same in either case: deprived of the use of symbols, the intellect cannot develop and function adequately. Before his illness, Edward must have repressed extensively many of the symbols already formed, and he confined his interests mainly to biology—substituting the plant and the animal for the human body. During the acute stage of his illness, the repressed returned with its characteristic equivalence of symbols and original objects.

After this digression I shall have to leave the subject of symbol formation, for it deserves a paper to itself, and return to my patient.

It is extremely difficult to give a coherent summary of the sessions we had at the nursing home. The material was disconnected; I often did not understand the patient's behavior, reactions and speech. Gradually, however, the picture became clearer. It seemed that the apparently disconnected material centered mainly around the two phantasies expressed already in his first hour with me: the phantasy that he was in prison and the phantasy that he and other people were changed.

Of course, the prison theme was not altogether a phantasy. One could hardly be more a prisoner than the mental patient in an old-fashioned military psychiatric hospital especially if, like Edward, the patient has to suffer days or weeks of solitary confinement. But in addition to this important element of reality, there was, in this case, a deeply ingrained, spontaneous delusion of being imprisoned.

In his own view, Edward's illness started when he was given work in the darkroom, the darkroom being the equivalent of a prison. To Edward, being imprisoned meant being treated like a criminal or like a child. Or rather, he felt imprisonment turned him into a child or a criminal. Through the failure to distinguish between that which was thought of and that which was, being treated like a child meant actually being a child; and child was equated with criminal.

These two main themes—imprisonment and changing—were often interconnected. For instance, in the nursing home, where Edward was treated well, he complained of being given nothing to do or to think about, of being supervised or fed too much. He felt as though he was nothing but a huge stomach, the limbs and head being irrelevant little appendages. He felt that all his thinking was done by his stomach, and that all this was due to his being imprisoned.

These phantasies were immediately followed by terrible anxiety that the world's food supply would disappear because everybody thought only of eating, and no one took the trouble to cultivate the earth and to plant new crops. Thus, imprisonment led to a change in him: he became a greedy child. His greediness in turn, led to the world's food supply being exhausted and to the world changing. This phantasy was depressive in its contents: the baby greedily empties the mother of food and babies but is incapable of a reparative genital relation. The feeling accompanying it, however, was persecutory. He did not feel guilty or responsible in any way, because his greed was forced on him by those who imprisoned him. His anger, like his greed, could change and destroy the world around him. Imprisonment led to anger; anger then made him into the child-criminal, led to imprisonment. The vicious circle was established.

Another important phantasy in which imprisonment and changing were connected was the phantasy of pregnancy. Usually when he spoke of changes he described destruction, damage, ruin. Occasionally, however, he would present a different picture. Things were growing out of all proportion, becoming distorted in a mysterious and terrifying way. The vegetation of India had changed, he said; it seemed to become enormous, luxurious, awe-inspiring. Clearly this referred to the mysterious changes in his mother's body during pregnancy.

A few months later, when I was analyzing him in his home, these anxieties became much clearer. He told me that he did not remember the birth of his next sibling, but he had been told that he was very jealous. He remembered the birth of the next baby when he was four, and he remembered feeling very angry and jealous. His first impression of the baby was that it was very greedy and very naughty. Gradually it became clear that he had felt envious of both the mother and the baby, and that he identified himself with both. Whenever I interpreted that, he would try to shift his ground and speak of his jealousy of either the father or of the older brother. Earlier on, in the nursing home, he had reacted by an increase in his feeling of persecution by male doctors.

My interpretations were felt to be actual castrations. For the wish to be a pregnant woman or a baby made him become a pregnant woman or a baby and that implied his not being a man. To interpret such a wish to him also meant castrating him.

In the pregnancy phantasy, the change in the external world, the mother, led to a change in himself. He was both the pregnant mother, the big tummy full of babies (full of voices) and the embryo imprisoned in her womb, castrated, helpless, all tummy and no limbs.

Of course, these phantasies and the links between them became clear only after months of analysis. From the start, however, some of his delusions could be recognized as phantasies familiar to every analyst. But I found that there was no point in interpreting them out of context. Edward's emotional life centered on the wish to be let out right away and on the fear of change and persecution. I had to bring these feelings into the transference, connect them with his phantasies and delusions and, finally, with his past. In trying to do that I met defense mechanisms of the most primitive kind: magic denial, splitting, and a series of rapid defensive introjections and projections.

In his changing world full of fear, he needed one unchanging good figure, and he tried to believe that I was this figure. But, to preserve this belief, he had to use all his defenses. In the first place, he had to deny that I had anything to do with his being kept in the hospital. If I frustrated him, he would deny the frustration and split me in to a good and a bad figure. The bad figure would be introjected as hostile voices or reprojected onto the hospital doctors. In effect, he felt acutely persecuted from within and from without.

Even the good figure was a very insecure possession. He could not love me any more than he could hate me, for love would lead to dependence and dependence to hatred. Love itself was often felt to be wholly bad. Giving me his love could give me his illness. As a result, I could be good and safe only if he withheld both hatred and love. He often expressed this by saying he wished I did not come to the nursing home where the voices would change me. I was much safer outside. The nursing home represented himself, and I could not be safe near to his madness. He could keep me good, but my goodness was of no avail, and his isolation was complete. His narcissism was a way of saving me from madness.

Whenever he gave me a chance, I interpreted to him his fear of involving me in his madness and the feeling of complete isolation when he successfully kept me out. His conscious fear of any change in me enabled me to bring into the transference some of his important phantasies. And though he rejected most of these interpretations, subsequent work convinced me that they had been effective.

After three months in the nursing home he was sufficiently improved to go home. At our first session in his parent's home, Edward was full of rage and despair. He spoke bitterly of his parents, reproaching them with their lack of warmth and their cruelty. But the real cause of his despair lay elsewhere. Having equated imprisonment in the hospital with his illness, he had hoped to leave the illness behind in the hospital where it belonged. He found that the delusions, the hallucinations, all his illness in fact, had followed him to his own home. And he was in despair.

Edward wanted reassurance. He wanted me to tell him that whatever was wrong was the fault of his parents and of the hospital. He wanted me to become his ally against the persecutors. I pointed out to him that he needed the reassurance so much because he was afraid that he was mad and that I was not an ally but the enemy—the doctor. Now that he was home I remained the only obvious link with the hospital. In his unconscious I was equated with all the hospital doctors. In a way, we were alone with madness: it was either in him or in me. If anyone was driving him mad it could only be I.

I had to bring this situation into consciousness, to substitute a conscious suspicion of me for blind acting out. Had I not done so, Edward's unconscious identification of me with the hospital might have led him to break off the treatment. Though he did not agree with my interpretations, he did not reject them altogether.

This raises a technical problem about which there is considerable controversy: should the analyst reassure a very ill patient at a moment of crisis and when the patient is craving reassurance? I have not done so, and I feel strongly that it would have been a mistake to give in to the patient's wishes. By giving sympathy and reassurance, the analyst becomes, for the time being, the good object, but only at the cost of furthering the split between good and bad objects and reinforcing the patient's pathological defenses. The unconscious suspicion of the analyst is then not analysed but is acted out, and sudden reversals may occur when God turns into the Devil and the negative transference may become unmanageable. And even while the "good" phase lasts, the progress of analysis is interfered with by the repression of phantasies about the "bad" analyst. Furthermore, whenever the analyst is artificially kept "good" someone else is chosen by the patient as the persecutor. Usually this is a member of his own family, someone obviously less adequately equipped than the analyst to cope with the patient's hostility.

After about three months' treatment at home, we decided that he should start coming to me for the analytic sessions. On his first visit he walked anxiously round the room investigating various objects and asking questions. When I interpreted his anxiety and distrust, Edward for the first time did not deny them. He admitted that he was afraid that I might imprison him again. He thought for a moment, and said, that a bottle on my table contained poison and that the little ivory skulls on my mantlepiece might be the skulls of patients I had killed. But he also said that he knew it was not, in fact, true. I had never before seen him distinguish between delusion and reality.

A few days later he lay on the couch for the first time. He was extremely anxious and his body looked quite rigid, but he did go on associating. Lying down reminded him of the hospital where he was kept in bed, and of his childhood, when being put to bed was a punishment. In his mind, bed and bad were equated; one was put to bed for having been bad and being in bed, in turn, made one bad. The humiliation and the frustration produced a rage which made him feel helpless against both the world and his own instincts. He remembered himself as a child in bed screaming in utter rage and despair. He freely acknowledged his fear that the same feelings might be reawakened on the analytic couch.

After that session, some of the particular difficulties of this analysis disappeared. In the first six months of treatment, my main concern was to establish an analytical situation. At the beginning of the analysis, the patient was detached from reality and unable to grasp the nature of the treatment. He appealed to me repeatedly to let him out of the hospital and would follow my footsteps when I was on my way out. He kept asking me to take him to the pictures or for walks, to arrange a means of escape for him. He was constantly demanding reassurance and, except at times when he was treating me ceremoniously like a neutral visitor, he was extremely curious and inquisitive.

My aim then was to retain the attitude of the analyst even without the cooperation of the patient. To achieve this, I had, first of all, to make him accept interpretations instead of the various gratifications he wanted, and to do it without appearing needlessly rude or cruel. I tried to show him in every interpretation that I understood what he wanted from me, why he wanted it at any particular moment, and why he wanted it so desperately. And I followed most interpretations of that kind with an interpretation of what my refusal had meant to him.

At that time, Edward was a deeply regressed psychotic with a disintegrated ego and his behavior was very infantile. When he went home later, he became more like a child in the latency period. He modeled in clay, remembered toys which his father used to make for him and tried to make similar ones. He wanted to make a flying machine with which prisoners could escape, knowing, yet somehow oblivious of the fact, that planes had already been invented. Finally, he developed a great cunning in concealing his delusions and hallucinations.

That, in itself, was partly a sign of progress. He recognized that delusions and hallucinations were not shared by everybody, and that he would be considered mad if he did not hide them. But it made a new difficulty in the analysis: he began hiding things from me consciously and deliberately. At the same time, he would fail to bring out material because of a lack of connection in his mind. He could tolerate ideas which naturally belonged together without either repressing or linking them, and I was not always able to discover if he was genuinely unaware of any particular omission.

On one occasion I remember, Edward became obsessed with the evil of money. He spent an entire hour speaking about it bitterly and vehemently. During this and the next hour I made several interpretations about his relation to money. But it soon became clear to me that there must have been an actual external cause which produced this outburst, and I told him that. He said he could not remember anything which would have made him think about money matters. I learned subsequently, and not from him, that he had received a letter from the Army authorities concerning his pay—a letter which he considered very humiliating. I am quite sure that he did not consciously conceal from me the existence of the letter but that he really failed to make a connection between the letter and his anger about money.

In the sixth month of treatment the formal analytic situation was finally established. The patient lay on the couch, associated and, at least consciously, expected nothing from me beyond analysis. From that time on, my problems were the same as those of the analysis of a neurotic, that is, the analysis of the patient's system of phantasies and defenses.

Edward's principal mechanisms of defense changed little. Splitting into an idealized and a persecuting object and magic denial continued. For weeks he would cooperate in the analysis of some important phantasies and then say happily, "Oh well, I don't think this can have anything to do with psychological reasons." Unconsciously, he felt certain that by saying "No." he could completely abolish any unpleasant experience. An interpretation could always be either split off and isolated, so that it was tolerated in consciousness but useless, or magically abolished by a conscious or unconscious "No" I always had to follow carefully his internal response to my interpretation to discover how far he was trying to invalidate it or do away with it.

The denial was often determined by a failure of symbolization which, at this stage, took a different form than it did at the beginning of the treatment. Then, consciously and unconsciously, the symbol and the thing symbolized were equated. Now the unconscious equation remained unchanged but consciously the symbolism had to be completely denied. A cigarette was a cigarette, and he would not accept that it might stand for a penis. For if he accepted that, it would mean that he was actually sucking and biting a penis—which would be madness. In effect, nearly every phantasy had to be totally denied.

With time, however, the rigidity of his defenses lessened and he gradually became capable of tolerating in his consciousness some phantasy and conflict.

Along with the analytic progress, a marked clinical improvement took place. Toward the end of the first year of treatment, all conscious delusions disappeared. Edward was in touch with reality, leading an apparently normal life, following a course at the university, working on some minor inventions and making himself useful in his country home. He was still preoccupied with phantasies about soil erosion, but now they gave rise to sublimations. He planted some very tall trees which had never before been successfully planted in this country. The planting and his later work on these trees (which he is still carrying on) was so successful that eminent biologists and experts in forestry wrote to him for information and advice. In this sphere, he tried realistically to become the father with the biggest penis (the tallest trees) returning to mother earth the food taken from the breast and the destroyed babies.

His relationships were better, he felt, than before his illness. He complained only of a recurring noise in his left ear which he called a "buzz" and of some difficulty of concentration. The improvement was in part genuine; but some of it seemed due to a magic denial of madness and to a splitting off and "encapsulating" of his illness in the insignificant little buzz, strictly localized in his ear.

His sex life remained unsatisfactory. He started having sexual relations for the first time during the analysis and it was a great relief to him to find that he was potent. He became a great flirt, always trying to have many girls to whom he could make love to and trying not to be dependent on anyone in particular. But he confined his sexual relations to prostitutes. In his mind he divided women into three categories: prostitutes, with whom to have intercourse, girls of his own social sphere to flirt with and to tantalize, and the ideal woman whom he would marry one day.

I shall now describe two incidents which happened approximately eighteen months after the beginning of the treatment. They show some of the schizophrenic mechanisms still operating, and the way in which these mechanisms were modified by analysis.

The first of these incidents led to the only recurrence of "voices" and, I think, might easily have brought a complete breakdown had the patient then not been in analysis. I have chosen this particular incident because it throws a light on some of the mechanisms of hallucinations. At the time when the patient was heavily hallucinated, it was impossible to follow these mechanisms in detail. In his temporary relapse he reproduced them in a mild and manageable form.

Two male relatives of Edward's mother died in quick succession. One, who had been ill for some time, died at the beginning of a week. Two days later, the other died suddenly in the street, on the way to an appointment with Edward's mother. Though he was very fond of both, he repressed all strong feelings and said that he was very sorry but not overwhelmingly so. His associations showed, however, that he identified himself with both of them.

The first relative had already come into the analysis in connection with his illness, and Edward admitted then to a strong identification and fears for his own health. When the relative died, Edward omitted telling me that it was the same man, obviously defending himself against the identification. He tolerated the thought of identification with his uncle's illness and of the latter's death, without making any connection between the two. Edward was not going to mourn the uncle, he said, because the man had been a cheerful person and would not wish to be mourned. About the second relative, he said that it had been a kind death and he himself would wish for a similar one.

Underneath the superficial detachment there was the identification, brought about partly through guilt and fear of retaliation, partly in order to influence the dead by sympathetic magic. He was saying, in fact, "If I had such a quick, kind death, I would not be angry; I would not persecute people with regrets and mourning. Therefore I am safe. The dead are not going to be angry with me and persecute me." When I pointed this out to him, he rejected the interpretation. Nor could he admit that he was afraid that the death of the two men—rivals in relation to his mother—proved his own omnipotence: that is, proved that at any moment now, his foremost rival, his father, might die.

During the weekend after his relatives' death, he attended an official function at his old school. He returned exultant. In contrast with his first visit, a year earlier, this time he had felt quite confident, free and happy. In the evening he had been out with a girl and was very pleased with himself. I interpreted his triumph in being young, strong and potent, while the fathers were old and dead. I pointed out to him his feeling that I, too, had died during the weekend which he had found so enjoyable.

On the following day, he lay on the couch silent for a long while and then said violently, "I wish that buzzing would stop." At first he denied that the "buzz" was worse than usual; he was merely expressing a general wish, he said. But after a while he admitted that, as he put it, the buzzing had become articulate. Slowly, and with many hesitations, he told me that he had been doing eye exercises the day before and, while he was counting them, an echo in his head counted together with him. To illustrate this point in the session, he counted aloud a number of times.

I shall not go into the details of the various defenses and evasions, associations and interpretations. The picture which emerged was this: the counting stood for competition with his older brother, in childhood, for control-keeping a check—killing as in the childish "counting out." It could also be used as a reassurance that all the relatives were still alive, and that all the limbs and members of his body were all right. Eye exercises stood for the wish to acquire omnipotent eyesight, so as to be able to see across the streets, which separated our houses, and to watch me in sexual intercourse. We were here on the very familiar ground of sexual curiosity; that much he eventually agreed to.

As he went on to describe the echo, it struck me that the echo had a mocking quality. Edward accepted this interpretation with unusual alacrity and seemed to find great relief in becoming aware of the pervasive persecution of this voice. Then I made a more complete interpretation. I reminded him of the death of his two relatives, his identification with them, his refusal to mourn them, and the triumph over them during the weekend. I suggested that, in performing eye exercises, he was watching the intercourse between his parents, and that he was killing the father or both parents, represented by the two relatives, by magic looking and magic counting. Finally he introjected the dead and triumphed over them. But apparently, they were not defeated; they came back to life inside him and mocked him, mocked particularly his magic looking and counting—the means by which, he thought, he had secured his triumph. Edward rejected this interpretation.

In the following session, Edward said that the articulate buzz was still there and had said "dreams, dreams." When I told him that it was I who had become the internal voice and was nagging him for dreams, he recounted a dream of the preceding night. He dreamed that he saw four people playing a very fast game of which he did not know the rules. This game was something halfway between tennis and squash. Then he saw two men, one black and one white, advancing in the distance. As they came nearer, the white man became more and more brown and he grew a stubble on his face.

Edward's first association was that he could not play squash. But what intrigued him most was the white man turning brown. It made him think of two things: (1) that in a film he had seen, a white man looked brown because of the way he had been photographed, and (2) of India, being brown with the sun and not shaving. The first reading of the dream made him accept the interpretations I gave in the preceding session. Watching the very fast game of which he did not know the rules, or knew them only in part (he could play tennis but not squash) meant watching intercourse. In his jealousy, he felt he had killed and introjected the parents, thereby changing them into feces, i.e. the approaching figures of a man who is brown and one who turns brown. These men were also the two dead relatives now representing the two parents. He made them brown by looking, that is, by photographing.

But the meaning of the dream does not end here. The white man turning brown was also himself; India always stood for his illness. The man turning brown represented the threat of an approaching breakdown. But the man was brown because of the way he had been photographed, which means that by showing Edward to himself in a bad light, by making him aware of his illness, I was magically making him ill. My evil eye changed him into feces, just as his own evil eye changed the copulating parents into feces.

This aspect of the dream gave us a link with the transference. As he tried to watch me in intercourse, while doing eye exercises, he swallowed me up in anger with his eyes and changed me into feces. (He watches; they turn brown.) Then, as the internal voice, I started persecuting him from the inside: "dreams, dreams." But reprojection occurs almost simultaneously. By looking, Edward also filled me with feces; then, in retaliation, my looking both swallowed him up and changed him into feces (by introjection) and filled him with feces (by projection). So that, by looking at each other, we put the excrements—illness and death—into each other.

This was the last session of the week. On the following Monday, he came to me with a very swollen face and immediately started assuring me that he had only been stung by a bee. When I said that he must have thought me very anxious to have to reassure me like that, he admitted that he did think I was anxious. He himself had had an excellent weekend. The buzz had disappeared and he felt very well. Obviously, he felt that he had projected the illness into me, so that he was free, but I became both the anxious and ill person and the external persecutor—the bee which had stung him and filled him with poison.

In Freud's view (1917), analysis meant essentially the analysis and resolution of a transference neurosis. Therefore, he saw in the schizophrenic narcissism a factor precluding analysis. Speaking in the *Introductory Lectures* of patients suffering from the narcissistic neuroses, Freud said, "They manifest no transference and for that reason are inaccessible to our efforts, not to be cured by us." The later work of Melanie Klein on internal objects has shown that narcissism is a complex phenomenon. There is in every case a relationship to phantasied internalized objects; and a state of narcissistic withdrawal can be approached in terms of a relation to internal objects.

In Edward's case, the object-relationship to the dead relatives broke down under the stress of anxiety and guilt. There came the splitting and introjection of injured and bad objects with the subsequent hallucinations and narcissistic withdrawal. But in the analytic situation, the patient experienced the internal persecution in the transference. My voice, asking for dreams, appeared in the hallucination. Canalized into the transference situation, the process became accessible to analysis.

I have chosen the second incident to illustrate how the splitting mechanisms lead to idealization and persecution, and how the analysis of these mechanisms reduces the split and makes possible a more realistic attitude.

During a holiday Edward was interested in two things. He milked cows in his country home, and he practiced sketching very quickly various items of botanical interest. He was very pleased with himself as he used to be very bad at drawing and had never tried milking cows before. He felt that when milking he was doing good; he was relieving the cow, providing milk for others and assuring himself of fresh milk every morning. Sketching represented to him an attempt at keeping things inside him unchanged—a new achievement.

But his attempt to get the milk inside him and keep it good there was not wholly successful. A day or two after his return to London, he developed a rash on his face. He found this embarrassing and extremely annoying. Simultaneously, he started working on the idea of sterilizing milk by ultraviolet rays, since he felt that it was impossible to keep the cowsheds clean enough to satisfy the requirements of health inspectors. Obviously he felt unconsciously that there was something hopelessly wrong with the milk, something that called for magic measures. When I interpreted this to him, he admitted that he had thought for a minute that he got the rash by infection, while milking a cow with a sore udder. The happy picture of his milking gave place to a persecutory one: the breast was sore, the milk dirty and infected, his own inside poisoned, and the poison coming out in the rash.

After the situation had become clear to him, Edward had a short but extremely violent dream in which he felt that he was torn open and possibly devoured—he did not know by whom or by what. He associated it with the fact that in India, he had used a goat as a decoy for a panther. The panther tore the goat's belly open and devoured it while he photographed the scene. He felt that in the dream he was like the goat. But the goat, which he threw to be devoured for the satisfaction of his own greed and ambition, repre-

sented the mother. Two things were telescoped here: his attack on the
mother's breast—the cow's udder—and his later attacks on her body, caused
mainly by curiosity and phallic ambition. He was identified with the
attacked and incorporated mother (the goat).

After this analysis the rash cleared up. Two nights later he dreamed that
he was imprisoned by the Russians and a young woman helped him to
escape. They travelled together, changing trains frequently because if they
stayed too long on any single train they would be caught. He immediately
associated the young woman with me and the Russians with any kind of
persecution. I was helping him to escape from it. But when he spoke of
Russia, it became clear that the Russians also represented me. The trains he
had to change represented trends of thought. If he followed a trend of
thought long enough he would be caught, that is, he would realize that his
ideal object is also the object which he had injured and the persecutor.

The dream also directly connected with his current sexual problems.
The journey on the train represented sexual intercourse with me, but he
could not go the whole way with me—the longed-for vagina would turn
into the dangerous and persecuting one. He could not go the whole way
with me, the ideal love object, and he had to sleep with prostitutes,
changing trains often for fear they would become dangerous.

Thinking about the cow led Edward to see that the milk he tried to
obtain and keep inside had poisoned him. Thinking about the Russians
made him see that I, who was to help him, had become the persecutor from
whom he was escaping. This recurring situation in which the very best
object turns out to be the most injured one and the worst persecutor was the
deepest tragedy in his internal world. Throughout his life he had to
"change trains quickly," never to go deeply into things or relationships, to
remain superficial, cold and detached, for fear the tragic situation would
become conscious. Here, again, we see the long history behind the narcissistic withdrawal.

In the following session Edward was sad. He thought it might be
because he was losing the ideal picture of the woman. But it appeared that
his feeling of persecution was giving way to depression. He told me that an
old servant was leaving on the same day. She had been kind to him when he
was a child and he was sorry to lose her and sorry that he had not always been
good to her. Toward the end of the hour, he brought up the first happy
memory of his childhood which he ever produced in analysis. At the age of
two he had been transferred from the washbasin to a real bath, and he had
been thrilled by the experience. These associations showed that after the
analysis of the splitting, the idealization and the persecution, he had

become free to accept a real good object, a real good experience and a real hope of growing out of babyhood.

The continued analysis of the splitting led to a gradual bridging of the gap between the persecuting and the idealized object. The process manifested itself in many ways. It showed in his dreams. The first dream he had in his analysis was of a panther in the central room of his home and of his terror. A year later, he dreamed that there was a bullock in the hall; it was behind bars, but the bars could easily be removed. And Edward was more sorry for the bullock than frightened of it. Clearly the internal persecutor (in the last analysis, identified with his own instincts) became more genital and more manageable. Another effect was the general improvement of his relationships, including the transference. While he became freer to admit that in his phantasies I appeared in various persecutory figures, his relationship to me became incomparably more confident and warmer. I think he felt that he had found in me a friend, and if that is so, this was the first intimate relationship that he had ever experienced in his conscious memory.

There is, I think, no doubt that the diagnosis of schizophrenia has been confirmed by the analysis. The patient, though apparently recovered, is still psychotic in his defenses.

The prognosis was relatively bad, in view of Edward's schizoid personality before the illness and of his rapid deterioration. In his favor was his youth (he was just twenty years old when the analysis started), and the short duration of his illness and of the psychiatric treatment (in this case, ill-treatment) which preceded analysis.

It will be seen that the analytic technique I used was different in many important respects from the technique used and described by the American analysts, particularly Frieda Fromm-Reichman and Paul Federn. They hold that the analyst must not give interpretations that would introduce into consciousness any new unconscious material, as the ego of the psychotic is anyway submerged by it. Federn (1943) has written, "The question as to whether one should use for further analysis the unconscious material produced by psychotics is answered. It is dangerous to call for still deeper layers and to introduce problems into the patient's mind."

I proceeded differently and I brought into consciousness new unconscious material whenever it was warranted. For instance, at the beginning of the treatment, Edward was very much under the sway of castration fears, which were much less repressed than is usually the case with neurotics. These fears did not diminish until I introduced new material into his consciousness. I had to interpret to him the underlying and entirely

unconscious phantasy in which he identified himself with both his pregnant mother and her unborn child. His castration fear was partly a result of
this phantasy in which he ceased to be a man and which his masculine self
felt as a castration. The castration fear also acted partly as a blind; he
forcibly drew my attention to his masculinity and the rivalry with his father
and brothers to cover up his rivalry with me, the woman.

I found that in Edward's analysis, as in any other analysis, understanding and progress were achieved only by making the patient aware of what
hitherto had been unconscious. The fact that many things are tolerated in
consciousness by the schizophrenic must not blind one to the necessity of
interpreting what is repressed. Schizophrenics, more than others, repress
the links between different trends of thought. They often tolerate in their
ego thoughts and phantasies which would probably be repressed in the
neurotic; but on the other hand they repress the links between the various
phantasies and between phantasy and reality. Those links have to be
interpreted whenever possible. Another important difference between the
neurotic and the schizophrenic is in the kind of material which becomes
conscious by the return of that which is repressed, although this mechanism
occurs in the psychotic and neurotic breakdown alike. The phantasies of the
psychotic, especially of the schizophrenic, are far more archaic and primitive. But that does not mean that in the psychotic repression does not
operate and does not have to be analyzed. For example, my patient produced
consciously primitive phantasies of being poisoned, overfed or starved.
These were not repressed, but what was repressed was the fact that these
phantasies referred to his mother in the past and to me in the present.
Secondly, they were believed to be largely the result of his own attacks on his
mother, exhausting her breast so that it was empty and he would starve, and
poisoning her milk with feces which would eventually poison him. Also, all
these phantasies were a regression from later depressive phantasies which
themselves were entirely repressed.

The delusions about being poisoned cleared up after those other
unconscious phantasies were interpreted and connected with the conscious
delusions.

The first important difference between the technique advocated by
Federn and the one I used in this case is as follows: I tried to analyze in this
psychotic all the important resistances and to interpret the unconscious
material at the level of the greatest anxiety, much as I would do with a
neurotic. The second important difference lies in the handling of the
transference situation. Federn (1943) wrote, "Psychotic patients offer the
positive transference to the analyst; the analysts must nourish it as some-

thing precious in order to preserve their influence: transference is helpful in the analysis of underlying conflicts of the psychosis but a positive transference itself must never be dissolved by psychoanalysis." He added in the same paper, "The general conditions which should be considered in every psychoanalytic treatment: establishment of positive transference, treatment to be interrupted when transference becomes negative."

I believe that this attitude must deepen the already deep pathogenic split characteristic of schizophrenia. I thought it worthwhile in the analysis of a schizophrenic to attempt that which Freud (1936) has shown to be the only way of attacking the roots of a mental illness, that is, not strengthening the defense mechanisms of the patient but bringing them into the transference and analyzing them.

In the early stages, Edward's analysis differed from the analysis of a neurotic in that I had to go and see him in the hospital and later at his home and he did not lie on the couch. I never explained the basic rule to him but from the start I maintained the analytic attitude. In other words, I interpreted defences and material with an emphasis on the transference, both positive and negative.

Edward has been in analysis nearly three years. In his case this approach has proved possible and, so far, entirely rewarding.

POSTSCRIPT 1980:
SOME ASPECTS OF THE ANALYSIS OF A SCHIZOPHRENIC

At the time I started analyzing this patient, there was no published account of a treatment of a schizophrenic by a purely psychoanalytic method so that I had very little guidance. Looking back on it, I think I did not pay enough attention to processes of splitting and fragmentation in his ego and, in particular, I did not see enough of the process described later by Bion (1957) as "pathological projective identification." It is maybe, because of this failure, that this analysis has not been entirely successful.

Soon after the time described in the paper, after some four years of analysis, the patient stopped it on a hypomanic swing. This interruption of his analysis, against my advice, was partly due to an internal and external pressure of his family tradition, which required that he attend a university outside London, and partly to the manic resistance to analysis. He remained well for some twenty years. He completed his university studies, married, had a family, and had an adventurous and varied—though not always successful—career in one of the major professions.

In 1968, under strong provocation of external events, he had another schizophrenic breakdown. He retained a sufficient internal link with me to evade rather cleverly his threatened certification and to come to me for help. As I had no vacancy at the time, I referred him to another analyst for further treatment, and he is doing well in his present analysis.

References

Bion, W. R. (1957). Differentiation of the psychotic from the non-psychotic personalities. *International Journal of Psycho-Analysis* 38:266-275. In W. R. Bion, *Second Thoughts*. New York: Jason Aronson, 1977.

Federn, P. (1943). Psychoanalysis of psychoses. *Psychiatric Quarterly* 17:3-19.

Freud, S. (1917). Introductory lectures on psycho-analysis: Part III. General theory of the neuroses. *Standard Edition* 16.

Klein, M. (1930). The importance of symbol-formation in the development of the ego. *International Journal of Psycho-Analysis* 11:24-39. In M. Klein, *Contributions to Psycho-Analysis 1921-1945* pp. 236-250. London: Hogarth, 1948.

9

Depression in the Schizophrenic

THE THESIS OF THIS CHAPTER is that in the course of development, schizo-phrenics reach the depressive position and, finding it intolerable, deal with it by projecting their depressive anxieties. This can be done only by projecting a large part of their ego into an object, that is by projective identification. I am speaking here of the depressive position as described by Melanie Klein. Briefly, this is a phase of development in which the infant's ego is integrated enough and the object synthesized enough for the infant to experience a whole object relation involving ambivalence, dread of loss, guilt, and the urge to regain and restore the object. By projective identifica-tion I mean that process in which a part of the ego is split off and projected into an object with a consequent loss of that part to the ego, as well as an alteration in the perception of the object.

In the course of psychoanalytic treatment of the schizophrenic, it is of great importance to put him in touch with his depressive feelings and the wish to make reparation which springs from them. As the treatment progresses and some of the paranoid anxieties, idealizing and splitting processes are analyzed, the patient comes more and more frequently to experience, for a short time, depressive anxieties. He usually tries to get rid of these anxieties by projective identification. Often it will be found that the depressive part of the patient's ego is projected into the analyst, and in order to achieve that projection the patient resorts to careful stage-managing of

121

the analytical situation. This is designed in such a way as to provoke depressive feelings in the analyst. It is of great importance, then, to find where and in what circumstances the part of his ego capable of experiencing depression has been projected and to interpret this to the patient.

I will illustrate what I mean by two examples taken from the analysis of a sixteen-year-old schizophrenic girl. She had suffered from hallucinations from the age of four or maybe earlier. She was an unusually gifted and intelligent child and for a long time retained something of her original brilliance, but there had been a progressive withdrawal and a steady, though slow, deterioration of her personality. At age sixteen when she started treatment she had a well-established, chronic hebephrenic schizophrenia.

First example. This happened in the February of the second year of this patient's treatment. Since the Christmas holiday she had been very silent, speaking one or two sentences at most during the hour and spending most of her time skipping round the room, biting her braids, her fingers, the cushions, or the couch. She also picked her nose a great deal, eating the pickings, and often collected and ate any odd bit of fluff or dust from the floor. I had interpreted her behavior mainly in terms of oral greed and aggression in relation to myself (standing for the breast) and in terms of her distress about the good food being changed into bad feces so that she had to feed on dirt from the floor and feces. During these hours, she had also experienced persecutory hallucinations which she betrayed by shaking her hands violently as though trying to get rid of something, tearing bits of her skin and clothing and throwing them out, listening in a frightened way to some internal voices, and occasionally shouting. I interpreted this behavior as evidence of her feeling that the food which had gone bad was attacking her, and that similarly now my interpretations were felt as bad food biting her or soiling her inside.

She had confirmed some of these interpretations verbally and referred to her babyhood, saying that as a baby she did nothing but bite and hate and cry. After some weeks of such behavior this patient came in one day, sat on the couch, and said in a composed and rational manner that Mummy took her to the doctor because she was very pale and thin and Mummy was worried. I asked her what she thought was the matter with her. She did not answer but started biting and again picking her nose and eating the pickings. So I connected her concern about herself with her feeling that she was destroying food, turning it bad and wasting it. But in this hour I obviously missed the gist of her anxiety, because in the following hour she came in and repeated the same behavior and the same statement as in the hour before. She put great emphasis on the words "pale and thin," looking at me intently and suspiciously, and then she put her hand to the base of her throat and gave herself two very slight scratches. Now, at the beginning of her treatment she used to have phases of being very voluble, and one of the things she talked about a great deal then was vampires and their supposed habits, about which she was very knowledgeable. I knew that vampires are supposed to bite their victims at the base of the neck and invariably to leave two small scratches. When I noticed the two scratches, I said that she felt she was pale and thin because she was being sucked by a vampire, and I drew her attention to the way she looked at me and said she suspected me of being that vampire.

This interpretation produced a number of associations about vampires and their habits. She directly confirmed my transference interpretation by saying that I could only make interpretations out of what she told me and she felt that I lived on her life and sucked out her brains and her blood. Such a direct verbal admission of feelings about me was most unusual in this patient.

The next day she came about ten minutes before the end of the session, and when I suggested that she was afraid to come for fear I should suck her blood out, she immediately started complaining of my dragging things out of her, doing it even in her dreams. Then she added that perhaps it was because of this that she had to fly to the "ideal people" inside herself. We knew by then that she had two kinds of hallucination, one of an extremely persecutory and one of a very ideal character.

In the following hour she came on time and continued to talk about the "ideal people" inside her. I knew from earlier material that many of her hallucinations were based on characters from books which she used to devour in order to create inside herself a hallucinatory world based on the book characters with whom she also identified. I interpreted to her that she treated me in a manner similar to that in which she treated books, taking in my interpretations and using them to create pleasurable hallucinations inside herself. She said that she knew that and added that she knew she was draining the life out of me. Then she gave me a long look and said that sometimes when vampires were in love they would not kill their victim outright but would do so slowly, by degrees, enjoying the sucking enormously.

In the next few sessions we could get at her various feelings about me in the situation of vampires. She had felt that her love for me, like her love for the breast, was as dangerous as hatred in its cruelty and its greed. She said that by being silent and making me talk she was sucking my life blood by slow degrees and building something wonderful inside herself that she was not sharing with me. While I was becoming emptied, I slowly became the vampire sucking life out of her, taking away her good hallucinations, persecuting her and threatening to kill her. She dreaded cure because being cured meant being exorcized, and being exorcized meant that it would be discovered that it was *she* who was the vampire to begin with and that she would be made to die. She felt that the situation could only end in death. At the end of a session following some working through of this material, the patient was sitting down very quietly on the couch. Deep in thought, she said, "Do you mean that all that vicious circle happens because I always took and ate and ate and did not do anything to rebuild anything good inside myself?" Throughout that session she looked concerned, depressed, thoughtful, and more sane than ever before.

The next day she met me in the waiting room, smiling and greeting me in an unusually open and friendly manner. She looked normal and composed. I also noticed that she wore an open-necked shirt which showed more of her chest than usual. As soon as she came into the consulting room there was an immediate change. She started behaving in an irrational and hallucinated way. She skipped and jumped around the room for a while, flapping her arms, behaving in a manic rather than a persecuted manner. Then she jumped on the couch and lay there muttering to herself and occasionally masturbating. She seemed to ignore me completely. This was a striking change compared with the preceding week when she had associated freely, and particularly compared with the preceding session in which she seemed so in touch with her feelings. After a time I realized that her behavior was symptomatic of a negative therapeutic reaction to the great progress in insight which she had gained in the last days. In the previous session, my patient had experienced the feeling that she had destroyed the breast that fed her and she was faced with the problem of reparation and rebuilding. This situation had obviously been intolerable to her, and she had acted in a way which would enable her to project these unbearable feelings onto me. To begin with, in the waiting room, she was the mother seducing me by showing me the breast, greeting me in a friendly manner, wanting to arouse my hopes; then in the consulting room she proceeded to frustrate me by ignoring me and exhibited to me the parental intercourse in her masturbation. She was the mother; I was to be the infant experiencing sexual excitement, greed, frustration, rage, and guilt. I remembered in this session that this patient's mother often lost her temper with her daughter and then felt absolutely crushed with guilt. And it struck me forcibly how subtly the patient must have managed to make her mother behave like an infant losing her temper. Then the mother had to carry the burden of guilt.

I first interpreted to the patient the meaning of her behavior, the identification with me as the mother who was frustrating her orally and exciting her rage by intercourse with father. Then I reminded her of the end of the previous session when she had been faced with her own feeling of guilt toward me as the feeding mother. I pointed out to her that she obviously could not bear those feelings inside herself. Therefore, she had to become the mother and I had to become the infant, so that she could put that part of herself which she could not bear, the guilty infant, into me. I could also show her that this was often the way she had behaved with her mother, both at present and in her early childhood. She listened to this interpretation carefully and said, with a sigh of relief and an expression of sanity returning to her face, "Of course, then I never need to be the child that depends."

In this series of sessions, I have tried to show a sequence of changes in my patient. After weeks of what had seemed wholly irrational and mad behavior, the patient had been enabled to verbalize in the transference her paranoid delusion about me as a vampire. Further analysis enabled her to relate this picture of me to her own sucking impulses and phantasies. Concurrently with that she had become aware that her ideal and persecutory figures were the split-off aspects of one object, the analyst standing for the breast or the feeding mother. At that point, her ego became more integrated and her objects more synthesized. The persecutory feelings lessened and the patient had to face her responsibility for her own impulses toward the breast and her feeling that she had to restore it, particularly that she had to restore the internal breast. She made this clear when she said, "Is it because I always took and ate and ate and did nothing to rebuild anything good *inside* myself?" At that point she was in touch with her feelings and with reality and she approached sanity. This, however, was unbearable to her and she immediately projected the depressed and more sane part of herself into me, thereby getting rid of it and becoming madder.

Second example. The second sequence that I want to describe happened in October of the same year. The patient had come back from the summer holiday remote and hallucinated. From her behavior I could gather that she was hallucinating God and the devil; they represented the good and bad aspects of the patient's father, who had committed suicide when she was fifteen. At times it was clear from her gestures and expressions that she was having intercourse now with God, now with the devil. There was a great deal of screaming, shouting, and attacking; at times she looked terrified. She was also continually picking threads from the cover of the couch and breaking them off angrily. I had interpreted to her mainly her relation to her father in terms of splitting, idealization, and persecution and related it to the transference, particularly in connection with the long summer holiday. I also paid a great deal of attention to her breaking off the threads from the couch cover, interpreting this behavior according to the context as breaking the threads of her thoughts, the threads of analysis, the threads connecting her internal world with external reality. Her violence gradually subsided, and although she was still picking off threads and breaking them, accompanied by a lot of biting, grimacing, and angry shaking, the change in her mood was noticeable. As time went on there was more skipping and dancing, more grace in her movements, less tension, and there was about her a general air of half gaiety, irresponsibility, and remoteness. Then one day, as she was dancing round the room, picking some imaginary things from the carpet and making movements as though she was scattering something round the room, it struck me that she must have been imagining that she was dancing in a meadow, picking flowers and scattering them. And it occurred to me that she was behaving exactly like an actress playing the part of Shakespeare's Ophelia. The likeness to Ophelia was all the more remarkable in that in some peculiar way, the more gaily and irresponsibly she was behaving, the sadder was the effect, as though her gaiety itself was designed to produce sadness in her audience, just as Ophelia's pseudo-gay dancing and singing is designed to make the audience in the theater sad. If she was Ophelia, she was scattering her sadness round the room as she was scattering the imaginary flowers, in order to get rid of it and to make me, the audience, sad. As the patient in the past had often identified with characters in books or plays, I felt on fairly secure ground in saying to her, "It seems to me that you are being Ophelia." She immediately stopped and said, "Yes, of course," as though surprised that I had not noticed it earlier, and then she added, sadly, "Ophelia was mad, wasn't she?" It was the first time she had admitted that she knew about her own madness.

I then connected her behavior with the previous material and with my interpretations about her relation to her father and showed her how she had felt guilty about the death of her father/lover whom she wished to kill and whom she thought she had killed for his having rejected her. I also told her how her present Ophelia-like madness was a denial of her feelings about his death and an attempt to put these feelings into me. As I was interpreting, she threw herself on the couch and let her head hang down from it. I said that she was representing Ophelia's suicide and showing me that she could not admit her feelings about her father's death, as the guilt and distress about it would drive her, like him, to suicide. But she did not agree with this and said Ophelia's death was not a suicide. "She was irresponsible, like a child, she did not know the difference. Reality did not exist for her; death did not mean anything."

I interpreted to her how putting into me the part of herself capable of appreciating the fact of the death of her father and the reality of her own ambivalent feelings and guilt resulted in her losing her reality sense, her sanity. She then became a person who "did not know the difference" any longer.

The patient came back the next day very hallucinated and persecuted, externally and internally. She was obviously having unpleasant hallucinations, and she also turned away from me in an angry and frightened way. She did a lot of grimacing, muttering, and biting. She again picked up and broke off threads. I reminded her of the previous session and how she was trying to get rid of her painful feelings by putting them into me. I drew her attention to the breaking of the threads and told her that in getting rid of those painful feelings she felt she was trying to break off and get rid of her sanity. At the same time she felt that I had become a persecutor because she put her painful feelings into me and now she felt that, in interpreting, I was trying to push those feelings back into her and persecuting her with them.

The next day she came looking sad and quiet. She again started picking threads out of the couch, but instead of breaking them off completely, she was intertwining them. When I made some reference to her Ophelia-like feelings, she said, "You know, when Ophelia was picking flowers it was not, as you said, all madness. There was a lot of the other things as well. What was unbearable was the intertwining." I said, "The intertwining of madness and sanity?" She said, "Yes, that is what is unbearable." I then told her that my interpretations about how she tried to put her sanity into me made her feel that she had regained the sane part of herself, but she felt it was unbearable because now that sane part of herself could appreciate and feel distress about the disintegration of the rest of herself. In the previous session she had tried to make me into the sane part of herself that was distressed at her own insanity. I pointed out to her how she was intertwining the threads that she was picking up and contrasted this with the earlier session in which she was breaking the threads. I interpreted to her that the breaking of the threads represented her breaking her sanity because she could not bear the distress, sadness, and guilt that sanity seemed to involve for her.

In the next session, the patient looked at me very carefully and said, "Do you ever smile or laugh? My Mummy says that she cannot imagine you doing either." I pointed out to her how much laughing and giggling she had done during the last weeks and said that she felt that she had stolen all my smiles and laughter. She had put into me all her depression and guilt, thereby making me into the sad part of herself. But in doing that she made me into a persecutor, because she felt I was trying to push this unwanted sadness back into her. Then she could not experience her guilt or her sadness as her own, but she felt it as something pushed into her by me in revenge and punishment. She felt that I had lost my laughter but she herself had lost the meaning and understanding of sadness.

In the sessions in February, one could see the emergence of depression following the analysis of the patient's vampire phantasies. In the sessions now described, in the patient's Ophelia-like behavior the depression was first observed by me in the projected form: I was obviously meant to be sad and depressed. The patient herself became aware of her depression only after interpretations which put her again in touch with this projected part of herself. There are other important differences in these two series of sessions. In February the patient was mainly preoccupied with the early feeding relation to the breast, and the depression, when it emerged, had a violent and ruthless character. The emotions projected onto the analyst were crude and primitive: oral love and greed, excited jealousy, rage followed by guilt and despair. In the October sessions, the patient was dealing with problems from a later stage of development and more related to the genital Oedipus complex. In keeping with that, the feelings projected were more complex, less primitive and more finely shaded, involving not only rage, guilt, and despair, but also sadness, grief, and pining. The similarities of the two situations, however, are important. Whenever the patient could be put in touch with her emerging depression, she became communicative in a sane manner, sanity and depressive feelings returning to her ego together. Whenever the depressive feelings became intolerable, reprojection occurred with the corresponding loss of reality sense, the return of mad behavior and an increase of persecutory feelings.

CONCLUSION

I have tried to show in these examples the emergence of depressive feelings in a schizophrenic patient and the use she made of projective identification as a defense against depression. The analysis of persecutory anxieties and schizoid defenses in the transference leads to a greater integration of the ego and the object. When this happens the patient becomes more sane and she begins to face the reality of her impulses, her depressive feelings, guilt and the need for reparation, as well as the fact of her own madness. For the schizophrenic, the guilt and distress in this situation is intolerable, and therefore, the steps that the patient has taken toward sanity have to be reversed.[1] The patient immediately projects the depressed part of the ego into the analyst. This constitutes a negative therapeutic reaction. The saner part of the ego is lost and the analyst becomes again the persecutor, since he is felt to contain the depressed part of the patient's ego and to force this unwanted depression back into the patient. In order to control this negative therapeutic reaction and to enable the patient to regain, retain, and strengthen the sane part of the personality, the whole process of the emergence of the depression and the projection of it has to be followed closely in the transference.

POSTSCRIPT 1980: DEPRESSION IN THE SCHIZOPHRENIC

Interestingly enough, this paper was read at the same Congress at which Bion read the paper "Differentiation of the Psychotic from the Non-Psychotic Part of the Personality," in which he described pathological projective identification and the creation of "bizarre objects." My patient was resorting to this mechanism as a defense against the depressive position: she split a part of her ego and the objects involved in the depressive relationship into minute fragments (the scattered flowers of Ophelia) and in projecting them into her object, she fragmented her object. It is a very important mechanism and a very dangerous one, leading to severe negative therapeutic reactions in the analysis of schizophrenics. If this process cannot be contained in the analysis, the patient may become more ill and more minutely fragmented than he had been at the inception of the treatment.

References

Bion, W. R. (1957). Differentiation of the psychotic from the non-psychotic personalities. *International Journal of Psycho-Analysis* 38:266-275. In W. R. Bion, *Second Thoughts*. New York: Jason Aronson, 1977.

Rosenfeld, H. (1955). Notes on the psycho-analysis of the superego conflict of an acute schizophrenic patient. In *New Directions in Psychoanalysis*, ed. M. Klein, P. Heimann, and R. Money-Kyrle, pp. 180-219. New York: Basic Books.

---

1. I do not propose to discuss in this paper why the depressive position is so unbearable to these patients. Some light is thrown on this problem in Rosenfeld (1955).

10

A Psychoanalytic Approach
to the Treatment
of Psychoses

THE PSYCHOANALYTIC APPROACH to the treatment of schizophrenia is based on the general assumption underlying all psychoanalytic thinking that psychological phenomena are amenable to understanding. The beginnings of psychoanalysis are in a way very modest. It started with Freud listening to the communication of his neurotic patients. Up to that time, the patient was classified, manipulated, maybe treated, but his communications were listened to in only a cursory manner and not considered material for examination. Psychoanalysis started with Freud's conviction that the verbal and nonverbal communications of his patients could be understood and should be examined with the intention of understanding. The pre-Freudian attitude to mental illness persits in many psychiatric approaches to psychotics. That is, psychotics can be classified, diagnosed as schizophrenic or manic-depressive, given treatment, etc., but their communications are considered either as not understandable or only marginally relevant to the understanding of the patient. In fact, it is often considered to be a diagnostic point that the content of the schizophrenic's psychotic communication is not understandable.

From the historical point of view, Freud tried to extend his attempts at understanding psychological manifestations into the area of psychosis as evidenced by his well-known analysis of the memoirs of President Schreber.

He never deliberately attempted, however, an actual psychoanalysis of a psychotic. His view was that since psychoanalysis depends on the work with the patient's transference, and since psychotics are wholly narcissistic and form no transference, he could not visualize how psychoanalytic work could be done with them. But for many who worked with psychotics in their ordinary psychiatric practice, this conclusion of Freud's did not seem to fit the facts.

To begin with, no one is completely psychotic. In every psychotic there are areas of personality which are neurotic and capable of forming an object relation, however flimsy. So a number of analysts did undertake treatment of psychotics, provided the healthy area was in sufficient evidence, and they tried to work on this healthier part of the patient's ego. They worked mainly in the positive transference with the aim of strengthening it enough to enable the healthier part of the ego to become dominant in relation to the psychotic part, a state of affairs which obtains in remissions. Frieda Fromm-Reichmann, Edith Jacobson, Harold Searles and others in America continued and developed work with psychotics on a similar basis. A completely different line of development was initiated by Melanie Klein, who continued Abraham's pioneering work in the analysis of psychotics, namely, manic-depressives. This work is also pursued by analysts trained by her. Bion (1967), Rosenfeld (1965), and I (chapters 4, 8, 9,) among others have produced a number of papers relating to the treatment of both acute and chronic states, and this is the approach I shall concentrate on here, since this is the one with which I have direct experience.

Melanie Klein's contribution to the theory and practice of psychoanalysis is rooted in her work with children. As a pioneer of child analysis, she discovered that small children can develop a transference, both positive and negative, of great intensity. In the analysis of children, she was impressed by the prevalence of the mechanisms of projection and introjection, more active and dynamic in the small child than repression. She discovered also that the infantile neurosis was a defensive structure, defending the child against primitive anxieties of a paranoid and depressive type which bear an obvious resemblance to those found in psychotic states. She herself did not analyze psychotic patients, with one exception—a four-year-old child who today would be diagnosed as autistic. She described this analysis in the paper "The Importance of Symbol Formation in the Development of the Ego" (Klein, 1930). In this paper, she showed how psychotic anxiety can block the process of symbol formation and the development of the ego and how the resolution of the anxiety can lead to a reestablishment of symbolic processes and ego development.

It is our contention that psychotic illness is rooted in the pathology of early infancy where the basic matrix of mental function is formed. By projection and introjection, splitting of the object into a good and bad one followed later by integration, introjection and identification with good objects, the ego is gradually strengthened and it acquires a gradual differentiation between the external and the internal world; the beginnings of superego formation and relation to the external objects are laid down. It is at this time also, in the first year of life, that symbol formation and the capacity to think and to speak develop. In psychosis, it is all these functions that are disturbed or destroyed. The confusion between the external and the internal, the fragmentation of object relationships and the ego, the deterioration of perception, the breakdown of symbolic processes, the disturbance of thinking: all are features of psychosis. Understanding the genesis of the development of the ego and its object relationships and the kind of disturbance that can arise in the course of that development is essential to understanding the mechanisms of the psychotic.

In order to undertake a psychoanalytic investigation of a psychotic patient, certain requirements of the setting and management must be satisfied. The management of the patient outside the sessions must be assured. The patient has to live between the sessions and his minimum needs at least must be satisfied. It is very helpful and at times essential that the management should be friendly to the analysis or at least neutral. It is a part of good management, for instance, to ensure that should the patient need hospitalization, the analytic treatment will not be interrupted at just the moment the patient needs it most. It is often through a failure of arranging a sufficiently stable management that the analytic treatment comes to grief. The analytic setting must provide for the patient the kind of holding environment in which his relationship to the analyst can develop without being broken up by the patient's psychosis. This necessitates, obviously, such things as reliability and regularity of the hours, a certain uniformity of the setting, a feeling of physical safety if the patient is violent, etc. But the analyst himself is a very important part of the setting. He must remain constant and not vary his role so that the patient's phantasies of omnipotent powers over objects can gradually undergo a reality testing. With secure management of the background and proper analytic setting, the analysis can proceed. Far from not developing a transference, the psychotic develops an almost immediate and usually violent transference to the analyst. The difficulty with the psychotic's transference is not its absence but its character—the difficulty both to observe it and to stand it. The apparent lack of transference or its peculiar nature when it manifests itself is due to the fact that the psychotic transference is based primarily on projective identification. By projective identification I mean here the patient's omnipotent phantasy that he can get rid of unwanted parts of himself into the analyst. This kind of transference is both violent and brittle. The psychotic tries to project into the analyst his terror, his badness, his confusion, his fragmentation and, having done this projection, he perceives the analyst as a terrifying figure from whom he may want to cut himself off immediately; hence the brittleness of the transference situation. The violence of his projective identification gives rise to a variety of phantasies and feelings. The patient may feel completely confused with the analyst and feel he is losing such identity as he still possesses; he may feel himself trapped, or that the analyst will invade him in turn. His experience of the transference is very concrete, as is his experience of the analyst's interpretation. When he is in the state of projective identification, and the analyst starts interpreting, the patient is apt to experience it as a projective identification in reverse, that is, to feel that the analyst is now putting into him, the patient, the analyst's own unwanted parts and driving him mad. This concreteness of experience, in which he feels that he is omnipotently changing the analyst and the analyst concretely and omnipotently changes him, is a technical point of utmost importance. It is essential for the analyst to understand that, when he interprets anxiety, the patient may feel that he is in fact attacking him, or if he interprets a patient's sexual feelings, the patient may experience it concretely as the analyst's sexual advances, toward him or her.

I cannot go at this point into the various aspects of why the experience is so concrete, which has to do with the failure of the patient's symbolic function. I have examined and described this failure in chapter 4. I emphasize this point here, however, in order to make it clear that it is useless to interpret to the psychotic as though he were a neurotic. Ordinary interpretations of the Oedipus complex for instance, could well be experienced as a sexual assault and in fact make the patient worse. It is the schizophrenic's language—with its concrete symbolization, its confusion between object and subject—his *psychotic* transference, that has to be the subject of the analysis.

I cannot even attempt to give a picture of the theory and practice of the analysis of a psychotic. The nearest I can come to it is to explain it by a model, based on Melanie Klein's concept of the paranoid-schizoid position and Bion's concept of the "mother capable of containing projective identification." In this model, the infant's relation to his first object can be described as follows: When an infant has an intolerable anxiety, he deals with it by projecting it into the mother. The mother's response is to acknowledge this anxiety and do whatever is necessary to relieve the infant's distress. The infant's perception is that he has projected something intolerable into his object, but the object was capable of containing it and dealing with it. He can then reintroject not only his original anxiety but an anxiety modified by having been contained. He also introjects an object capable of containing and dealing with anxiety. The containment of the anxiety by an internal object capable of understanding is a beginning of mental stability. This mental stability may be disrupted from two sources. The mother may be unable to bear the infant's projected anxiety and he may introject an experience of even greater terror than the one he had projected. It may also be disrupted by excessive destructive omnipotence of the infant's phantasy. In this model, the analytic situation provides a container. Into the setting, the patient projects his intolerable anxieties and impulses, but the setting itself cannot produce a change. The analyst, who is capable of tolerating and understanding the projected parts, responds by an interpretation which, at its best, is felt by the patient to contain the projected elements made more tolerable and understandable. The patient can then reintroject these projected parts made more tolerable, together with the functions of the analyst with which he can identify, allowing for the growth of a part of himself capable of containment and understanding.

This is, I think, as much as I can say in such a short paper to try to indicate what I, as a psychoanalyst, see myself doing when confronted by a psychotic patient. The question arises—Of what value is this procedure? Quite clearly psychoanalytic treatment, so very time-consuming and lengthy, does not give the answer to the social problem posed by schizophrenia. If all the psychoanalysts in the world were expert in the analysis of schizophrenics and devoted themselves solely to this task, it would statistically do very little for the world problem of the treatment of psychosis. What then is the value of psychoanalytic treatment? I think we have to differentiate here between the value to the patient and the value to the community. To take the patient first: It is my conviction that in the rare cases where all the conditions are right, psychoanalytic treatment is the treatment that gives the most hopeful therapeutic prognosis for the individual patient, and that, when successful, it is the treatment that deals with the very root of the disturbance of his personality; and I would not refrain from recommending it to an individual patient on the grounds that it is not a social solution, any more than I would withhold kidney machines or grafts from patients to whom they may be available, just because they are not universally available. From the point of view of society, the value of psychoanalysis of psychotics lies mainly in its research aspect. Psycho-analysis is basically an investigation, a method that throws light on the actual psychopathology of the illness. It is on such knowledge of the psychopathology that all other psychotherapeutic endeavours, such as management, group therapy, individual psychotherapy, or community care must be based. As Alanen (1975) has made clear, psychoanalytic research can also contribute here to methods of prevention which we hope one day will take precedence over treatment. Another aspect of the research on psychotics is the light it throws on mental phenomena in general. In every analysis of the neurotic, and even more so of borderline or delinquent patients, we have to deal with psychotic anxieties and mechanisms, and it is in the treatment of psychotics that one can observe these phenomena at their greatest intensity. But the research aspect and what we derive from it is not confined here to the treatment of illness. In the same way in which Freud's psychoanalysis of neurotics enabled him to formulate a general theory of mental development and function, it is analysis of psychotics with their disturbances of thinking, perception, symbolic function, object relations, etc., that enables us now to formulate much more precisely processes that go into these functions.

References

Alanen, Y. (1975). In *Studies of Schizophrenia* (Chapter 15). Ashton, Kent: Headley Brothers.

Bion, W.R. (1967). *Second Thoughts*. London: Heinemann Medical Books; New York: Jason Aronson, 1977.

Klein, M. (1930). The importance of symbol-formation in the development of the ego. *International Journal of Psycho-Analysis* 11:24-39. In M. Klein, *Contributions to Psycho-Analysis* 1921-1945 pp. 236-250. London: Hogarth, 1948.

——— (1946). Notes on some schizoid mechanisms. *International Journal of Psycho-Analysis* 27:99-110. Rosenfeld, H. (1965). *Psychotic States*. London: Hogarth.

11

Schizoid Mechanisms Underlying Phobia Formation

I WOULD LIKE to present some material from a patient who suffered from severe and extensive probias in order to illustrate some connections between early psychotic anxieties and defenses, and a common neurotic symptom. I shall try to show that certain paranoid schizoid mechanisms, particularly disintegration of the ego and projective identification, described by Melanie Klein in 1946, underlie my patient's probias.

My patient was a woman in her late thirties who had had severe difficulties from childhood onward as far back as she could remember, particularly social difficulties, feeding difficulties, and numerous phobias. By the time she sought analysis she was gravely ill.

Her symptoms, of which I shall mention only a few, could be divided into three categories:

1. Personality disturbances: She often felt depersonalized and unreal. She could form no relationship except on the basis of totally controlling her objects. She could not lead her own life and she was severely inhibited in work. I have described these last two aspects of her personality and their relation to projective identification in chapter 16. This patient is referred to as Patient D.

2. Various hypochondriacal and hysterical symptoms which had led in the past to numerous surgical interventions.

137

3. Extensive phobias, particularly of crowds, and a phobia of food, leading to such severe anorexia that prior to her analysis the patient had to be hospitalized. She had a great fear of restaurants, i.e. crowded places where one eats food.

In the first two years of her analysis certain features were prominent, especially the violence of her transference feelings and their markedly delusional character, varying between extremes of persecution and idealization. There was also a total inability to bear frustration in any form. She felt that if I were at her bedside giving her food at the moment she woke up, she would be able to eat it: but if she had to wait for it for a few minutes, or if the other person giving her food was not sufficiently representative of myself as a good object, the food would become poisonous and she could not eat it. In that way, any waiting or frustration in relation to food became a threat of never-ending starvation and death.

From the start, this patient made very extensive use of projective identification. She had been in analysis previously with Dr. Z., who later left her by emigrating from this country. For the first few days of the analysis with me, my patient could make no contact, feeling only acutely anxious, empty, and depersonalized. After some interpreting on my part, she told me the following dream: "Dr. Z. was sitting in an armchair in a foreign-looking flat and her belly was enormous, as though she was pregnant with a monstrous baby." I interpreted that the monstrous baby was herself, and that she had put herself into Dr. Z. and traveled with her to the foreign-looking flat. After this interpretation the patient became less depersonalized and could establish contact with me.

The second year of her analysis brought some material which seemed crucial in solving some of her major problems. The patient started a session by telling me, "Oh, I had another of those packing dreams!" In fact, she had never mentioned any packing dream before. When I pointed this out she said that she often dreamed of packing and that in the dreams she could never manage to pack. She had been very anxious about packing ever since her childhood. She thought, however, that to begin with it was only in a specific situation, namely, when she had to go to boarding school, that is, leave her mother. I interpreted to her that she put bits of herself into her mother to prevent separation, and that her inability to pack expressed her inability to collect the bits of herself from inside her mother and to reintegrate herself sufficiently to be able to leave her. Then she remembered more of the dream. She was in a large room with her mother, and her particular difficulty was that her things were all muddled up with her mother's things and she could not disentangle them. I took this as a confirmation. I also interpreted to her that in the transference, she felt I knew all about her packing dreams though she had never mentioned them before, because she projected parts of herself into me, as she did into her mother. Her dreams were inside me and therefore I knew all about them.

The next day she said she had had a terrible night. She had had "scattered dreams." She could not remember any of them but felt that they had been scattered all about the room inside and outside of her. Now and then she would wake and find herself saying in an imploring voice, "O God, don't let me be hungry, I must not be hungry." I interpreted to her that she had tried to overcome her overwhelming fear of hunger, which to her meant death, by splitting herself into bits and scattering them. The scattered dreams represented the scattered bits of herself, when she was disintegrating to avoid experiencing the peril of hunger and death. She then said, "That must be it, because when I woke up I thought, I scatter, I splutter and I sink." After a short silence, she added, "But now I can remember a bit of the dream. My daughter Ruth and her friends were doing a harlequinade in the dream and I was helping and directing them." She told me about a play in which her daughter was taking part and she, the patient, was helping. It was clear that though she had started with the genuine wish to help she had ended by trying to control and bully the children. Particularly, she wanted them to do a harlequinade instead of the play which they intended to do. I interpreted her need for controlling the situation, and pointed out to her how in the dream she had control in that the children were doing a harlequinade as she had wanted them to. She then said, "But later it rather changed. The children became more like puppets." I took this as a confirmation of my interpretation. I then reminded her of the scattering of herself and of the previous material on packing, and I suggested to her that the scattering of herself served a further purpose. Not only was she avoiding feeling anxiety, but also by scattering she was putting bits of herself into everybody in order to control them like puppets.

She then remembered a further bit of the dream: "Now that you mention packing, I remember further that there were kind of packing-tables in the room and that I was somehow manipulating these children-puppets into the packing-tables and then they were disappearing." After hesitating, she added, "It has nothing to do with packing, but I felt as though they were disappearing into me and I felt all wooden." I interpreted that, having projected herself into so many different people in order to control them, then, to reintegrate herself, she had to swallow all these people, that is, wooden puppets. She laughed and said, "Yes, I feel I often look as though I was a picture painted by Picasso."

The patient then remembered yet another part of the dream: "Ruth, or she, herself, was in hospital, and somebody was losing blood." She associated this part of her dream to her own loss of blood during an abdominal operation she had had. I knew that at the time she had been severely anxious, fearing what the surgeon had, unknown to her, taken out or put into her. She also had poor control over her urine and feces and suffered a feeling which she called "profound disgrace." I interpreted that she had projected her illness into her daughter Ruth, and I reminded her of the anxieties at the time of her operation. I suggested that when she lost control of her urine and feces and felt so profoundly disgraced, it was not only her excrements but bits of herself projected into the excrements that she felt she was scattering around.

The following day, a Friday, she told me that she had taken two pink pills to avoid another scattered night. She spent at least ten minutes describing in glowing terms the virtue of the pink pills. I interpreted to her that the pink pills represented the two ideal breasts, which should protect her from hunger and disintegration and pointed out her intense need for introjecting me as good breasts, i.e. food. I reminded her of her desperate cry the night before: "God, don't let me be hungry." I also pointed out to her the intense idealization that was apparently needed before she could take me in. She then said that, in fact, she always distrusts colored foods, particularly pink. As a child she loved pink sugary pills, until one day she opened one and to her horror found that inside they were full of a disgusting brown stuff, and she realized that what she was actually given was a sugar-coated purgative. I interpreted that the brown mass was felt by her as horrible feces that she was given to eat, that it was attacking her from inside and giving her diarrhea. She idealized my breasts and pretended they gave her complete comfort but, in fact, she felt persecuted by my interpretations the day before and felt I was filling her with horrible fecal stuff. She then remembered two bits of dreams from the previous night: the first one had to do with a "bunged-up" lavatory, and in the second one "she saw a child peeing into the soup." I reminded her of the end of the previous session—her splitting herself into bits and putting all these bits in the form of urine and feces into me, standing for her mother. The child peeing into the soup was herself peeing into me in her anger at the frustration of the coming weekend, as well as in an attempt to control me by filling me with bits of herself. The bunged-up lavatory was myself, bunged-up by her excrements and all the bits of herself projected into me; but, if so, then the food that my breasts gave her became a horrible fecal and urinary mass. And by introjection, she herself became a bunged-up lavatory. Her intense idealization of the breasts (pink pills) was a denial of her attacks and of the resulting feeling of internal persecution and depression.

She then started talking about her fear of restaurants. She was invited out to lunch and was terrified.

I was then able to link up this analysis of her relation to the breasts with her phobia of restaurants. I reminded the patient of her childhood fear of wetting her pants in the restaurant and connected it with the dream in which the child pees into the soup. I interpreted her terror of the restaurant as a result of her projective identification, the restaurant standing for the feeding mother. She felt that she had thrown her urine and feces and parts of herself into all the people in the restaurant as well as into the food. She, therefore, became depersonalized, afraid of the people containing bad parts of herself, and of the food bunged-up with her excrement. Then she had to avoid the restaurant so as not to have to reintroject this mess.

This session preceded a three-day break. During this break, the patient had an acute experience of her phobia of crowds. She belonged to an organization, the members of which come from two London districts: St. John's Wood and Hampstead. This weekend that organization had its annual meeting. My patient suddenly conceived the notion that the Hampstead people had too much control in the organisation, and she decided to have them removed from all important posts. Though she was not conscious of it at the time, it appeared in the analysis that she pictured the situation as follows: the St. John's Wood people were English, decent, working-class people; the Hampstead people were intellectual, Jewish, and communist. She got her charwoman, a member of the same organization, to propose her (the patient's) husband for President. At the meeting, however, she felt very anxious, and when the Chairman called upon her to speak for her husband she felt empty and terrified, surrounded by a hostile crowd— overwhelmed by panic. She said, "Oh, but I don't support him." When she returned home, she felt profoundly disgraced by her disloyalty and for the following days confined herself to the house, afraid that she might meet a crowd in the street. She managed, however, to come to her analytic session.

I shall summarize briefly the meaning of this acting out. Both she and I live in St. John's Wood. St. John's Wood stands, therefore, for the good me when I am present, hard-working, feeding her and looking after her like her charwoman and her husband. I am then simple and decent, i.e. complete, unspoilt, without conflict. But I am so good only when I am always present and when she has complete control of me. Both her charwoman and her husband did as she told them. Hampstead is where I do not live. It represents what I become when I am not present. Then, in her mind, I become split into millions of dangerous fecal bits. The Jews have, for her, a very fecal meaning. I also become dangerous, greedy and vindictive (her feelings about communists). So one of the things which happened during that weekend was that she split me into a good object—charwoman and husband—and into a bad one, which was felt as the crowds of communists, Jews, intellectuals. But that is not the whole story. St. John's Wood represents a good part of herself united with me, while Hampstead undoubtedly also represents an aspect of herself. She is often deeply identified with Jews: it is she who is a professional intellectual, and it is she, in fact, who had been a member of the Communist Party. Hampstead not only represented me in bits, but I was in bits because she projected into me all the bad fecal, split-off, disintegrated and disowned parts of herself. The meeting was to her a battle between her good self and object, put into her husband, and her bad disintegrated parts and objects projected into the crowd. When called upon to speak for her good object, the patient had to face the crowd, that is, her own projected disintegration and evil, as well as the destroyed and therefore bad objects. She was overwhelmed by it and threatened by madness. In phobically avoiding crowds she was avoiding the come-back of her projected disintegration.

The material described here took a long time to work through. Its analysis enabled the patient to integrate herself more. Through a lessening of the projective identification, the horrors of introjection diminished so that the patient was able to introject a good object and experience ambivalence and depression. Since the acting out described, she has not had any major phobic symptoms. Her analysis was, unfortunately, interrupted after about three years through external circumstances. She was not cured, but the considerable improvement she derived from her analysis has been steadily maintained.

To summarize: I suggest that this patient was basically fixated in a paranoid-schizoid position. When she was threatened by ambivalent feelings she regressed to the schizoid level. In this primitive stage of the ego any frustration was felt as an actual threat of death. She had to defend herself by disintegration of the ego, which she described as "scattering, spluttering and sinking," and by an extensive use of projective identification. In the analytic situation she projected bits of herself into me to prevent separation, to hurt and to damage and control me. As a result, she felt persecuted, afraid of crowds and of food. She defended herself against this persecution by an unsuccessful attempt at idealization: "the pink pills." At the peak of her anxiety, she felt threatened by madness: her ego was disintegrated, she lost large parts of it by projective identification, she felt persecuted by bad disintegrated objects from within and without.

The formation of a phobia averts such catastrophic situations. The patient projects her phantasies and binds them in definite external situations, which she is then able to avoid.

In conclusion, I suggest that my patient's phobias of food and crowds are due to the operation of schizoid anxieties and defenses, and that they serve the purpose of averting an acute schizophrenic illness.

This patient was admittedly a borderline case, showing many schizoid features. Her phobias, however, were typical hysterical formations. In the analysis of other less ill patients I uncovered similar mechanisms in the formation of phobias and I find that in order to dissolve these neurotic symptoms it is of particular importance to analyze the underlying psychotic fears. This conclusion is in keeping with one of the basic contentions of Melanie Klein, namely, that the infantile neurosis is a means of working through earlier psychotic anxieties of both a paranoid-schizoid and manic-depressive nature. It is, therefore, of importance to analyze psychotic anxieties in order to dissolve neurotic manifestations.

POSTSCRIPT 1980:
NOTES ON SCHIZOID MECHANISMS UNDERLYING PHOBIA FORMATION

This paper presents phobia formation from both the theoretical and technical point of view. From the theoretical point of view, it describes the process of fragmentation of a part of the ego, combined with violent projection. This was later described by Bion (1957) as pathological projective identification, a hallmark of the psychotic process.

I would say today that to a phobic, the crowd represents a conglomeration of bizarre objects. I think that I have described correctly the basic mechanisms of phobic formation.

On the other hand, looking back on this paper twenty-five years later, I find my technique very poor. I thought I was analyzing the transference when I was interpreting to the patient her phantasies about me. Now I think I completely failed to analyze the transference properly. Her projective identification was not just a phantasy; I seem to have been quite unaware of the way in which it was happening in these sessions. In the session before the weekend, she was obviously placating me, idealizing me and thereby both controlling me and feeling controlled by me. Today I would be more concerned with showing her what she was actually doing in the session in the moment-to-moment interaction between us. I would concentrate less on the detailed content of her phantasies and dreams.

References

Bion, W. R. (1957). Differentiation of the psychotic from the non-psychotic personalities. *International Journal of Psycho-Analysis* 38:266-275. In W. R. Bion, *Second Thoughts.* New York: Jason Aronson, 1977.

Klein, M. (1946). Notes on some schizoid mechanisms. *International Journal of Psycho-Analysis* 27:99-110.

PART V

OTHER
CLINICAL ISSUES

12

Manic Reparation

I PROPOSE TO DISCUSS in this paper some problems connected with the use of manic reparation as a defense against insight.

Reparation proper, in the definition of Melanie Klein, arises out of feelings of loss and guilt experienced in the depressive position. Reparation is based on the love for the object and the wish to restore and regain it. The reparative drives contribute to the development of the ego and the object relationships; they cannot be considered as a defense since reparation does not aim at denying psychic reality but is an endeavor—realistic in psychic terms—to resolve depressive anxiety and guilt.

Manic trends in reparation, on the other hand, aim at denying guilt and responsibility and are based on an omnipotent control of the object. The defense against anxiety and guilt is paramount and love and concern for the object—the hallmark of genuine reparation—are relatively weak.

As I have encountered it, there are two types of patients in whom manic reparation presents a particular problem. To the first type belongs the patient whose whole life structure seems to depend on a manic defense system with manic reparation as its most constant characteristic. Very frequently, breaches in the defense appear in mid-life crisis. what follows is a fairly typical example of how a case history may present itself.

147

The patient was in his late thirties. He had a great deal of drive and ambition and was a successful doctor devoted to his patients. The profession is characteristic (helping the sick). He came to the analysis suffering from a gastric ulcer, feelings of inability to cope and depression, a depression which was more paranoid than appeared at first sight. The symptom he presented was his wife. According to him, she was withdrawn and cold, partially frigid, and drove him to distraction. It soon became clear that an important aspect of his relationship with his wife had to do with her illness. He was aware of her difficulties when he married her but convinced that his relationship to her, basically his sexuality, would cure her. Gradually, her lack of response undermined his confidence, and he began to hate her and to experience paranoid rages at her, sometimes quite murderous. He felt that she was giving him nothing, exploiting him, frustrating him and robbing him. The analysis revealed quite clearly that what he felt so robbed of was his phantasy of an imaginary, omnipotent, curative penis. One of his earliest memories of childhood was of a little potato patch on his father's farm; he was convinced that this was the source of food for the whole family. As an adult, he recognized it to be a phantasy, but for quite a few years he maintained in the analysis that he was, as a little boy, the one who helped his mother do all the housework. He believed this to be a reality even in his adult life until, while in analysis, he suddenly realized that at the age at which he supposedly did this, age two-and-a-half to about age four, he could not possibly have done any actual work for her and that, in fact, this was the way in which mother kept him busy and happy.

When the patient was about seven and a sibling was born, he was sent away for more than a year to an aunt. There he was quite happy and did not seem to miss his home. Far from admitting any feelings of rejection, he felt himself very wanted and needed. His aunt was childless and a widow, and he thought he was sent to her to relieve her loneliness. Here again, he was the provider. His leading memory of that phase of his life was how he got up at the crack of dawn to collect the milk for his aunt. He presented a lot of material that looked like an idealization of breasts. He saw himself as a great lover of women and particularly of breasts. It was the breast in a woman that attracted him most. He often complained that he vested all his interest in the maternal breast and it let him down. One day, in associating to a dream, he had a phantasy of an empty breast which he was filling with his tongue. The experience was lovely. This phantasy was the basis of all his relationships to women. The ideal breast for him was an empty breast, which he, the baby was feeding with his tongue and later with his penis, urine and semen. If, in such a position, the idealization of the magic powers of his tongue or his penis failed, he faced the breast as a vengeful abyss. As a young man he could maintain this position up to a point. He was the benevolent physician—father, husband, provider. He was never exposed to envy, jealousy, rage or deprivation. Bad feelings were projected into the objects who depended on him and denied in them, for he felt he could satisfy them all.

Around middle age, his idealization of himself as the provider began to collapse, and persecution made its appearance. Slowly, it dawned on him that his siblings resented him because he got the best of the parental inheritance; the same was true of his colleagues whom he thought envied him because of his rapid promotion. Most of all, his wife did not respond to his ministrations. She was experienced by him as this abyss of the empty breast defying his claims of the magic curative powers of his penis. Another internal abyss was opening right in his very stomach (his ulcer). He was bewildered. Here he was, so good to patients, wife, children—all to no avail.

Patients of this kind do not usually come into analysis unless the defenses are already breaking down. I think this is so even if the apparent reason for starting an analysis is professional, for instance, becoming a candidate. The fact that the defense is breaking down, or on the point of breaking down, makes the task of the analyst easier, even though the patient will battle desperately to re-establish the defense. The patient I have referred to openly longed to be the way he was ten or twenty years ago. The cry was "But it worked, why doesn't it work now?"

I think a more difficult technical problem arises when the manic reparation emerges in the analysis partly as a result of an improvement which allows the patient to start emerging from the paranoid-schizoid position, and then it is apt to be organized into a formidable defense against any further progress. A central European woman, who started analysis also in her middle thirties, had been suffering for a long time from a state of disintegration, fragmentation of personality, hypochondriasis and very vague and diffuse paranoia.

Gradually, this stage of diffusion and disorganization lessened; the patient became more coherent. She could go back to work as a nursery teacher (another helping profession, you will notice) and even started working for a higher qualification. She became more aware of her feelings and relationships, and some genuine depressive feelings began to emerge. These were immediately counteracted by a flurry of activities, felt by her as reparative, taking the form of acting out, and interfering with any further development of insight. This had appeared intermittently earlier in her analysis as depressive anxieties were approached, but a new phase of her analysis started when manic reparative activities seemed to bring her analysis to a standstill. This phase was ushered in by a dream. She was very excited because a Mr. X from abroad, who had certain contacts in the psychiatric world, was going to visit her and her husband. The following week, her brother was also visiting them in London. In her dream, she had lots of visitors in her kitchen; men, women and children. She was feeding them pink cakes and chocolate cakes. She felt very good and very excited. In the corner of the kitchen, there was a paper bag of sugar with very little sugar left and that spilled on the floor. Her associations were first to the exciting visits of Mr. X and her brother. When I drew her attention to the bag of sugar toward the end of the session she remembered that the bag was exactly like the one used by her mother. The meaning of the dream was that she was giving an exciting sexual and anal meal to all, while her mother's breasts, empty and discarded, were pushed into a corner. This expressed very well her feeling toward the analytic breasts at that time. She paid a great deal of lip service to how marvellous her analyst was and how the analysis had helped her, but, in fact, the analyst was completely disregarded and the interpretations were used only to produce her own "food"; and her child, husband and friends were treated to quite regal helpings of my interpretations intended for the patient herself.

Soon after the kitchen dream, the patient's father died, and his death contributed very much to the manic trend. She came back from his funeral very elated by the marvelous religious service with the hymn singing, etc. Though feeling herself an agnostic, she felt that through these observances the spirit of her father was kept alive. She had a dream of a man and his family under water and she saw in the dream that, though some people might think that they had drowned, they were, in fact, perfectly happy. After some interpretion of her denial and idealization of death, she started associating to a patchwork quilt that was made by her father's mother and which always moved her to tears. She referred to something which she had spoken about in the past, about her idea of her father having a very good internal mother as a source of goodness and strength. She herself noticed that this idealization of her father's mother contrasted very much with her feelings about father's wife, her own mother. In connection with her idealization of the dead objects, that is, the man and the family under the water, I reminded her that her father's mother died when he was very little, and she agreed that the main point was that the *ideal* mother was a dead mother, not her own while she was still alive. Her other associations were to the quilt. It represented the patchwork of her own activities, and it emerged fairly clearly that her activities were concerned with an object mother or father, felt to be dead, but covered up by a quilt of patchy, colorful activities.

This association was followed by a few days of quieter feelings about her father and some reawakened mourning for her mother. She also resisted acting out in a ready-made situation. She was visiting her mother-in-law, old and ailing. The old woman was lighting a fire, slowly and painfully, but lighting the fire was her great pride. The patient was longing to make her sit down while she lit the fire for her; she felt like screaming with impatience. But she resisted the temptation, and she let the old lady get on with it. Two points emerged clearly from this situation: first, her difficulty in sympathizing with or containing a damaged object ("If I had a handicapped child, I would kill it"); and second, her insistence that she must be the giver of light and warmth, that all life must come to the objects from her ("I wanted to treat her as though she were a mummy"). This insight led to some quietening in her acting out, but it did not last long. She was full of ideas about translating a book of her father's into English, neglecting her own work and her own analysis. True to her patchwork quilt tendencies, a day or two later, she was planning to do some research into the battered children syndrome. One Friday, she came a quarter of an hour late, very excited. She thought she had had a very good talk with the mother of a pupil, one of "my evacuated mothers"; maybe she could combine research into battered children and evacuated mothers. I drew her attention to the fact that currently I was being an evacuated mother by her quarter-of-an-hour lateness and interpreted the evacuated mother as the mother, myself, changed into feces and evacuated. The battered babies of the mother were being treated in a similar way. As was typical with her, she reacted to the interpretation with a kind of persecuted collapse and the comment, "I thought I had a good interview." A day or two previously, she had a similar reaction when her husband made a critical remark about her plan for redecorating the kitchen: "When E. said that, it all collapsed, and I had thought it was such a good plan."

The next week ushered in two more great reparative plans. Her father's book, battered babies and evacuated mothers disappeared from the scene and a threatened park in the country suddenly emerged as the object to be rescued. The patient had read in the papers that the owner of a famous hilly park had died and she decided that it would be wonderful to make it into a national park. She wrote to the paper and to her M.P. Here the paranoid element came more clearly to the fore. The park had to be saved from the "Edwards." This was her name for get-rich-quick exploiters, because Edward is the name of a young businessman relative. Further, at the time of her mother's illness and after her mother's death, the mourning for her mother was quite inaccessible to the patient. All her emotions then were switched into a paranoia about Edward, who was accused of exploiting her parents and making her mother's life and death a misery. Her parents had been, in fact, fond of Edward and she could never bear this blindness in them. The rescue of the park from the "Edwards" represented a situation in which her dead and idealized mother had to be rescued from her brothers, into whom the patient projected all her own exploitation and ruthlessness toward mother.

Simultaneously, the patient was defending the school in which she worked against exploitation by a child psychologist fraudulently representing herself as an analyst. With all these rescuing operatons of the good mother (the park) and the good analysis at the school, she regularly forgot all her dreams; she came late and did not retain any links with the previous day's analysis. When this was pointed out to her, she reacted with a violent feeling of being attacked; and she accused the analyst of confusion and of not being able to distinguish between her and the people she was describing, the "Edwards" and the fraudulent child psychologist. The paranoia, however, was of much shorter duration than in the past.

A few days later, the patient was again a quarter-of-an-hour late and in the same excited mood as when she was dealing with the evacuated mothers. An old tree in the school playground was being cut much too short, and she started a tremendous agitation in the school to get a protest to stop this process. In doing this, the patient got into a paranoid quarrel with two of her colleagues. She said that she thought she was at last undoing the damage she had done to me in the past. Indeed, in the past the tree represented a good father's analytic penis, and she was identified with children damaging it. But this rescue operation left her confused. It got her into a new quarrel and, in fact, as I pointed out to her, cut the analytic hour short.

I have given here a long and rather anecdotal account of this phase of the patient's analysis to bring out the feeling of the relentless repetitiveness of her acting out.

As it is, I gave only some examples; I left out many concurrent intermittent activities imbued with the same excitement. Most of those activities included the following elements: a good object has to be preserved or rescued as is the Park from the "Edwards," the school from the fraudulent psychologist, the tree from the school authorities. This threatened good object could be her father (the book), the penis (the tree), or mother (the school or the hilly park).

The villains varied. Her brothers, represented by the "Edwards," were seen as villains. But often, this switched to her father if the object of rescue was her mother; or her mother became the villain if her father or brother were to be rescued. All the patient's own bad impulses were projected into the villains. However, interpretations of projections were lapped up by the patient without making the slightest therapeutic change. She was quite aware that the villains contained projected bad aspects of herself, but she felt that this was all the more reason to stamp them out.

The only approach which made an impact on her was that of constantly pointing out to her how these phantasies and activities were to be a rescue of the good analysis but were, in fact, an unremitting attack on analytic work. The phantasies were both escapes from facing the analysis and her internal world and a positive attack on the analyst's capacities and the analysis. Thus, when the patient was planning to save the evacuated mothers, she was actually evacuating her analyst, in her lateness. And while she was saving the tree from being cut too short, she was actually cutting her session short.

It could be shown to the patient that she felt, in fact, that her internal objects were dead; if the analyst, who represented them, showed any signs of effective functioning, that functioning was immediately cut short and deadened. This, of course, was found to be very persecuting; it was a different kind of persecution from that by the "Edwards" and similar objects. It was far more devastating in two ways: first, it was the persecution by the dead, unrestored internal parents; and second it was experienced as an attack on her goodness, on what she felt was best in her, her love and reparation.

Interpretations on these lines, though rejected by the patient, brought some shift. The internal objects and the analysis showed some life, and dreams reappeared.

The patient dreamed about a broken vase; she was trying to put it together and I was helping her; it was the first time during that phase of the analysis that she had had a dream in which she allowed me to help her. Then, in the dream, she was putting two coats on me, one blue, one brown. Her associations were that the blue coat belonged to her mother, and the other to the maid Maisie, who had looked after her when she was a child. Her mother was admired but felt as unhelpful; the maid was helpful but despised, a borderline mental defective. The patient thought that it was the first time that she had brought these two aspects of mother together.

As dreams reappeared, the acting out continued but with a lessened intensity and she was more aware of its interference with the analysis. Her father, who was an eminent politician in his own country, left some memoirs. She no longer thought of publishing them, but her sister wrote to her asking her for ideas for the foreword to the book. This excited her greatly.

A few days after the dream of the two coats, she came very elated. She started the session by saying that she had been super-efficient that morning. She had visited a journalist friend and discussed with him ideas for the foreword. She had even written her reports at school and had put her watch on the table to watch the time and not to be late for the session. But halfway to the consulting room, she realized that she had left the watch in the office. She was very despondent about this because the watch belonged to her father-in-law and was treasured by her husband. It also reminded her that not long ago she had lost her own father's watch. She had to put the watch on the table because the strap of the watch was broken. (The breaking of the strap of the watch was a regular event: even a steel strap she got for her last watch broke on the second day. When the strap was broken, it did not take long for her to lose or mislay the watch.) She had a dream. In the dream, the analyst was present in the background, but it was Maisie, the maid, who was really her companion. She was very surprised because in the dream it seemed that she had written a book about mental deficiency but she had not known that she had written it. She was surprised and disbelieving. In another part of the dream, she was giving a lift to Mrs. X somewhere in the wilderness. Mrs. X was indicating where she wanted to go and what direction the patient should take. She thought it was incredible cheek from a person to whom she was giving a lift, and she stopped the car, deciding to go on strike. Her associations were mainly to Mrs. X. She thought that Mrs. X was a kind of superior nanny person; in fact, she must have been a nanny or a nursery teacher before her marriage. Nevertheless, the patient had to admit that Mrs. X had published some very good research on deprived children.

I shall not go into the detailed interpretations, but the dream is obviously a continuation of the 'two coats' dream. What appeared in the two coats dream as an integration between mother and nanny became more clearly a denigration of myself and mother as an internal object. Her super-efficiency is obviously at the expense of the analyst, who is turned into a mentally deficient nanny in the internal world, about whom the patient writes a book. (A very similar thing happens, of course, with her father's book. By virtue of her foreword, the book becomes her book at the expense of her father.) The breaking of the strap and the losing of the watch represented a break in contact with the analyst as mother or father as a helpful figure. In the part of the dream about Mrs. X, some rehabilitation of the analyst occurs. She was a superior kind of nanny, and the patient has to admit her grudging respect; but at the thought of dependence on this internal figure, which told her the direction to take, she revolted and went on strike.

In spite of the rather hectic excitement at the beginning of the session, the patient quieted down a great deal and cooperated much better than in the previous month. Toward the end of the session, however, she was evidently preoccupied with something. In fact, I had a cold that day, though by no means a bad one. Suddenly in the middle of my interpreting her going on strike against Mrs. X, she burst out with the exclamation, "But you should not be working at all now; you should be in bed, being looked after and given hot drinks!" It is very difficult to convey the subtlety and impact of what she did at that moment, but I had no doubt that she was making a mental defective out of me. She was interrupting my adult mental functioning as the parent in relation to her as the child and wanting me to become a helpless baby in bed. But from the connections to the dream and the impact of this sudden interruption on the analytic process, I think it was more making me into an idiot than into a baby. I do not remember how I formulated the interpretation, but, rather surprisingly for her, she did not react with injured innocence and saw the point that an adult working person, who would collapse and retire to bed to be looked after because of a touch of cold, would be rather deficient.

It is significant that when this type of pseudo-reparative feeling is brought directly into the transference, it invariably becomes an attack on the analyst's functioning and the analysis itself. It never takes the form of actually helping the analyst to function by bringing material or dreams or providing links, but it strips the analyst of his powers of functioning. The direct reparative thoughts in relation to myself in this patient took usually one of two forms: either I was ill and helpless and being looked after by her, or, particularly early in her analysis, she had phantasies of buying material, making clothes, and dressing me, almost like a doll.

The following day, she again had a dream and quite rich associations, showing further mobilization of her internal world. She came five minutes late and said that she had again been very efficient but something went wrong. She put my fee, which she was going to bring me, and the key of the car into a bag and then mislaid the bag. She added, "It's funny. When I put things in the bag, I feel I have done what I ought to do. I need not concern myself with it anymore; the job is done. I forget I still have to bring it here." She then spoke of how efficient she was in arranging the painting of a room in her house. I was able to interpret to her, using some additional past material, that the bag represented all the external jobs and activities into which she put things from the analysis, breaking links with me and not bringing anything back into the analysis. I connected the analysis with the internal world which remained unreplenished and the internal Maisie/

mother. That reminded her of a dream which was in two parts. First, she was clambering, she did not know where, into a clock, or down a clock, but she could not see the clock face. She thought, "I must be able to get in, because there must be an exit." Inside the clock there were some very beautiful objects, like delicate ornaments on a mantlepiece, but then, as she was climbing down, everything seemed to be in the usual muddle, her husband, her child, school children, all sorts of bits and pieces in confusion. Then, she was again giving a ride to Mrs. Z. (Mrs. Z is a doctor and the wife of an analysand of mine.) She took a violent turn which could have led to a fatal accident. She then tried to reassure herself that they were both not frightened or hurt, but she was not convinced. She noticed that there was a further rehabilitation to the woman to whom she was giving a ride: first to Maisie, then Mrs. X, the superior nanny, now Mrs. Z, the object of frank admiration and envy as a woman doctor standing for the analyst. I pointed out to her that with the rehabilitation of the object goes increased violence. Maisie is unharmed; with Mrs. X, she goes on strike, but she wants to smash Mrs. Z in the car. She protested that she only wanted to show off but then admitted that the feeling in the dream was quite murderous and that this murderous feeling was part of the showing off of her superior power and strength. She then came back to the clock and remembered a book she had read as a small child, called *The World Behind the Clock*. She had also had a grandfather clock in her home which intrigued her greatly. She thought of all my interpretations in the past about clocks and watches and her inability to look at a watch and the connections I had made in the past between the watch and the breast. The clock part of the dream showed an important aspect of her relation to the object. The getting inside the breast and the confusion that arose, for instance, between the entrance and the exit, had, at one time, played a much more prominent role in her analysis. In this context, I think it was mainly an indication of how she got possession of the car in which she gave rides. She got inside the breast, partly messing it up, the muddle below in the clock representing her mother's messed up internal objects, and she got control of the nipple as a kind of steering wheel. But she also felt completely cut off from the real world and drove blindly. The super-efficiency in her control of the nipple was constantly interrupted either by confusion or by persecution coming to her from the breast inside of which she resides or by identification with the mentally deficient, depleted internal object. The so-called reparative activities—her wild, controlling driving in this dream—appeared more clearly here as an envious attack and taking over from mother.

This theme became still clearer the following week. A new ploy was

looking after Jean. Jean was a schizophrenic girl in analysis with Miss B.
My patient's sudden excited interest in her was due to the fact that Jean's
parents were friends of a friend of the patient's. This friend of the patient
was Dr. O, who had died recently. The patient wanted to arrange for Jean to
go to her nursery school as a kind of occupational therapy. She was furious
when I pointed out her rivalry with Miss B and her cutting Miss B out by
never checking whether this kind of occupation was suitable for her patient.
The next day, she said that she had had a dream which made her furious
because it made her think that my interpretation was right. She was giving a
party in what might have been her mother's house, but there were a lot of
analysts there, so it might have been mine or Miss B's, but it was *her* party.
She was wearing a peculiar floppy hat. She thought the dream confirmed
that she was in rivalry with Miss B and me, and was taking over our house
and practice. The floppy hat had associations to Dr. O and, she thought, it
meant that she had a secret relation to his penis. As usual in this kind of
dream, she was very distraught because there was no food and everything
was in a muddle. There was no one to help her arrange things. This dream
was like a synthesis of the dream about the clock and the dream about Mrs. Z.
Here clearly, she got inside the mother's body, in envy and competition. She
took over the nipple and the penis (floppy hat). Jean was the projected mad
child, herself, whom she insisted she could look after better than her mother.
In fact, the concern for Jean was minimal even in that context, so minimal
that, a few days later, when the plans were coming to fruition and everything was arranged, she forgot to take Jean to the school.

It is, of course, characteristic of manic reparation that love for the
apparent object of concern is shallow and unreal. The external object is
there to distract attention from the internal situation.

In the patient described, the internal situation underwent a certain
rehabilitation. At the beginning of the term, her internal objects were felt to
be dead. Later, the mother appeared first as a mentally deficient nanny, then
as a superior nanny, and finally as the admired and envied Mrs. Z, and the
patient's hostility and envious attacks were more openly acknowledged. She
could then see more clearly the functions of her compulsive manic reparation: first, the denial of the deadness of the object through maintaining a
flurry of activity; second, a denial of her own hostility and envy by taking
over the place of the mother and constantly doing good, and third, the
projection of badness into the villains. All this defended her against guilt.
At the same time, a continuing attack was being made on the internal
objects kept dead or deficient and triumphed over. In the transference, this

became a continuous attack on the analyst's functioning, either by keeping the analysis defeated and dead or by demonstrating that every intervention of the analyst was an attack on the patient's reparative capacities.

Only the ceaseless analysis of this process in the transference can lessen the omnipotence of these mechanisms and lead to a gradual restoration of a good internal object.

POSTSCRIPT 1980: MANIC REPARATION

In this paper I try to emphasise two points; one is theoretical, trying to show the links between envy and manic reparation. The patient was in despair because her internal objects were dead or destroyed, largely because of her envious attacks. She was frantic to restore them, but her reparative activities had to be compatible with her envy and because of that they failed in relieving the guilt—the objects remained in subjection.

The other point I make is technical. It is very dangerous to go along with the patient's manic reparation, as it does not solve the vicious circle of despair, but the analysis of the underlying internal situation does bring relief, and I show in the paper the gradual rehabilitation of the patient's internal objects.

13

A Note on Internal Objects

THE AIM OF this short communication is to show in a patient's session a relationship to her introjected object and the role played by this relation in her character and her life.

The patient came to analysis because of a character disturbance. This disturbance threatened the stability of her marriage, interfered with her relation to her children and her work. The underlying psychopathology was predominantly of a manic-depressive type but not amounting to a psychosis. The material that I shall present comes from a time when her analysis was fairly advanced. In the weeks preceding the session the patient was particularly preoccupied with difficulties at her work. She was a university lecturer. She complained of deficiencies in her memory and difficulties of concentration. What disturbed her most was that recently she had completely forgotten her own past work. She had to review the literature on a certain topic in preparation for her lectures. She consulted a bibliography and was horrified to find that she had herself published work on the topic—a fact she had totally forgotten. Another theme linked with her difficulties emerged: a great idealization of the contents of her mind and a great anxiety about committing to paper any of her thoughts for fear of their being criticized and found wanting. During that week she also

159

spoke with some guilt about her neglect of her daughters. The session I am
going to report is a mid-week one.

When I went to the waiting room, I noticed that the patient was
furtively hiding something in her handbag and blushing. Once on the
couch, she told me she had been eating an apple but didn't want to be seen
by me so she quickly stuffed it into her bag. But as she had already bitten
into it, she was now worried that it would be turning brown and starting to
smell in her bag. She then went on to say that she thought things were
beginning to open up in her analysis and she was coming to grips with
herself. She had a dream in which she was breaking down barriers. She then
related the dream. The first part was very vague. She was in a field, breaking
down fences, and she felt anxious. On waking, she thought that the fences
must represent her defenses and that this must mean progress. But she found
the second part of the dream depressing. She dreamed that she had five
lodgers in her London apartment. She tried to look at them but they were in
semi-darkness and she couldn't see them clearly. She thought she had
neglected them shamefully and that she must really start looking after them.
In the third part of the dream she was walking with me and we were talking
in a friendly manner, but she thought she must take good care not to look at
me as it would be against the psychoanalytic rules. Her associations turned
first to the lodgers. She said she could understand why she had dreamed of
lodgers. She ought to pay more attention to them. (In the small university
town in which she taught, she had in fact a few lodgers.) But she was puzzled
why it was so clearly stated in the dream that it was her London apartment. I
pointed out to her that it is her children who live in London and that she
spoke of them the previous week. Her worry about her lodgers was not in
fact realistic, it was the effect of the displacement from her children about
whom she did have cause to feel guilty. This kind of displacement was very
characteristic. She agreed with this comment but wondered why there were
five. Neither her lodgers nor her children numbered five. She had five
sessions a week and she thought that may be the five lodgers represented the
five sessions, since the previous week we talked a great deal about her
forgetting the content of the sessions. I agreed with her that the five lodgers
were the sessions and added that they must also represent the internal
perception she had of me and the difficulty she has in perceiving me clearly
in the semi-darkness of her inner world. I reminded her that in the third
dream she did not look at me. She laughed and said, "I knew that I was
cheating. Even in the dream I knew that it wasn't because of analytic rules,
but because of anxiety that I didn't want to look." But she did have a
glimpse of my face in the dream, and since she felt very troubled by it and

didn't want to talk about it, she had managed to forget about it up until then. When she did have a glimpse of it, my face was more yellow than usual and my hair much more black. She thought it looked like the behind of a chinese baby. This thought tormented her on waking because she liked my face and particularly my cheeks.

In the past, my cheeks frequently represented breasts. I reminded her that she ate an apple in the waiting room and that she was anxious that it was going to get brown and rotten in her bag. Also, she didn't want me to see her eat. I interpreted that she experienced me, the analyst, as the breast—my two cheeks—and that she felt the session to be a secret eating of those breasts. But once inside her, they were devalued and in her phantasy, the breasts became buttocks and the milk, feces. This filled her with an anxious guilt which made it hard for her to look into her inner world. Not looking at the objects in her internal world made it hard to look after them. She groaned, "Oh, not that—not the shit again. I so hoped we wouldn't get the shit today, so that I won't have to tell you that it happened again. I was constipated and had again to pull the shit out with my fingers. Why is it always like that? Why can't I let go? And writing my lecture is just the same—constipated." She went on to associate partly to her feces and to her disgust with herself for the manual extraction of her feces and partly to her difficulties with her work. Eventually, she remembered that when she was little she and her siblings played many games with the stools in the potty. They called them "our pudding," and when it was cold and the excrements produced some vapor, they called them "steam pudding." I linked this material with what was going on the previous week and I interpreted to her that she took the analyst into her like a breast, but once in her inner world, she proceeded to attack it and turn it into feces. Confronted with this internal breast turned into shit, she then idealized it as her own wonderful food, the "steam pudding." I reminded her here of contemptuous and denigrating remarks she made about me and my interpretations in the previous week. (Denigration and contempt mostly due to an envious competition with me was a recurring characteristic of her relationship to me. The attacks were sometimes frank and open but often very secret, subtle and hard to get at.) Then she apparently changed the subject: "There is something else that I was hiding from you these last few weeks, and I really don't understand why. There is a Rhodesian student just liberated from a concentration camp whom we want to bring over. I have been very efficient. I managed not only to get him a visa but also a scholarship. He is due to arrive in a day or two. His wife and child are still detained in another camp, but we shall be able to get them out too. I really can't understand why I kept pushing it out of my mind. Surely there is nothing guilty or shameful in what I was doing. I am even sure that you will approve." I pointed out to her that she mentioned the young black who had been detained in a concentration camp immediately after my interpretation dealing with her feces, which were retained in her behind and idealized. If she wanted to hide these activities that, on the face of it, were not objectionable, it must have been because this black youngster represented a piece of feces in her behind which she idealized, did reparation to and probably used for sexual purposes. Such an object had to be hidden from me.

That was the end of the session. In the following session it became quite clear that in her unconscious phantasy, the Rhodesian represented a fecal penis. She had anal sexual phantasies about him and she had great difficulty subsequently in relating to him and his family as real people.

I think that this session illustrates certain theoretical points. It shows how this patient introjected an object, attacked it internally, and then abandoned it. She abandoned attempts at reparation because in order to look after this object, she had to look at it and experience the depressive pain. She either got rid of this object by a mental defecation (the forgetting) or she retained it in the form of feces and idealized it. She then could not produce her work for fear of discovering that it was idealized shit. She also acted out this relation by projecting it onto external objects. An attractive, charming woman, she easily picked up acquaintances and friends but then dropped them and forgot about them. The same phantasy was active at the most primitive level where the object was felt to be incorporated physically, the apple representing the analytic breast. And her real feces could become a problem. At this level, her phantasy gave rise to a psychosomatic symptomatology affecting her digestive apparatus. Her relation to the young Rhodesian showed the beginning of a typical mode of manic reparation. In her mind, people easily changed into feces and then, in relation to those black and despised feces, she could do reparation. She idealized them and, at the same time, used them as fecal sexual objects.

This session marked a turning point in a difficult phase in her analysis. The previous weeks were characterized by constant acting out and acting in. There were constant attacks, overt or secret, against me. The analyst was mocked, the content of sessions regularly forgotten. She refused to look at her own material, secretly idealizing her own thoughts and ideas. Outside her analysis, she quarelled constantly with her colleagues and had the greatest difficulty in writing her lectures. In this session, on the other hand, she could communicate to me her dreams and thoughts and express her phantasies instead of acting them out. I believe that the session gives some idea of the depressive situation lived through by this patient, this situation being the result of her attack on her internal object (the lodger in her world) and the manic mechanisms used as defenses: denial (she doesn't look at my face), evacuation of the contents of her mind (the forgetting), alternating with the retention and idealization of a destroyed fecal object.

POSTSCRIPT 1980: ON INTERNAL OBJECTS

At first sight my technique seems as faulty as in chapter 11. The patient and I seemed too much in agreement about the meaning of the material. The situation, however, was completely different. The patient's acting in in the transference had been analyzed for weeks, and the session reported was the result of work already done and represents real progress of insight in the patient.

14

A Necrophilic Phantasy

IN THIS CHAPTER I intend to describe a phantasy which was brought to light in the analysis of a patient, and I shall try to show its crucial importance for the patient's whole personality. I shall have to leave out a general description of the man, his background, the course of his analysis, as such a description would be beyond the scope of the present short communication.

One day my patient, M, a man in his late forties, told me the following dream: "He was lying in bed with a woman on a kind of balcony inside a room near the ceiling. The husband of the woman was lying on the floor above; he and the woman were lying head to foot. At some point he uncovered her to make love to her, and he then realized that she was a wooden doll. He noticed especially her wooden legs.

To the woman in bed he associated an old and very rich woman of his acquaintance. He would have liked to marry her for her money, but he was terrified of how possessive and sexually demanding she would be. The thought of her "old, empty, stinking vagina" made him shudder.

M associated the balcony near the ceiling with my former consulting room. The man on the floor above was my husband. He wondered what my husband would do if he found us together on the couch. He also thought that I might prefer my husband to him, a thought which he found quite unbearable and brushed away.

The position, head to foot, he associated to being in bed with a young boy when he himself was younger, also with another situation involving an older man. In his associations, he referred to his fears of his own homosexuality which had come up often in his analysis. He was aware of strong homosexual tendencies in himself but viewed them with great horror.

At that point, I summarized his associations and suggested that he was beset by fears: if he slept with the old and rich woman she would exhaust him; if he attempted to sleep with the young and married one, he risked either rejection or the vengeance of the husband; he could not sleep with men because of his fear of their penises. Driven by these fears, he could only enjoy an object when it was completely immobilized, like a wooden doll.

He then said that his favorite song was "I wish I had a paper doll to call my own." For years he used to sing this little song to himself. He started singing it to me and became sentimental and maudlin about it. I then remembered a frankly necrophilic phantasy which he had had a few days previously, and I suggested that the doll was a corpse. He agreed to this immediately, indeed, with such eagerness that I wondered whether I had been wrong in my interpretation. But it seemed from his later reactions that his eagerness was partly due to insight and partly to manic enjoyment of the phantasy itself. He started by immediately telling me a joke: "A man and his wife," he said, "were spending the first night of their honeymoon in a sleeper. The man was in the upper berth. When the woman asked, 'Shall I come up?' he said, 'Don't bother, just hand it up.'" He then started extolling the virtues of a corpse as a sexual object. He described with relish the feeling of power and security that he could enjoy in making love to a corpse: it is there when wanted; you put it away when finished with it; it makes no demands; it is never frustrating, never unfaithful, never reproachful; persecution and guilt, he said, could be quite done away with.

I then suggested that he tried to make real people conform to this ideal, and when I gave some examples of such behavior, he himself added many more. He did, indeed, try to get people to behave like this idealized corpse. In sexual relations he wanted absolute compliance in his partner. He was intolerant of any demur, or, conversely, of any demand. The woman should be ever-willing, responsive in intercourse, but she should not have an orgasm, not derive any enjoyment other than for his sake. He indulged in various sexual practices demanding immobility and compliance. In non-sexual relations, he had to have similar power. For instance, if he wanted his girl friend, he telephoned her and she had to come immediately. The slightest delay sometimes gave rise to a severe attack of anxiety or depression; but the moment he was tired of her she had to go at once. He had even sent her home in the middle of the night when she had already fallen asleep in his bed. His relation to other people was similar: they must come and go as he wanted; he could not bear anybody's presence for long. He drew my attention to the pleasures of giving and withholding life. He liked to feel that he infused life into people as though he were animating corpses. He would lend them money, set them up in business, look after them, console them; he felt that he gave them life. But to feel secure he must have the conviction that the moment he withheld his love, interest, money, they would again become lifeless, inert; when he withheld his wish to see them they would disappear. It was also extremely important to M that people should not mind any pain which he inflicted on them; they should indeed welcome it. Previously we accounted for this feature of his sadism by his need for an ideal mother who would welcome the child whatever he did. It was also a denial that the person minded pain, or indeed that he himself minded inflicting pain. But this demand that the object should not mind became more understandable in terms of the necrophilic phantasy; to be acceptable, the object had to behave like a corpse, and corpses do not mind whatever you do to them.

All M's relations to people proceeded in terms of this phantasy. And the elaboration of that theme brought, to begin with, no anxiety or guilt, only a feeling of relish, pleasure and excitement. The way he described his relation to the doll/corpse at that point was reminiscent of Winnicott's description of the child's relation to its transitional objects: "notoriously ill-used," yet surviving it; non-retaliating, non-guilt-producing. The feeling toward me in the transference was one of triumph and omnipotence. He was extremely co-operative in associating, and himself spotted various aspects of his relationships in which people were treated by him as corpses. He was boasting of the fact that he so nearly fulfilled his phantasy in real life. He was indeed showing me that he was like God who could give and withhold life, and I was inert clay which he was animating with his own ideas and associations.

It was only gradually, and weeks later, that the underlying deprivation, persecution, and guilt could be admitted by him. In the dream he was, indeed, wholly deprived. Whatever object he turned to; women, old and young, boys, men all were unavailable to him. They were either rejecting or threatening. He could only have a corpse. Behind the boast of how ideal the corpse is as a sexual object, there was the complaint and the despair of having only a corpse with which to live. There was also a mixture of guilt and persecution due to the feeling that, by virtue of his ruthlessness and greed, he turned his objects into corpses as soon as he approached them. His first association to the dream was about wanting to marry a rich woman in order to exploit her. He then had to turn her into the doll to protect himself from retaliation and guilt. He had to turn people into corpses as soon as he thought of exploiting them. But the corpse, itself, was a persecutor: he idealized it so intensely in order to deny his overwhelming fear of disintegrating, stinking, putrid corpses, their bits and pieces forever attacking him and claiming his very life. There was a hint of that feeling in the first associations to his dream. The old woman's vagina was "empty and stinking." When this idealization of the corpse was analyzed, the doll/corpse bore little resemblance to a normal child's transitional object.

In the midst of his manic elation after telling me the dream in the session there were already present feelings of quite a different nature. Toward the end of that session, he remembered a forgotten detail of the dream. He remembered that he took the woman's wooden leg between his own legs and he felt that it became his penis. The doll had, as it were, castrated him; his penis became dead in identification with his dead object. This association was followed by actual sensations of deadness in the penis; it felt to him like a lifeless, foreign body, and he was very disturbed by this feeling. In later hours this theme was followed up. His penis was dead unless life was infused into it. He said that he resented the presumption of the woman expecting him to approach her with an already erect penis; he wanted the woman to caress his genital first and bring it to life for him. He also had to wait little before attempting intercourse, as if waiting for inspiration. Analysis brought to awareness his waiting for the father's penis to enter him and animate his own genital. In the dream, the man on the floor above was not only his rival but also the man whose presence was necessary for M to achieve intercourse.

The feelings in his penis were transferred to different parts of his body, predominantly to his head and to his mind, and he felt his mind to be a bodily thing, a part of his head. He used to complain of his head being "dead," "useless." He could have no ideas; he had to be stimulated, animated. He felt that without stimulation from outside, his mind would disappear altogether. His feet were a dead-weight and he had to wear special shoes to keep them in shape or they would disintergrate. He needed special collars, coats and spectacles. He said that he was like an inanimate object, a puppet, held together by endless special contraptions. His hypochondria affected all his organs. No part of him was felt to be alive by itself; he had to watch all his organs, to rest them, to give them gentle exercise, to make blood flow through them. He took phenobarbital to put himself to sleep and benzedrine to wake himself up. Nothing was a going concern; every part of him had to be kept alive artificially and with infinite care.

In subsequent hours one could follow three trends of thought, all of which were started by the dream. First the object was the corpse; then his own penis and the various organs identified with it; and finally, by identification with either his penis or his object, he himself was dead.

When he was the corpse, his relationships acquired a peculiar quality of lifeless dependence. He described to me a paralyzed man whom his wife had to lift, lay on herself and then jump up and down during intercourse. He felt completely identified with the paralyzed man. He was the corpse, and I was to animate him by intercourse. In this situation in the transference, there was an enormous longing to be loved by me like a baby, the wish for me to rock him, to jump him up and down, to kiss him, to blow life into him. But this wish to be a baby took the distorted form of his being a corpse animated by me. He felt that he was a deadweight to me, that he was a millstone round my neck. He would very often begin his analytic hours by saying, "Yesterday was a good hour, you gave me life," or "You allowed me to live," or conversely, "That was a bad session, I was quite dead," or "I could not think, or talk, or work." He would repeat constantly that if I ever stopped analyzing him he would just stop living. "I am like a lamp that you have to light every day." One of his recurring expressions was, "I live only by other people's permission." By other people's permission meant really by other people lending or giving him, their own life. In this situation every frustration was felt as a threat of death from a hostile object. He would say of his friend, "She did not come when I rang her, she really wants my death," and he really meant and believed it. His greed was limitless. He came to me lifeless; if I frustrated him he died; if I gratified him he stole my life and I died. His greed also made him feel quite incapable of discrimination; I was pouring something into him to animate him, but he had no means either of controlling his intake or of discovering the nature of what I was giving him. So he lived in constant suspicion of the content of that with which I filled him.

As we progressively unravelled his phantasies and fears, it became clear that the basic situation was that in any relation either he or I had to be a corpse. There was one life between us and one death, as it were, represented by the concrete form of the corpse, and we were constantly identified with one another by projection and introjection. The various complicated relations we had on various levels were endless attempts at solving the problem of how to share one life between the two of us. This phantasy was at the very basis of the structure of his personality and relationships.

It would be beyond the scope of this paper to attempt to describe fully the endless ramifications of this phantasy and the way in which it was used as a defense against other phantasies. To mention only one instance: being a corpse was a defense against pain, anxiety, madness, disintegration, and the threat of dying, since corpses are immune from death.

Up to that point, the analysis had not brought to light enough childhood material to enable me to unravel the origins of this persistent phantasy. Certainly the fact that my patient was the youngest of a big family and remained the smallest when they grew up, as well as the fact that his parents were poor and old by the time he was born must have done a great deal to confirm this feeling that there was not enough life left for him. It seems to me, however, that he was caught in a vicious circle that must have started very early on in his life. The primitive quality of the mechanisms, the massive use of projective and introjective identification seem to suggest a fixation at a very early level. In her paper "Notes on Some Schizoid Mechanisms," Melanie Klein (1946) suggests that there are two main sources of anxiety: the operation of the death instinct and external bad experiences, like the trauma of birth and frustrations. These two factors interact constantly. The death instinct is deflected outward and is felt as a threat of annihilation coming from outside. External frustrations are also experienced as threats of annihilation by bad objects, but the bad objects are internalized and reinforce the fear of the death instinct within.

I think that my patient was fixated in this paranoid phase described by Melanie Klein, and that his phantasy can be understood only in terms of these very early anxieties and mechanisms. I have the impression that M must have suffered a severe deprivation at the very start of his life. This deprivation was felt to be, or maybe indeed was, a threat to his very existence. It must have lead to an overwhelming destructiveness and greed. He felt that in phantasy he emptied his mother of all life and she became the corpse; he introjected this corpse and identified it with himself. He said once, "If I could remember so far back, I know what my first memory would be: I would remember realizing my mother's existence and feeling that 'It is either you or I'." And to this day this emotional situation persists in the form of his necrophilic phantasy.

Reference

Klein, M. (1946). Notes on some schizoid mechanisms. *International Journal of Psycho-Analysis* 27:99-110.

15

Fear of Death:
Notes on the Analysis
of an Old Man

THIS CHAPTER is based on the analysis of a man who came to treatment at the age of seventy-three and a half and whose analysis was terminated just before his seventy-fifth birthday. He had suffered an acute psychotic breakdown when he was nearing the age of seventy-two. Following the usual psychiatric treatments (electric shocks, etc.), he settled down to a chronic psychotic state characterized by depression, hypochondria, paranoid delusions, and attacks of insane rage. When no improvement occurred, and when the psychiatrists in Rhodesia, where he lived, gave a hopeless prognosis, his son, who resided in London, brought him for psychoanalytic treatment. This was nearly two years after the beginning of his overt illness.

His treatment with me lasted eighteen months. It was not, of course, a completed analysis, but it dealt sufficiently with the patient's outstanding problems to enable him to resume a normal life and activity and to achieve, for the first time in his life, a feeling of stability and maturity. Eighteen months later he was enjoying good health back in Rhodesia and had resumed his business.

In his analysis, I came to the conclusion that the unconscious fear of death, increasing with old age, had led to his psychotic breakdown. I believe that the same problem underlies many breakdowns in old age.

I cannot give here a complete picture of the patient's history or

173

psychopathology, and I shall mention only such points as are relevant to my theme. The patient came from a little ukrainian village. His family was extremely poor and orthodox Jewish. His childhood was marked by fear of starvation and freezing during the long cold winters. He had seven siblings and was on bad terms with most of them. His description of his family showed a very clear and rigid splitting. His eldest brother was admired and loved; the next two were described as devils. One of his two sisters was remembered as having loved him, fed him, looked after him; of the other, he remembered only rejections and attacks. His mother was, to begin with, portrayed as greatly favoring his older brother, while he himself was a favorite of the father. In contrast to the mother, who was felt as cold and rejecting, the father was idolized but also greatly feared. Following his father's death, the patient, then seventeen, fled from the Ukraine; and after a long hard struggle, he eventually established himself in Rhodesia as a middleman salesman. He had not tried to keep any contact with his family, who remained in the Ukraine. He also largely broke away from Jewish orthodoxy. He married and had two daughters and one son. He idealized his new family but in his business relations he was suspicious and persecuted. Further, some splitting of the family members was evident. His two daughters corresponded exactly to his two sisters: one adored and gratifying, the other one a source of constant bitterness and complaints. For several years he had been addicted to secret drinking.

The circumstances of his breakdown are relevant to my theme. It became apparent early in his analysis that there were three precipitating factors of his illness. The first was his first visit to his son, who was studying medicine in London. During this visit, the second precipitant occurred; he met with his younger brother, from whom he learned that all the members of his family who had remained in Europe had perished in Hitler's camps during the war. The third and immediately precipitating factor was an incident which happened when he returned to Rhodesia. He had for several years given bribes to a man in order to get business from his firm. During the patient's absence, this man had been caught in another dishonest deal. As soon as the patient heard this, he felt terrified that his own bribery would be discovered, and within a matter of hours he was in a state of acute psychosis with delusions of reference and persecution, centering, to begin with, on his fear of his deal being discovered and of his being punished and ridiculed. He believed, for instance, that newspapers contained articles about him, that radio broadcasts were being made, that people laughed at him in the streets.

I suggest that my patient was unconsciously terrified of old age and death, which he perceived as a persecution and punishment. His main defenses against this fear were splitting, idealization, and denial. His visit to London had shaken his defenses. His idealization of his only son broke down. The news he received about his family had broken down his denial of his family's death and the result was guilt and fear of retaliation. When he returned to Rhodesia, he was faced with the fear of punishment, which, at that point, represented death to him.

First phase of the analysis. From the point of view of the patient's anxiety about death, the analysis could be divided into three phases. The first was characterized by complete denial of aging and of the fear of death. He described himself as having always been very young for his age, working and looking like a young man until the beginning of his illness, which he felt had robbed him of his youth and health. He unconsciously expected that his treatment would give him back his youthfulness. It soon became apparent that this denial was made possible by the patient's idealization of his son, who represented to him another self, young and ideal, into whom he had projected all his own unfulfilled hopes and ambitions. The patient used to send his son parcels every week, and on these parcels all his interest and love centered. He put himself into these parcels, sending them to his son, in whom he lived untouched by age. This relationship to his son was partly a repetition and partly a reversal of his relation to his own father. The father appeared early on in the analysis, particularly as a loving and feeding father and the patient developed an unconscious, intensely idealized, oral, homosexual relationship to him. He was the father's favorite, and he felt that as long as he had his father's love and could orally incorporate his penis, he would be protected from starvation and cold and ultimately from death. With his son, he partly repeated and partly reversed this relationship. He identified himself with his father and projected himself, the favorite son, into his own son, thereby prolonging his own life. This projective identification of his young self into his son kept fears of persecution and death at bay. At times, he also projected his ideal father into the son and expected to be fed and kept alive by him forever.

　　Accompanying this idealization was a great deal of split-off persecution. Parallel to his ideal son was a son-in-law, like a black twin, his main persecutor. In the past the father had been perceived mainly as loving, while the brothers, with the exception of the eldest, were remembered for bullying and terrifying him. Any feeling of persecution that pertained to his father was immediately split off and projected onto his older brothers. In the background, there was a picture of an unloving and cold mother. The feeling of persecution by her had been mainly transferred onto the various countries he lived in, which he completely personified, and invariably described to me as treating him badly, exploiting him, and refusing to give him a livelihood. At the beginning, none of this split-off persecution could be mobilized in the transference. I represented mainly his ideal father and son, occasionally merging with an ideal feeding mother. All the ideal figures, including his ideal self, he projected into me. The bad feelings and figures he projected on to remote persecutors, either remote geographically—in Rhodesia—or remote in time—far in the past. As long as he could maintain this idealization of me, I would protect him from persecutors and he would be safe.

Second phase of the analysis. The second phase of the analysis was ushered in by the first holiday, which the patient acutely resented; when he came back, it was more possible to make him aware of his feelings of deprivation. The splitting lessened; the persecution came nearer to the transference. The bad countries of the past stopped playing such a role in his analysis, and the persecution now centered on the very cold English winter which was going to kill him. Death was no longer denied; it seemed to be there, around the corner. The split between his son-in-law and his son also narrowed. To begin with, he could maintain opposite feelings quite simultaneously: that his son brought him to London, where he was going to be made completely well again because he had his wonderful analysis, and, at the same time, that his son-in-law sent him to London to die of cold. Gradually it became possible to point out to him how much his son-in-law was the other aspect of his son, and how much the cold climate and country that was going to kill him was the other aspect of the analytic treatment and of me. One day, for instance, he ended the session in a very adoring way typical of his idealizing, "Doctor, when you look at me with your kind eyes I can feel you drawing the illness out of me and throwing it out of the window." He started the next session by describing vividly how he felt attacked outside my house as soon as he left the consulting room: "You can't imagine how it got into me, how it squeezed me, how it burned me." ("It" being the usual way of describing his hypochondriacal symptoms.) He could not deny the interpretation that the same kind doctor who drew the illness out of him seemed to have thrown it at him outside the window.

At that point, his disappointment in his son during the first visit to London came to the fore. He admitted that his son had not lived up to his expectations. He kept repeating, "It wasn't the same Harry, it wasn't what I meant for Harry." He admitted that he had felt completely robbed: having put his potency, his life, his love into his son and then losing the son meant losing his own potency and life and facing death alone. Having to recognize that his son, though devoted to him, in fact led a life of his own, was experienced as the loss of his greatest hope, namely that his son would give him a new lease of life.

At this stage, it became clear to the patient that his ideal and his persecutory object were one and the same person. In the past he had split off his fear of his father onto his brothers. Now he saw clearly that it was his father's retaliation that he feared. He feared that his son would leave him to his persecutors and to death and disown him, as he had left and disowned his family. Earlier on in the treatment, he said that before he left the Ukraine he had to put a stone on his father and worked very hard to earn the few shillings to purchase this stone for the grave. To begin with, it appeared as an act of mourning and piety; now it became clearer that he had to keep under the stone a very frightening and revengeful ghost of his father. In the transference, it also became clear how much he had either to placate me or to control me in order to prevent me from becoming a persecutor. The persecution by his mother also came vividly to the fore: it was experienced as cold and starvation and as being abandoned or actively poisoned. He remembered that his younger brother was fed by a Christian wet-nurse. One day this girl squirted some milk in his face and he fled terrified, feeling soiled and poisoned. Being burned up or broken inside (a frequent description of his hypochondriacal symptoms) was also felt as somehow connected with his mother. As his experiences of persecution were becoming more explicit and more connected with the real objects—me in the transference, his son, and finally his experiences with his early family—it was also becoming clearer that these persecutions, which he was either expecting or currently experiencing, were felt by him as punishments. With this admission of these fears of persecution and punishment, he could overtly admit fear of death. He felt that his idealization of me was his only protection against death. I was the source of food, love, and warmth, but I was equally the killer, since I could bring him death by withdrawing these qualities. Idealization and placation of me alternated with only thinly-veiled persecutory fears.

Third phase of the analysis. As this split in his perception of me lessened so did the projection, and gradually he was able to admit his aggression in relation to me. This ushers in the third phase of his analysis, during which the persecution and idealizations gradually gave place to ambivalence, a sense of psychic reality and depressive anxieties. Slowly he was beginning to realize that if his symptoms now appeared only during breaks and weekends it was not simply because I, the ideal object, abandoned him to his persecutors; he was beginning to realize that everything I had given him—interpretations representing the good breast and food or the good penis—became, in my absence, the bad burning, poisonous, and persecutory substances, because when he was away from me, hatred welled up in him and turned everything bad. He began to admit more freely how greedy he was for the analysis and for my presence and how impatient and angry he was when away from me. His son and I were becoming more and more in his eyes the oedipal couple, always together when we were not with him. His son represented now the father, now his younger brother—a partner of me standing for his mother. He recalled vividly the birth of his younger brother and the absolute fury he experienced not only in relation to the baby and the mother but also to the father who gave mother this new baby. We reconstructed that he was weaned at the birth of this brother when he was about two. He relived it intensely in the transference. For several years, this patient had suffered from a fine tremor of his hands diagnosed as senile parkinsonism. In the session in which he was describing his feelings at the birth of his brother, he lifted his hands and shook them with fury, shouting, "How did they dare to have a new one! How did they dare to have a new one when they could not feed the ones they had!" Following this session, the tremor of his hands disappeared completely and permanently. One could gauge then the strength of his repressed fury.

He remembered soon after that that there was a fire which destroyed nearly the whole village, after which his family had been practically homeless, living in one room in an inn. It became clear that this fire was felt by him to be a result of his own urinary attacks. These were relived with such intensity that for a few nights he actually became incontinent.

We could now trace the beginning of his secret drinking to the beginning of the war in 1939. The beginning of the war unconsciously meant to him the destruction of his family. He admitted that, had he thought of it, he might have brought his family over to Rhodesia and saved their lives. He felt that he had had all the luck; he took the father's penis and then he turned against his family in anger, superiority, and contempt, leaving them behind to be burnt and destroyed. He unconsciously internalized them and carried inside himself the concentration camp with its burning and breaking up. But, unable to bear his depression and guilt, he split off and denied it and turned to drink. We then understood more about his drinking: he drank only brandy, never any other drink, nearly always alone and secretly. He remembered that when he first came to Rhodesia at the time of his greatest poverty he fainted in the street with hunger and a soldier revived him with a glass of brandy. Thus, brandy acquired the meaning of the magic life-giving drink from father. It was significant that his only occasional companion in brandy-drinking was the man involved in the business deal which led to the patient's breakdown. Thus, as in the past, he had turned away from his depression to an ideal homosexual relationship with his father, but in this escape he repeated his guilt: he was again taking the best from father and deserting and neglecting the rest of the family. His dread of the discovery of his dishonest deal in business included the dread of all the guilt of this unconscious situation coming to light.

When he began to face in his analysis what the beginning of the 1939 war meant to him, the patient experienced a great deal of guilt in relation to his family and particularly to his mother. His previous valuation of her had become very altered. He realized what a hard struggle she had had to keep the family alive, and that the bad relations that existed between him and her were at least partly due to the way in which he treated her. With anger and contempt he turned from her to the idealized homosexual relation with his father, thereby robbing her of both himself and the father. He then experienced mourning about his family and particularly about his mother. And with it relived his early weaning situations with her, his deprivation, jealousy, envy and urinary attacks on her which he felt had left her empty and bad and unable to feed his younger brother. Together with this changed relation to his mother and family came a very altered relation to the idea of his own death. The end of the treatment had then been already fixed and symbolized for him his approaching death, of which he now spoke very freely. It appeared to him as a repetition of weaning, but now, not so much as a retaliation and persecution, but as a reason for sorrow and mourning about the loss of something that he deeply appreciated and could now enjoy: life. He was mourning the life that he was going to lose together with his analysis that was ending, and for the first time he was mourning fully the mother and the breast that he had lost in the past. He also felt some longing for death, expressed mostly in his wish to go back to Rhodesia to meet his old friends again, which symbolized his wish to die and to meet his dead parents of whom he was no longer frightened. But the mourning and sadness were not a clinical depression and seemed not to interfere with his enjoyment of life. In fact, he began to feel that if this life, this life-giving breast was something that he was going to mourn for so much, then, as he told me, he might as well enjoy it and do his best with it while he could. In the last weeks, particularly in the last days of his analysis, he repeated some main themes in his associations, but not in symptoms, and I here select a few associations from the last week. The first day he spoke angrily about somebody who behaved like a cow; he gave a bucket of milk and then kicked

it. I interpreted that I was the cow who gave him the analysis, like the
mother who gave him the breast. But by sending him away, I was kicking it
and spoiling it all. Thus I was responsible for "kicking the bucket," that is
for my own and his deaths. The next day he came back to this association
and said in a dejected way that it was he, in relation to his mother, who often
behaved like the cow that kicked the bucket. Later he said that she was the
cow and he kicked the bucket that fed him; and he accepted my interpretation that his anxiety was that when he had to leave me he would be so angry
that he would kick me inside him and spoil and spill out all the good
analysis, as he felt he had done with his mother's breast, and that he would
be responsible for my death inside him and for his own death. On the third
day he spoke about a jug. He said that one must not judge a drink by the jug
it is carried in. He associated that he was the jug—old and unprepossess-
ing—but the stuff that he contained could be good; it could be beer, he said,
or milk. In associations it became quite clear that the beer and milk
represented the good breast and the good penis, the mother and father, and
me in both roles inside him. He felt that he had re-established his good
internal objects.

At this point in his analysis he felt hopeful. He felt that his life was
worth living and that, however old he was, his internal objects were
rejuvenated and worth preserving. It was also clear that his children and
grandchildren were no longer felt by him as projections of himself but as his
objects that he loved. And he could enjoy the thought of their living on and
growing after his own death.

CONCLUSION

I suggest that my patient had been unable in infancy, childhood, and
later to face his ambivalence and the resulting depressive anxiety.

He could not face the death of his objects and the prospect of his own
death. He protected himself against those anxieties by denial of depression,
splitting and projective identification. Those defense mechanisms,
however, intensified his unconscious anxiety, in that all situations of
deprivation or loss were unconsciously perceived as persecution. Idealization and denial were therefore intensified as a defense against both depression and persecution. In old age when he had to face the prospect of
approaching death, the loss of his life appeared to him primarily as a
situation of acute persecution and retaliation. He tried to counteract it by
intensifying mechanisms of projective identification, denial and idealization. When his denial and idealization broke down during his visit to

London, the persecution became unbearable and he became insane. The analysis of those anxieties and defense mechanisms in the transference enabled him to experience ambivalence, to mobilize the infantile depressive position and work through it sufficiently to enable him to re-establish good internal objects and to face old age and death in a more mature way.

POSTSCRIPT 1980: FEAR OF DEATH

I had a long and satisfying follow-up of this analysis after the patient had finished his treatment at the age of seventy-four and a half. Both he and I thought that, having made a better relation with his internal objects, and having come to terms with his fear of death, he was returning to his own country to die in peace. This proved an unduly cautious expectation: in fact he lived another eleven years.

He resumed his work, though not full-time, and led a vigorous life. On several occasions he looked after his family, particularly his wife when she suddenly became very ill.

He had a few phases of mild depression, but when a physician wanted to give him pills he said that he could cope with his feelings, and if he found he could not, then he would return to London to have more analysis. He remained in excellent health up to the time of his death in his eighty-fifth year.

The events preceding his death, as reported to me by his son, are of interest. The last day of his life he was in good health and active as usual. In the evening, he started a long conversation with his wife in which he was concerned about establishing with her help the exact whereabouts of various members of his family and their present occupations. Sometime later in the evening he said, "It's funny, in the past I often tried to reassure myself that so-and-so was here-or-there: say, that Harry was in London; but however often you told me or I told myself, it never seemed real. I never quite believed it. Now I know they are there and it is quite real to me."

I think that unconsciously that evening he must have felt approaching death and was preparing for it. (Possibly the thought was even conscious but he did not communicate it to his wife.) The preparation consisted in "placing his objects in reality." I think it signified a relinquishing of omnipotent control and allowing these objects to live on without him. It also probably had the significance of placing them correctly in his internal world, without coercion or control.

He went to sleep as usual but woke up in the night, telling his wife that he was very hungry. She gave him a drink of milk and a sandwich and he went back to sleep, not to wake up again. I think the hunger was his experience of dying—the dreaded starvation—but apparently experienced with a minimum of persecution and anguish.

This analysis has illuminated for me the problems of old age. Certainly it has altered my views on the prognosis of analysis at an advanced age.

PART VI

ARTISTIC CREATIVITY

16

A Psychoanalytic Approach
to Aesthetics

IN 1908 FREUD WROTE: "We laymen have always wondered greatly—like the cardinal who put the question to Ariosto—how that strange being, the poet, comes by his material. What makes him able to carry us with him in such a way and to arouse emotions in us of which we thought ourselves perhaps not even capable?" And as the science of psychoanalysis developed, repeated attempts were made to answer that question. Freud's discovery of unconscious phantasy life and of symbolism made it possible to attempt a psychological interpretation of works of art. Many papers have been written since, dealing with the problem of the individual artist and reconstructing his early history from an analysis of his work. The foremost of these is Freud's book on Leonardo da Vinci. Other papers have dealt with general psychological problems expressed in works of art and show, for instance, how the latent content of universal infantile anxieties is symbolically expressed in them. Examples are Freud's "The Theme of the Three Caskets" (1913), Ernest Jones's "The Madonna's Conception Through the Ear" (1914), and Melanie Klein's "Infantile Anxiety-Situations Reflected in a Work of Art and the Creative Impulse" (1929).

Until recently such papers were not mainly concerned with aesthetics. They dealt with points of psychological interest but not with the central problem of aesthetics, which is: What constitutes good art and in what essential respect is it different from other human works, from bad art in particular? Psychological writers attempted to answer such questions as: How does the poet work? What is he like? What does he express? In the paper "The Relation of the Poet to Day-dreaming" (1908) Freud has shown how the work of the artist is a product of phantasy and has its roots, like children's play and dreams, in unconscious phantasy life. But he did not attempt to explain why we should derive such pleasure from listening to the daydreams of a poet. How he achieves his effects is to Freud the poet's "innermost secret." Indeed, Freud was not especially interested in aesthetic problems. In "The Moses of Michelangelo" (1914) he says "I have often observed that the subject-matter of works of art has a stronger attraction for me than their formal and technical qualities, though to the artist their value lies first and foremost in these latter. I am unable rightly to appreciate many of the methods used and the effects obtained in art" (p. 257).. He was also aware of the limitations of analytical theory in approaching aethetics. In the preface to the book on Leonardo he says that he has no intention of discussing why Leonardo was a great painter, since to do that he would have to know more about the ultimate sources of the creative impulse and of sublimation. This was written in 1910. Since that time the work of Melanie Klein has thrown more light on the problem of the creative impulse and sublimation, and has provided a new stimulus to analytical writers on art. In the last fifteen years a number of papers have appeared dealing with problems of creation, beauty, and ugliness. I would mention, in particular, those by Ella Sharpe, Paula Heimann, John Rickman, and W.R.D. Fairbairn in this country, and H. B. Lee in the U.S.A.

Maybe it is possible now, in the light of new analytical discoveries, to ask new questions. Can we isolate in the psychology of the artist the specific factors which enable him to produce a satisfactory work of art? And if we can, will that further our understanding of the aesthetic value of the work of art, and of the aesthetic experience of the audience?

It seems to me that Melanie Klein's concept of the depressive position makes it possible at least to attempt an answer to these questions.

The "depressive position," as described by Melanie Klein, is reached by the infant when he recognizes his mother and other people, and among them his father, as real persons. His object realtions then undergo a fundamental change.[1] Where earlier he was aware of "part objects" he now perceives complete persons; instead of "split" objects—ideally good or

---

1. For the description of the preceding phase of development see Klein (1948) and Rosenfeld (1952).

overwhelmingly persecuting—he sees a whole object both good and bad. The whole object is loved and introjected and forms the core of an integrated ego. But this new constellation ushers in a new anxiety situation: where earlier the infant feared an attack on the ego by persecutory objects, now the predominant fear is that of the loss of the loved object in the external world and in his own inside. The infant at that stage is still under the sway of uncontrollable greedy and sadistic impulses. In phantasy his loved object is continually attacked in greed and hatred, is destroyed, torn into pieces and fragments; and not only is the external object so attacked but also the internal one, and then the whole internal world feels destroyed and shattered as well. Bits of the destroyed object may turn into persecutors, and there is a fear of internal persecution as well as a pining for the lost loved object and guilt for the attack. The memory of the good situation, where the infant's ego contained the whole loved object and the realization that it has been lost through his own attacks, give rise to an intense feeling of loss and guilt, and to the wish to restore and re-create the lost loved object outside and within the ego. This wish to restore and re-create is the basis of later sublimation and creativity.

It is also at this point that a sense of inner reality is developed. If the object is remembered as a whole object, then the ego is faced with the recognition of its own ambivalence toward the object; it holds itself reponsible for its impulses and for the damage done to the external and to the internal object. Where, earlier, impulses and parts of the infant's self were projected into the object with the result that a false picture of it was formed, that his own impulses were denied, and that there was often a lack of differentiation between the self and the external object, in the depressive phase a sense of inner reality is developed and in its wake a sense of outer reality as well.

Depressive phantasies give rise to the wish to repair and restore, and become a stimulus to further development only insofar as the depressive anxiety can be tolerated by the ego and the sense of psychic reality retained. If there is little belief in the capacity to restore, the good object outside and inside is felt to be irretrievably lost and destroyed, the destroyed fragments turn into persecutors, and the internal situation is felt to be hopeless. The infant's ego is at the mercy of intolerable feelings of guilt, loss, and internal persecution. To protect itself from total despair the ego must have recourse to violent defense mechanisms. Those defense mechanisms which protect it from the feelings arising out of the loss of the good object form a system of manic defenses. The essential features of manic defenses are denial of psychic reality, omnipotent control, and a partial regression to the paranoid position and its defenses: splitting, idealization, denial, projective identification, etc. This regression strengthens the fear of persecution and that in turn leads to the strengthening of omnipotent control.

But in successful development the experience of love from the environment slowly reassures the infant about his objects. His growing love, strength, and skill give him increasing confidence in his own capacities to restore. And as his confidence increases he can gradually relinquish the manic defenses and experience more and more fully the underlying feelings of loss, guilt, and love, and he can make renewed and increasingly successful attempts at reparation.

By repeated experiences of loss and restoration of the internal objects they become more firmly established and more fully assimilated in the ego.

A successful working through of the depressive anxieties has far-reaching consequences: the ego becomes integrated and enriched through the assimilation of loved objects; the dependence on the external objects is lessened; and deprivation can be better dealt with. Aggression and love can be tolerated, and guilt gives rise to the need to restore and re-create.

Feelings of guilt probably play a role before the depressive position is fully established; they already exist in relation to the part object, and they contribute to later sublimation; but they are then simpler impulses acting in a predominantly paranoid setting, isolated and unintegrated. With the establishment of the depressive position the object becomes more personal and unique and the ego more integrated, and an awareness of an integrated internal world is gradually achieved. Only when this happens does the attack on the object lead to real despair at the destruction of an existing complex and organized internal world and, with it, to the wish to recover such a complete world again.

The task of the aritst lies in the creation of a world of his own. In his introduction to the second Post-Impressionist Exhibition, Roger Fry writes: "Now these artists do not seek to give what can, after all, be but a pale reflex of actual appearance, but to arouse a conviction of a new and different reality. They do not seek to imitate life but to find an equivalent for life." What Roger Fry says of post-impressionists undoubtedly applies to all genuine art. One of the great differences between art and imitation or a superficial "pretty" achievement is that neither the imitation nor the "pretty" production ever achieves this creation of an entirely new reality.

Every creative artist produces a world of his own. Even when he believes himself to be a complete realist and sets himself the task of faithfully reproducing the external world, he in fact only uses elements of the existing external world to create with them a reality of his own. When, for instance, two realistic writers like Zola and Flaubert try to portray life in the same country, and at very nearly the same time, the two worlds they show us differ form each other as widely as if they were the most fantastic creations of surrealist poets. If two great painters paint the same landscape we have two different worlds.

> . . . and dream
> Of waves, flowers, clouds, woods,
> Rocks, and all that we
> Read in their smiles
> And call reality.

How does this creation come about? Of all artists, the one who gives us the fullest description of the creative process is Marcel Proust—a description based on years of self-observation and the fruit of an amazing insight. According to Proust, an artist is compelled to create by his need to recover his lost past. But a purely intellectual memory of the past, even when it is available, is emotionally valueless and dead. A real remembrance sometimes comes about unexpectedly, by chance association. The flavor of a cake brings back to his mind a fragment of his childhood with full emotional vividness. Stumbling over a stone revives a recollection of a holiday in Venice which, before, he had vainly tried to recapture. For years he tries in vain to remember and re-create in his mind a living picture of his beloved grandmother. But only a chance association revives her picture and at last enables him to remember her, and to experience his loss and mourn her. He calls these fleeting associations *intermittences du coeur,* but he says that such memories come and then disappear again, so that the past remains elusive. To capture them, to give them permanent life, to integrate them with the rest of his life, he must create a work of art. "Il fallait . . . faire sotir de la pénombre ce que j'avais senti, de le reconvertir en un équivalent spirituel. Or ce moyen qui me paraissait le seul qu'était-ce autre chose que de créer une oeuvre d'art?" ("I had to recapture from the shade that which I had felt, to reconvert it into its psychic equivalent. But the way to do it, the only one I could see, what was it—but to create a work of art—?")

Through the many volumes of his work the past is being recaptured; all his lost, destroyed, and loved objects are being brought back to life: his parents, his grandmother, his beloved Albertine. "Et certes il n'y aurait pas qu'Albertine, que ma grandmère, mais bien d'autres encore dont j'aurais pu assimiler une parole, un regard, mais en tant que créatures individuelles je ne m'en rappellais plus; un livre est un grand cimetiére ou sur la plupart des tombes on ne peut plus lire les noms effacés." ("And indeed it was not only Albertine, not only my grandmother, but many others still from whom I might well have assimilated a gesture or a word, but whom I could not even remember as distinct persons. A book is a vast graveyard where on most of the tombstones one can read no more the faded names.")

And, according to Proust, it is only the lost past and the lost or dead object that can be made into a work of art. He makes the painter, Elstir, say: "On ne peut recréer ce qu'on aime qu'en le renoncant." ("It is only by renouncing that one can re-create what one loves.") It is only when the loss has been acknowledged and the mourning experienced that re-creation can take place.

In the last volume of his work Proust describes how at last he decided to sacrifice the rest of his life to writing. He came back after a long absence to seek his old friends at a party, and all of them appeared to him as ruins of the real people he knew—useless, ridiculous, ill, on the threshold of death. Others, he found, had died long ago. And on realizing the destruction of a whole world that had been his, he decided to write, to sacrifice himself to the re-creation of the dying and the dead. By virtue of his art he can give his objects an eternal life in his work. And since they represent his internal world too, if he can do that, he himself will no longer be afraid of death.

What Proust describes corresponds to a situation of mourning: he sees that his loved objects are dying or dead. Writing a book is for him like the work of mourning in that gradually the external objects are given up, they are reinstated in the ego, and re-created in the book. In her paper "Mourning and its Relation to Manic-Depressive States" (1940), Melaine Klein has shown how mourning in grown-up life is a reliving of the early depressive anxieties; not only is the present object in the external world felt to be lost, but also the early objects, the parents; and they are lost as internal objects as well as in the external world. In the process of mourning it is these earliest objects which are lost again, and then re-created. Proust describes how this mourning leads to a wish to re-create the lost world.

I have quoted Proust at length because he reveals such an acute awareness of what I believe is present in the unconscious of all artists: namely, that all creation is really a re-creation of a once loved and once whole, but now lost and ruined object, a ruined internal world and self. It is when the world within us is destroyed, when it is dead and loveless, when our loved ones are in fragments, and we ourselves in helpless despair—it is then that we must re-create our world anew, reassemble the pieces, infuse life into dead fragments, re-create life.

If the wish to create is rooted in the depressive position and the capactiy to create depends on a successful working through it, it would follow that the inability to acknowledge and overcome depressive anxiety must lead to inhibitions in artistic expression.

I should now like to give a few clinical examples from artists who have been inhibited in their creative activities by neurosis, and I shall try to show that in them it was the inability to work through their depressive anxieties which led to inhibitions of artistic activity, or to the production of an unsuccessful artistic product.

Case A was a young girl with a definite gift for painting. An acute rivalry with her mother made her give up painting in her early teens. After some analysis she started to paint again and was working as a decorative artist. She did decorative handicraft work in preference to what she sometimes called "real painting," and this was because she knew that, though correct, neat, and pretty, her work failed to be moving and aesthetically significant. In her manic way she usually denied that this caused her any concern. At the time when I was trying to interpret her unconscious sadistic attacks on her father, the internalization of her mutilated and destroyed father, and the resulting depression, she told me the following dream: She had seen a picture in a shop which represented a wounded man lying alone and desolate in a dark forest. She felt quite overwhelmed with emotion and admiration for this picture; she thought it represented the actual essence of life; if she could only paint like that she would be a really great painter.

It soon appeared that the meaning of the dream was that if she could only acknowledge her depression about the wounding and destruction of her father, she would then be able to express it in her painting and would achieve real art. In fact, however, it was impossible for her to do this, since the unusual strength of her sadism, her resulting despair, and her small capacity to tolerate depression led to its manic denial and to a constant make-believe that all was well with the world. In her dream she confirmed my interpretation about the attack on her father, but she did more than this. Her dream showed something that had not been in any way interpreted or indicated by me: namely, the effect on her painting of her persistent denial of depression. In relation to her painting the denial of the depth and seriousness of her depressive feelings produced the effect or superficiality and prettiness in whatever she chose to do—the dead father was completely denied and no ugliness or conflict was ever allowed to disturb the neat and correct form of her work.

Case B was that of a journalist aged a little over thirty, whose ambition was to be a writer, and who suffered, among other symptoms, from an ever increasing inhibition in creative writing. An important feature of his character was a tendency to regress from the depressive to the paranoid position. The following dream illustrates his problem: He found himself in a room with Goebbels, Goering, and some other Nazis. He was aware that these men were completely amoral. He knew that they were going to poison him and therefore he tried to make a bargain with them; he suggested that it would be a good thing for them to let him live, since he was a journalist and could write about them and make them live for a time after their death. But this stratagem failed and he knew that he would finally be poisoned.

An important factor in this patient's psychology was his introjection of an extremely bad father-figure who was then blamed for all that the patient did. And one of the results was an unbearable feeling of being internally persecuted by this bad internal father-figure, which was sometimes expressed in hypochondriacal symptoms. He tried to defend himself against it by placating and serving this bad internal figure. He was often driven to do things that he disapproved of and disliked. In the dream he showed how it interfered with his writing: to avoid death at the hands of internal persecutors he had to write for them to keep them immortal; but there is, of course, no real wish to keep such bad figures alive, and consequently he was inhibited in his capacity for writing. He often complained, too, that he had no style of his own; in his associations to the dream it became clear that he had to write not only for the benefit of the persecutors, and to serve their purposes, but also at their command. Thus the style of his writing belonged to the internal parental figure. The case, I think, resembles one described by Paula Heimann (1942). A patient of hers drew a sketch with which she was very displeased. The style was not her own—it was Victorian. It appeared clearly during the session that it was the result of a quarrel with another woman, who stood for her mother. After the quarrel the painter had introjected her as a bad and vengeful mother, and, through guilt and fear, she had to submit to this bad internal figure; it was really the Victorian mother who had dictated the painting.

Paula Heimann described this example of an acute impairment of an already established sublimation. In my patient his submission to a very bad internal figure was a chronic situation preventing him from achieving any internal freedom to create. He was basically fixed in the paranoid position and returned to it whenever depressive feelings were aroused, so that his love and reparative impulses could not become fully active.

All the patients mentioned suffered from sexual maladjustments as well as creative inhibitions. There is clearly a genital aspect of artistic creation which is of paramount importance. Creating a work of art is a psychic equivalent of pro-creation. It is a genital bisexual activity necessitating a good identification with the father who gives, and the mother who receives and bears, the child. The ability to deal with the depressive position, however, is the precondition of both genital and artistic maturity. If the parents are felt to be so completely destroyed that there is no hope of ever re-creating them, a successful identification is not possible, and neither can the genital position be maintained nor the sublimation in art develop.

This relation between feelings of depression and genital and artistic problems is clearly shown by another patient of mine. C, a man of thirty-five, was a really gifted artist, but at the same time a very ill person. Since the age of eighteen he had suffered from depression, from a variety of conversion symptoms of great intensity, and from what he described as "a complete lack of freedom and spontaneity." This lack of spontaneity interfered considerably with his work, and, though he was physically potent, it also deprived him of all the enjoyment of sexual intercourse. A feeling of impending failure, worthlessness, and hopelessness marred all his efforts. He came to analysis at the age of thirty-five because of a conversion symptom: he suffered from a constant pain in the small of his back and the lower abdomen, a pain aggravated by frequent spasms. He described it as "a constant state of childbirth." It appeared in his analysis that the pain started soon after he learned that the wife of his twin brother was pregnant, and he actually came to me for treatment a week before her confinement. He felt that if I could only liberate him from the spasm he would do marvelous things. In his case, identification with the pregnant woman, representing the mother, was very obvious, but it was not a happy identification. He felt his mother and the babies inside her had been so completely destroyed by his sadism, and his hope of re-creating them was so slight, that the identification with the pregnant mother meant to him a state of anguish, ruin, and abortive pregnancy. Instead of producing the baby, he, like the mother, was destroyed. Feeling destroyed inside and unable to restore the mother, he felt persecuted by her; the internal attacked mother attacked him in turn and robbed him of his babies. Unlike the other three patients described, this one recognized his depression and his reparative drive was therefore very much stronger. The inhibition both in his sexual and artistic achievements was due mainly to a feeling of the inadequacy of his reparative capacity in comparison with the devastation that he felt he had brought about. This feeling of inadequacy made him regress to a paranoid position whenever his anxiety was aroused.

Patient D, a woman writer, was the most disturbed of the patients here. A severe chronic hypochondriac, she suffered from frequent depersonalization and endless phobias, among them food phobias leading at times to almost complete anorexia.

She had been a writer, but had not been able to write for a number of years. I want to describe here how her inability to experience depression led to an inhibition of symbolic expression.

One day she told me the following dream: She was in a nursing home and the matron of this home, dressed in black, was going to kill a man and a woman. She herself was going to a fancy dress ball. She kept running out of the nursing home in various fancy disguises, but somehow something always went wrong, and she had to come back to the nursing home, and to meet the matron. At some point of the dream she was with her friend Joan.

Her friend Joan was for my patient the embodiment of mental health and stability. After telling me the dream she said: "Joan was not in a fancy dress, she was undisguised, and I felt her to be so much more vulnerable than me." Then she immediately corrected herself: "Oh, of course I meant she was so much less vulnerable than me." This slip of the patient gave us the key to the dream. The mentally healthy person is more vulnerable than my patient, she wears no disguises and is vulnerable to illness and death. My patient herself escapes death, represented by the matron, by using various disguises. Her associations to this dream led us to a review of some of her leading symptoms in terms of her fear of, and attempted escape from, death. The disguises in the dream represented personifications, projective and introjective identifications, all three used by her as means of not living her own life and—in the light of the dream—not dying her own death. She also connected other symptoms of hers with the fear of death. For instance, her spending almost half her life lying in bed, "half-dead," was a shamming of death, a way of cheating death. Her phobia of bread, her fear of sex, appeared to her now as ways of escaping full living, which would mean that one day she would have "spent her life" and would have to face death. So far, she had almost lived on "borrowed" life. For instance, she felt extremely well and alive when she was pregnant—she felt she lived on the baby's life; but immediately after the baby's birth she felt depersonalized and half-dead.

I mention here only some of her striking symptoms, which all pointed in the same direction—to a constant preoccupation with the fear of death. The analyst, represented by the matron, tears off her disguises one after another and forces her to lead her own life and so, eventually, to die.

After some three sessions completely taken up with the elaboration of this theme, she started the next one with what appeared to be a completely new trend of thought. She started complaining of her inability to write. Her associations led her to remember her early dislike of using words. She felt that her dislike was still present and she did not really want to use words at all. Using words, she said, made her break "an endless unity into bits." It was like "chopping up," like "cutting things." It was obviously felt by her as an aggressive act. Besides, using words was "making things finite and separate." To use words meant acknowledging the separateness of the world from herself, and gave her a feeling of loss. She felt that using words made her lose the illusion of possessing and being at one with an endless, undivided world: "When you name a thing you really lose it."[2] It became clear to her that using a symbol (language) meant an acceptance of the separateness of her object from herself, the acknowledgment of her own aggressiveness, "chopping up," "cutting," and finally losing the object.

In this patient the loss of the object was always felt as an imminent threat to her own survival. So we could eventually connect her difficulties in using language with the material of the earlier sessions. Refusing to face this threat of death to her object and to herself, she had to form the various symptoms devised magically to control and avoid death. She also had to give up her creative writing. In order to write again, she would have to be stripped of her disguises, admit reality, and become vulnerable to loss and death.

I shall now briefly describe a session with the same patient two years later.

She had known for some time that she would have to give up her analysis at the end of the term, through external circumstances. She came to this session very sad, for the first time since it became clear that she would end her analysis. In preceding sessions she felt nausea, felt internally persecuted and "all in bits and pieces." She said at the beginning of the session that she could hardly wait to see me for fear that her sadness would turn into a "sickness and badness." She thought of the end of her analysis, wondered if she would be able to go on liking me and how much she would be able to remember me. She also wondered if she in any way resembled me. There were two things she would wish to resemble me in: the truthfulness, and the capacity to care for people which she attributed to me. She hoped she may have learned these from me. She also felt I was an ordinary kind of person, and she liked that thought. I interpreted her material as a wish to take me in and identify herself with me as a real "ordinary" feeding breast, in contrast to an earlier situation when an idealized breast was internalized, which subsequently turned into a persecuting one.

She then told me the following dream: A baby has died or grown up—she didn't know which—and as a result her breasts were full of milk. She was feeding a baby of another woman, whose breasts were dry.

2. This theme was later linked with the Rumpelstiltskin theme of stealing the baby and the penis, but I cannot follow it up here.

The transference meaning of that dream was that I weaned her—my breast was dry—but she acquired a breast and could be a mother herself. The baby who "died or grew up" is herself. The baby dies and the grown woman takes its place. The losing of the analyst is here an experience involving sadness, guilt (about the rivalry with me in relation to the baby), and anxiety (will she be able to go on remembering me?). But it is also an experience leading to the enrichment of her ego—she now has the breasts full of milk and therefore need no longer depend on me.

Toward the end of the hour, she said: "Words seem to have a meaning again, they are rich," and she added that she was quite sure she could now write, "provided I can go on being sad for a while, without being sick and hating food"—i.e., provided she could mourn me instead of feeling me as an internal persecutor.

Words acquired a meaning and the wish to write returned again when she could give up my breast as an external object and internalize it. This giving up was experienced by her as the death of the breast, which is dried up in the dream, and the death of a part of herself—the baby part—which in growing up also dies. Insofar as she could mourn me, words became rich in meaning.[3]

This patient's material confirmed an impression, derived from many other patients, that successful symbol formation is rooted in the depressive position.

One of Freud's greatest contributions to psychology was the discovery that sublimation is the outcome of a successful renunciation of an instinctual aim; I would like to suggest here that such a successful renunciation can happen only through a process of mourning. The giving up of an instinctual aim, or object, is a repetition and at the same time a reliving of the giving up of the breast. It can be successful, like this first situation, if the object to be given up can be assimilated in the ego, by the process of loss and internal restoration. I suggest that such an assimilated object becomes a symbol within the ego. Every aspect of the object, every situation that has to be given up in the process of growing, gives rise to symbol formation.

In this view, symbol formation is the outcome of a loss; it is a creative act involving the pain and the whole work of mourning.

If psychic reality is experienced and differentiated from external reality, the symbol is differentiated from the object; it is felt to be created by the self and can be freely used by the self.

---

3. I have given here only the transference meaning of the dream in order not to detract from my main theme. The transference situation was linked with past experiences of weaning, birth of the new baby, and the patient's failure in the past to be a "good" mother to the new baby.

I cannot deal here extensively with the problem of symbols; I have brought it up only insofar as it is relevant to my main theme. And it is relevant in that the creation of symbols, the symbolic elaboration of a theme, is the very essence of art.

I should now like to attempt to formulate an answer to the question whether there is a specific factor in the psychology of the successful artist which would differentiate him from the unsuccessful one. In Freud's words: "What distinguishes him, the poet, the artist, from the neurotic day-dreamer?" In his paper "Formulations Regarding the Two Principles in Mental Functioning" (1911), Freud says that the artist "finds a way of return from this world of phantasy back to reality; with his special gifts he moulds his phantasies into a new kind of reality" (p. 19). Indeed, one could say that the artist has an acute reality sense. He is often neurotic and in many situations may show a complete lack of objectivity, but in at least two respects he shows an extremely high reality sense. One is in relation to his own internal reality, and the other in relation to the material of his art. However neurotic Proust was in his attachment to his mother, his homosexuality, his asthma, etc., he had a real insight into the fantastic world of the people inside him, and he knew it was internal, and he knew it was phantasy. He showed an awareness that does not exist in a neurotic who splits off, represses, denies, or acts out his phantasy. The second, the reality sense of the artist in relation to his material, is a highly specialized reality assessment of the nature, needs, possibilities, and limitations of his material, be it words, sounds, paints, or clay. The neurotic uses his material in a magic way, and so does the bad artist. The real artist, being aware of his internal world, which he must express, and of the external materials with which he works, can in all consciousness use the material to express the phantasy. He shares with the neurotic all the difficulties of unresolved depression, the constant threat of the collapse of his internal world; but he differs from the neurotic in that he has a greater capacity for tolerating anxiety and depression. The patients I described could not tolerate depressive phantasies and anxieties; they all made use of manic defenses leading to a denial of psychic reality. Patient A denied both the loss of her father and his importance to her; Patient B projected his impulses onto an internal bad object, with the result that his ego was split and that he was internally persecuted; Patient C did the same, though to a lesser extent; Patient D regressed to the schizoid mechanisms of splitting and projective identification, which led to depersonalization and inhibition in the use of symbols. In contrast to that, Proust could fully experience depressive mourning.

This gave him the possibility of insight into himself, and with it a sense of internal and external reality. Further, this reality sense enabled him to have and to maintain a relationship with other people through the medium of his art. The neurotic's phantasy interferes with his relationships, in which he acts it out. The artist withdraws into a world of phantasy, but he can communicate and share it. In that way he makes reparation, not only to his own internal objects, but to the external world as well.

I have tried, so far, to show how Melanie Klein's work, especially her concept of the depressive position, the reparative drives that are set in motion by it, and her description of the world of inner objects, throws new light on the psychology of the artist, on the conditions necessary for him to be successful, and on those which can inhibit or vitiate his artistic activities. Can this new light on the psychology of the artist help us to understand the aesthetic pleasure experienced by the artist's public? If, for the artist, the work of art is his most complete and satisfactory way of allaying the guilt and despair arising out of the depressive position and of restoring his destroyed objects, it is but one of the many human ways of achieving this end. What is it that makes a work of art such a satisfactory experience for the artist's public? Freud says that he "bribes us with the formal and aesthetic pleasures."

To begin with, we should distinguish between the aesthetic pleasure and other, incidental pleasures to be found in works of art. For instance, the satisfaction derived from identification with particular scenes or characters can also arise in other ways, and it can be derived from bad as well as from good art. The same would apply to the sentimental interests originating in memories and associations. The aesthetic pleasure proper, that is, the pleasure derived from a work of art and unique in that it can only be obtained through a work of art, is due to an identification of ourselves with the work of art as a whole and with the whole internal world of the artist as represented by his work. In my view all aesthetic pleasure includes an unconscious reliving of the artist's experience of creation. In his paper "The Moses of Michaelangelo" (1914), Freud says: "What the artist aims at is to awaken in us the same mental constellation as that which in him produced the impetus to create."

We find in Dilthey's philosophy (Hodges 1944) the concept *nacherleben*. This word denotes for him our capacity to understand other people from their behavior and expression. We intuitively reconstruct their mental and emotional states, we live after them; we re-live them. This process is, he says, often deeper than introspection can discover. His concept is, I think, equivalent to unconscious identification. I assume that this kind of unconscious reliving of the creator's state of mind is the foundation of all aesthetic pleasure.

To illustrate what I mean I will take as an example the case of classical tragedy. In a tragedy the hero commits a crime: the crime is fated, it is an "innocent" crime, he is driven to it. Whatever the nature of the crime, the result is always complete destruction—parental figures and child figures alike are engulfed by it. That is, at whatever level the conflict starts— *Oedipus Rex*, for instance, states a genital conflict—in the end we arrive at a picture of the phantasies belonging to the earliest depressive position where all the objects are destroyed. What is the psychological mechanism of the listener's *nach-erleben?* As I see it, he makes two identifications. He identifies himself with the author, and the whole tragedy with the author's internal world. He identifies himself with the author while the latter is facing and expressing his depression. In a simplified way one can summarize the listener's reaction as follows: "The author has, in his hatred, destroyed all his loved objects just as I have done, and like me he felt death and desolation inside him. Yet he can face it and he can make me face it, and despite the ruin and devastation we and the world around us survive. What is more, his objects , which have become evil and were destroyed, have been made alive again and have become immortal by his art. Out of all the chaos and destruction he has created a world which is whole, complete, and unified."

It would appear, then, that two factors are essential to the excellence of a tragedy: the unshrinking expression of the full horror of the depressive phantasy and the achieving of an impression of wholeness and harmony. The external form of classical tragedy is in complete contrast with its content. The formal modes of speech, the unities of time, place, and action, and the strictness and rigidity of the rules are all, I believe, an unconscious demonstration of the fact that order can emerge out of chaos. Without this formal harmony the depression of the audience would be aroused but not resolved. There can be no aesthetic pleasure without perfect form.[4]

---

4. Roger Fry says: "All the essential aesthetic quality has to do with pure form," and I agree; but he adds later: "The odd thing is that it is, apparently, dangerous for the artist to know about this." Roger Fry feels that it is odd, I think, because of an inherent weakness of the formalist school he represents. The formalists discount the importance of emotional factors in art. According to Fry, art must be completely detached from emotions, all emotion is impurity, and the more the form gets freed from the emotional content the nearer it is to the ideal. What the formalists ignore is that form as much as content is in itself an expression of unconscious emotion. What Fry, following Clive Bell, calls *significant form*, a term he confesses himself incapable of defining, is form expressing and embodying an unconscious emotional experience. The artist is not trying to produce pretty or even beautiful form; he is engaged on the most important task of re-creating his ruined internal world, and the resulting form will depend on how well he succeeds in his task.

In creating a tragedy, I suggest, the success of the artist depends on his being able fully to acknowledge and express his depressive phantasies and anxieties. In expressing them he does work similar to the work of mourning in that he internally re-creates a harmonious world which is projected into his work of art.

The reader identifies with the author through the medium of his work of art. In that way he reexperiences his own early depressive anxieties, and through identifying with the artist he experiences a successful mourning, reestablishes his own internal objects and his own internal world, and feels, therefore, reintegrated and enriched.

But is this experience specific to a work of art that is tragic, or is it an essential part of any aesthetic experience? I think I could generalize my argument. To do so I shall have to introduce the more usual terminology of aesthetics and restate my problems in new terms. The terms I need are *ugly* and *beautiful*. For Rickman, in his paper "On the Nature of Ugliness and the Creative Impulse" (1940), the ugly is the destroyed, the incomplete object. For Ella Sharpe (1930) ugly means destroyed, arythmic, and connected with painful tension. I think both these views would be included if we say that ugliness is what expresses the state of the internal world in depression. It includes tension, hatred, and its results—the destruction of good and whole objects and their change into persecutory fragments. Rickman, however, when he contrasts ugly and beautiful, seems to equate the latter with what is aesthetically satisfying. With that I cannot agree. Ugly and beautiful are two categories of aesthetic experience and, in certain ways, they can be contrasted; but if beautiful is used as synonymous with aesthetically satisfying, then its contradictory is not ugly, but unaesthetic, or indifferent, or dull. Rickman says that we recoil from the ugly; my contention is that it is a most important and necessary component of a satisfying aesthetic experience. The concept of ugliness as one element in aesthetic satisfaction is not uncommon in the tradition of philosophical aesthetics; it has been most strikingly expressed, however, by the artists themselves. Rodin writes: "We call ugly that which is formless, unhealthy, which suggests illness, suffering, destruction, which is contrary to regularity—the sign of health. We also call ugly the immoral, the vicious, the criminal and all abnormality which brings evil—the soul of the parricide, the traitor, the self-seeker. But let a great artist get hold of this ugliness; immediately he transfigures it—with a touch of his magic wand he makes it into beauty."

What is beauty? Taking again the beautiful as but one of the categories of the aesthetically satisfying, most writers agree that the main elements of the beautiful—the whole, the complete, and the rhythmical—are in contrast with the ugly. Among analytical writers, Rickman equates the beautiful with the whole object, while Ella Sharpe considers beauty essentially as rhythm and equates it with the experience of goodness in rhythmical sucking, satisfactory defecation, and sexual intercourse.. To this I should add rhythmical breathing and the rhythm of our heartbeats. An undisturbed rhythm in a composed whole seems to correspond to the state in which our inner world is at peace. Among nonanalytical writers, Herbert Read comes to a similar conclusion when he says that. what we find rhythmical are simple arithmetical proportions which correspond to the way we are built and our bodies work. But these elements of beauty are in themselves insufficient. If they were enough we would find it most satisfactory to contemplate a circle or listen to a regular tattoo on a drum. I suggest that both beauty, in the narrow sense of the word, and ugliness must be present for a full aesthetic experience.

I would reword my attempt at analyzing the tragic in terms of ugliness and beauty. Broadly speaking, in tragedy ugliness is the content—the complete ruin and destruction—and beauty is the form. Ugliness is also an essential part of the comic. The comic here is ugly in that, as in caricature, the overstressing of one or two characteristics ruins the wholeness—the balance—of the character. Ugly and tragic is also the defeat of the comic hero by the sane world. How near the comic hero is to the tragic can be seen from the fact that outstanding comic heroes of past ages are felt, at a later date, to be mainly tragic figures; few people today take Shylock or Falstaff as figures of fun only; we are aware of the tragedy implied. The difference between tragedy and comedy lies, then, in the comic writer's attempt to disassociate himself from the tragedy of his hero, to feel superior to it in a kind of successful manic defense. But the manic defense is never complete; the original depression is still expressed and it must therefore have been to a large extent acknowledged and lived by the author. The audience relives depression, the fear of it, and the aggression against it which are expressed in a comedy and its final successful outcome.

It is easier to discover this pattern of overcoming depression in litera-ture, with its explicit verbal content, than in other forms of art. The further away from literature the more difficult is the task. In music, for instance, we would have to study the introduction of discords, disharmonies, new disorders which are so invariably considered to be ugly before they are universally accepted. New art is considered difficult; it is resisted, misun-derstood, treated with bitter hatred, contempt; or, on the other hand, it may be idealized to such an extent that the apparent admiration defeats its aim and makes its object the butt of ridicule. These prevalent reactions of the public are, I think, manifestations of a manic defense against the depressive anxieties stirred by art. The artists find ever new ways of revealing a repressed and denied depression. The public use against it all their powers of defense until they find the courage to follow the new artist into the depths of his depression, and eventually to share his triumphs.

The idea that ugliness is an essential component of a complete experience seems to be true of the tragic, the comic, the realistic—in fact, of all the commonly accepted categories of the aesthetic except one. And this single exception is of great importance.

There is, undoubtedly, a category of art which shows to the greatest extent all the elements of beauty in the narrow sense of the word, and no apparent sign of ugliness; it is often called "classical" beauty. The beauty of the Parthenon, of the Discobolos, is whole, rhythmical, undisturbed. But soulless imitations of beauty, "pretty" creations, are also whole and rhythmical; yet they fail to stir and rouse anything but boredom. Thus classical beauty must have some other not immediately obvious element.

Returning to the concept of *nach-erleben,* of experiencing along with another, we may say that in order to move us deeply the artist must have embodied in his work some deep experience of his own. And all our analytical experience as well as the knowledge derived from other forms of art suggests that the deep experience must have been what we call, clinically, a depression, and that the stimulus to create such a perfect whole must have lain in the drive to overcome an unusually strong depression. If we consider what is commonly said about beauty by laymen, we find a confirmation of this conclusion. They say that complete beauty makes one both sad and happy at the same time, and that it is a purge for the soul—that it is awe-inspiring. Great artists themselves have been very much aware of the depression and terror embodied in works of classical beauty which are apparently so peaceful. When Faust goes in search of Helen, the perfect classical beauty, he has to face unnamed terrors, to go where there is no road:

> Kein Weg! Ins Unbetretene
> Nicht zu Betretende; ein Weg ins Unerbetene,
> Nicht zu Erbittende.

He must face endless emptiness:

> —Nichts Wirst du sehn in ewig leerer Ferne,
> Den Schritt nicht horen den du tust,
> Nichts Festes finden, wo du ruhst.

Rilke writes: "Beauty is nothing but the beginning of terror that we are still just able to bear."

Thus to the sensitive onlooker, every work of beauty still embodies the terrifying experience of depression and death. Hanns Sachs, in his book *Beauty, Life and Death*, pays particular attention to the awesome aspect of beauty; he says the difficulty is not to understand beauty but to bear it, and he connects this terror with the very peacefulness of the perfect work of art. He calls it the static element; it is peaceful because it seems unchangeable, eternal. And it is terrifying because this eternal unchangeability is the expression of the death instinct—the static element opposed to life and change.

Following quite a different trend of thought I come to similar conclusions about the role of the death instinct in a work of art. Thus far my contention has been that a satisfactory work of art is achieved by a realization and sublimation of the depressive position, and that the effect on the audience is that they unconsciously relive the artist's experience and share his triumph of achievement and his final detachment. But to realize and symbolically express depression the artist must acknowledge the death instinct, both in its aggressive and self-destructive aspects, and accept the reality of death for the object and the self. One of the patients I described could not use symbols because of her failure to work through the depressive position; her failure clearly lay in her inability to accept and use her death instinct and to acknowledge death.

Restated in terms of instincts, ugliness—destruction—is the expression of the death instinct; beauty—the desire to unite into rhythms and wholes— is that of the life instinct. The achievement of the artist is in giving the fullest expression to the conflict and the union between these two.

This is a conclusion which Freud has brought out in two of his essays, though he did not generalize it as applicable to all art. One of these essays is that on Michelangelo's Moses (1914), where he clearly shows that the latent meaning of this work is the overcoming of wrath. The other essay is his analysis of the theme of the three caskets (1913). He shows there that in the choice between the three caskets, or three women, the final choice is always symbolic of death. He interprets Cordelia in *King Lear* as a symbol of death, and for him the solution of the play is Lear's final overcoming of the fear of death and his reconciliation to it. Freud writes: "Thus man overcomes death, which in thought he has acknowledged. No greater triumph of wish-fulfilment is conceivable" (p. 254).

All artists aim at immortality; their objects must not only be brought back to life, but that life must also be eternal. And of all human activities art comes nearest to achieving immortality; a great work of art is likely to escape destruction and oblivion.

It is tempting to suggest that this is so because in a great work of art the degree of denial of the death instinct is less than in any other human activity, that the death instinct is acknowledged, as fully as can be borne. It is expressed and curbed to the needs of the life instinct and creation.

POSTSCRIPT 1980: AESTHETICS

Looking back on this paper, the first one I presented in the Society in 1947, although it was published much later, I still find myself in agreement with its main thesis, namely, that the essence of the aesthetic creation is a resolution of the central depressive situation and that the main factor in the aesthetic experience is the identification with this process. I should, however, now emphasize more the role of the idealization arising from the paranoid-schizoid position. I am in agreement here with Adrian Stokes (1965), who says that the artist seeks the precise point at which he can maintain simultaneously an ideal object merged with the self, and an object perceived as separate and independant, as in the depressive position.

I would also have liked to link my work with the paper of Elliot Jaques (1965) on the midlife crisis, and to describe in more detail the difference between a pre-midlife and a post-midlife crisis type of creativity. I think that before the midlife crisis the artist seeks more the ideal object, and that past the midlife crisis he is more in search of the re-creation of the object as seen in the depressive position.

References

Ehrenzweig, A. (1948). Unconscious form-creation in art. *British Journal of Medical Psychology* 21:88-109.

Fairbairn, W. R. D. (1938). The ultimate basis of aesthetic experience. *British Journal of Psychology* 29:167-181.

Freud, S. (1908). The relation of the poet to day-dreaming. *Collected Papers* 4:173-183.

——— (1910). Leonardo da Vinci and a memory of his childhood. *Standard Edition* 11:57-137.

——— (1911). Formulations regarding the two principles of mental functioning. *Collected Papers* 4:13-21.

——— (1913). The theme of the three caskets. *Collected Papers* 4:244-256.

——— (1914). The Moses of Michelangelo. *Collected Papers* 4:257-287.

Fry, R. (1920). *Vision and Design*. London: Chatto and Windus.

——— (1926). *Transformations*. London: Chatto and Windus.

Heimann, P. (1942). A contribution to the problem of sublimation and its relation to processes of internalization. *International Journal of Psycho-Analysis* 23:8-17.

Hodges, H. (1944). *Wilhelm Dilthey: An Introduction*. London: Routledge and Kegan Paul; New York: Howard Fertig, 1969.

Jaques, E. (1965). Death and the mid-life crisis. *International Journal of Psycho-Analysis* 46:502-514.

Jones, E. (1914). The Madonna's conception through the ear. In E. Jones, *Essays in Applied Psycho-Analysis* 2:266-357. London: Hogarth, 1951.

——— (1916). The theory of symbolism. In E. Jones, *Papers on Psycho-Analysis*. 2nd ed. London: Ballière, Tindall and Cox, 1918.

Klein, M. (1929). Infantile anxiety-situations reflected in a work of art and the creative impulse. *International Journal of Psycho-Analysis* 10:436-443. In M. Klein, *Contributions to Psycho-Analysis* 1921-1945. pp. 227-235. London: Hogarth, 1948.

——— (1935). A contribution to the psychogenesis of manic-depressive states. *International Journal of Psycho-Analysis* 16:145-174. In M. Klein, *Contributions to Psycho-Analysis 1921-1945*, pp. 282-310. London: Hogarth, 1948.

——— (1940). Mourning and its relation to manic-depressive states. *International Journal of Psycho-Analysis* 21:125-153. In M. Klein, *Contributions to Psycho-Analysis 1921-1945*, pp. 311-338. London: Hogarth, 1948.

Lee. H. (1939). A critique of the theory of sublimation. *Psychiatry* 2:239-270.

——— (1940). A theory concerning free creation in the inventive arts. *Psychiatry* 3:229-293.

Listowel, Earl of. (1933). *A Critical History of Modern Aesthetics*. London: Allen and Unwin.

Read, H. (1931). *The Meaning of Art*. London: Heinemann.

——— (1934). *Art and Society*. London: Heinemann.

Rickmann, J. (1940). On the nature of ugliness and the creative impulse. *International Journal of Psycho-Analysis* 21:294-313. In J. Rickman, *Selected Contributions to Psycho-Analysis*, pp. 68-89. New York: Basic Books, 1957.

Sachs, H. (1940). Beauty, life and death. *American Imago* 1:81-133. In H. Sachs, *The Creative Unconscious: Studies in the Psychoanalysis of Art*, pp. 147-240. Cambridge, Mass.: Sci-Art, 1942.

Sharpe, E. (1930). Certain aspects of sublimation and delusion. *International Journal of Psycho-Analysis* 11:12-23. In E. Sharpe, *Collected Papers on Psycho-Analysis*, pp. 125-136. London: Hogarth, 1950.

——— (1935). Similar and divergent unconscious determinants underlying the sublimations of pure art and pure science. *International Journal of Psycho-Analysis* 16:186-202. In E. Sharpe, *Collected Papers on Psycho-Analysis*, pp. 137-154. London: Hogarth, 1950.

Stokes, A. (1965). *The Invitation in Art*. London: Tavistock.

tional Journal of Psycho-Analysis 21:294-313. In J. Rickman, *Selected Contributions to Psycho-Analysis*, pp. 68-89. New York: Basic Books, 1957.

Sachs, H. (1940). Beauty, life and death. *American Imago* 1:81-133. In H. Sachs, *The Creative Unconscious: Studies in the Psychoanalysis of Art*, pp. 147-240. Cambridge, Mass.: Sci-Art, 1942.

Sharpe, E. (1930). Certain aspects of sublimation and delusion. *International Journal of Psycho-Analysis* 11:12-23. In E. Sharpe, *Collected Papers on Psycho-Analysis*, pp. 125-136. London: Hogarth, 1950.

——— (1935). Similar and divergent unconscious determinants underlying the sublimations of pure art and pure science. *International Journal of Psycho-Analysis* 16:186-202. In E. Sharpe, *Collected Papers on Psycho-Analysis*, pp. 137-154. London: Hogarth, 1950.

Stokes, A. (1965). *The Invitation in Art*. London: Tavistock.

17

Delusion and Artistic
Creativity

THIS ESSAY has no pretensions to literary criticism, nor is it an attempt to "psychoanalize" a book, or through the book, its author. It is an attempt to use the material of a novel to further a psychoanalytic investigation into the origin and the nature of artistic endeavor. It is a continuation of a trend of thought I started in chapter 16. In particular, it is concerned with the shadowy area in which originate both the psychotic delusion and the artistic creation.

The Spire, a novel by William Golding (1964), is the story, set in the Middle Ages, of the endeavors of Jocelin, Dean of the Cathedral, to build a 400-foot spire, as he has heard that this has been done in France. Despite the opposition of his chapter and advice that such a spire cannot be built because the church has no foundations and the structure no strength, he is certain that he can translate his vision into reality. He has been vouchsafed a vision which convinces him that he has been chosen by God for this task. His conviction that he has been so chosen is also nourished by the fact that his promotion to his present position has been miraculously fast. He is supported by an angel, who "warms his back." Roger Mason is the only man capable of building such a spire, but he is, to begin with, doubtful, and later is completely opposed to the plan. Jocelin must compel him to do the building.

Apart from Jocelin, there are four main protagonists: Roger Mason and his wife Rachel, Pangall, an old servant of the cathedral, and his beautiful young wife, Goody. Jocelin compares them to the four pillars of the cathedral: "My spire will stand on them as on the four pillars." Pangall is old and crippled, Goody young and beautiful and Jocelin's favorite—his "golden child." He had arranged her marriage to Pangall, but the marriage is sterile because, as becomes clear later, Pangall is impotent. Roger Mason is the powerful builder, Rachel his earthy counterpart. But that marriage too is sterile, as Rachel later confesses to Jocelin, because "she always laughs at the crucial moment."

When the novel starts, we are carried by Jocelin's exultation. He is full of power and conviction about his mission; he radiates a god-like patronizing love toward his enemies as well as his friends. But right from the start one can feel the underlying anxiety and tension, and his mood very quickly becomes irritable as his plans are opposed or his authority seems flouted.

He exults in his imagination of his cathedral. He contemplates the model:

> The model was like a man lying on his back. The nave was his legs placed together, the transepts on either side were his arms outspread. The choir was his body; and the Lady Chapel, where now the services would be held, was his head. And now also, springing, projecting, bursting, erupting from the heart of the building, there was its crown and majesty, the new spire. They don't know, he thought, they can't know until I tell them of my vision!

Four portraits of Jocelin are to adorn the four faces of the spire.

From the beginning of the book, he meets with opposition from his chapter, from Pangall and from Roger Mason. Pangall accuses him of ruining and defiling the cathedral, built by Pangall's fathers and fore-fathers, and he complains of the workmen's desecration of the cathedral and mockery of himself. Mason opposes the building of such a tall tower because, according to him, the structure of the cathedral has no strength to support it. But Jocelin ignores the chapter's and Pangall's complaints, as well as Mason's realistic warnings. He has noticed Mason's interest in Goody and realizes that this gives him power over the man. With guilt and exultation, he thinks, "I've got him in a net."

The story of the building and, possibly, final collapse of the spire is marked by several climaxes which make the underlying symbolism of the story clearer. The first climax comes when Roger Mason, having decided to dig to the foundation of the cathedral to gauge its strength, opens up a pit. Slowly the cathedral starts filling with the stench of the dead. There is no foundation, and when the floors are removed, the subterranean waters start moving. And the earth creeps. There is a dramatic moment when the foundations begin to collapse. Pangall complains to Jocelin that he is the butt of the workmen's mockery. Just before the waters start moving, Jocelin gets a glimpse of the workmen chasing Pangall, one of them holding the model of the cathedral between his legs, with the spire "sticking out obscenely." He half-sees Pangall pushed about and later disappearing into the pit. He also has a glimpse of Goody, part naked, covered by her flaming red hair. But he immediately represses the sight, is unclear about what he has seen, and becomes confused. After the pit has been opened Pangall disappears and Roger again begs to be let go. But Jocelin is more convinced than ever of his mission: if the cathedral has no foundations it is but further confirmation that it is miraculous. He also realizes that with Pangall's disappearance Roger is finally caught in the net. He sees Roger and Goody "as in a tent."

From the moment the pit has been opened, Jocelin's folly becomes more apparent. His confusion increases. He spends more and more time on the building's tower watching the building of the spire. Somewhere on the tower Roger has his "swallow's nest," in which Goody visits him. Another climactic moment occurs when Jocelin overhears their intercourse and becomes acutely aware of his jealousy and his guilt.

Parallel to his angel, Jocelin has also his devil, and the devil torments him with sexual feelings and attains more power. He has a masturbatory phantasy in a state of semi-sleep. Upon waking, he realizes with horror his sexual feelings toward Goody as well as his homosexual feelings toward the young sculptor who is engaged on his portrait. He feels his angel begins to exhaust him by recurring and increasing hotness in his back, and at times the angel becomes indistinguishable from the devil. He is occasionally threatened by the emergence of the memory of what he saw at the pit but inevitably represses it again and becomes more confused. The structure of the spire begins to collapse, and another climax is reached, when Jocelin finds Goody in the throes of childbirth— red hair and red blood fusing in his mind—a dramatic childbirth which leads to the death of Goody and the child. His guilt at what he has done to Goody and Roger begins to break through, but more than ever it is important to finish the spire, to justify such sacrifice: "This I have done for Him through love." Roger works gloomily now on the spire, having nowhere else to go, but things progressively deteriorate: the cathedral is deserted, the workmen take part in devil worship; the countryside is desolate; and the pillars of the cathedral begin to sing. Jocelin pins his hopes on the Nail from the Cross that was promised to him by the bishop. But when the bishop comes and offers him the Nail, his main business is a court of inquiry into Jocelin's fitness to continue as Dean.

Simultaneously, he receives a visit from his aunt. The aunt has been the king's mistress, and it was largely her money that provided for the building of the spire. In exchange, she wanted to be buried in the cathedral; Jocelin manipulates for the money but refuses her request, since to him it would be defiling the cathedral. Now, however, she is alarmed by reports about his health. The crucial moment in their conversation comes when he says, "After I was chosen by God. . . ." And she laughs, saying, "Who chose you— God? *I* chose you." She describes how after a particularly happy love-making she and the king wanted to spread their happiness; they then decided to elevate him to his post. At that moment, the basis of Jocelin's conviction is shaken: he has not been chosen by God but by this sinful, despised couple. From that moment a complete collapse sets in. His doubts and guilt break through and illness "breaks his spine." Crippled by illness he crawls on all fours to Roger Mason to beg his forgiveness, but Roger, lying drunk and despairing in his digs, only curses him. In a semi-confused state, but with an awful clarity, he confesses that the pit, "the cellarage knew it all." It knew that he had made Goody marry Pangall because he knew of the man's impotence. He also knew that Pangall was murdered at the pit.

He is brought home and nursed physically and mentally by Father Adam, whom he always called Father Anonymous because of his humility. And it is only then that he describes the details of his vision in which the spire represented his prayer reaching Heaven, to which Father Anonymous replies sadly, horrified, "They never taught you to pray."

A synopsis is always very unsatisfactory. For those who know the book it must seem a very thin account of the real thing. To those who have not read it, it hardly conveys the richness and complexity of the themes.

I have chosen only such elements of the narrative as will illustrate my own view of it. The cathedral obviously represents Jocelin himself. This is clear from his first seeing the model of the cathedral as a human body; and it is his own face that will adorn the spire. That the erect spire represents the penis and potency becomes even clearer when the workman pursuing Pangall sticks the spire "obscenely between his legs." The sexual phantasies involved in the building of the spire are both clear and complex. Heterosexually, the spire-penis is meant to reach Heaven-mother (after Goody's death Jocelin has a phantasy of the spire reaching Goody in heaven and she is confused in his mind with the Virgin Mary). Seen homosexually, the spire is an offering to God the Father. His relationship with God is felt in quite physical terms. The angel that warms his back, and becomes later indistinguishable from the devil, is felt as a sexual penetration by God. Toward the end, when the angel and devil fuse, he feels that the angel "kicks him in the arse." There is also a homosexual relationship in which he does not submit to God or the angel, but *is* God to another man. The sculptor, who sculpts his face and follows him around, is a dumb young man with a permanently open and humming mouth; and it is his face and mouth that get confused with Goody's genital in Jocelin's masturbation phantasy. The spire, however, represents not only his potency but also his omnipotence. He represents it to himself as an offering to God, but it is clear throughout that it is his own penis-spire that is to dominate the landscape, to reach heaven and to stand forever as an object of universal admiration.

This building of his own self and his own omnipotent potency is done on the basis of the total destruction of his parents. He says with anguish, "How many people at that moment are built into this cathedral!" His parents are represented by the two sterile couples: Pangall and Goody, Roger and Rachel. In one couple, the man is impotent; in the other, the woman. As his plan develops, he further destroys these couples, allowing the murder of Pangall and the unfaithfulness of Roger. As Roger tells him, the four pillars are hollow; they cannot support his spire. The hollow pillars are the hollow, sterile marriages representing what he has made in his phantasy of his parents' sexuality. But to build his own potency he must reconstruct in his internal world a potent father and marriage; so he brings Roger and Goody together to form a couple. This bringing of the sexual parents together is done, however, entirely under his control. They are in his "tent." He overcomes his extreme jealousy by acquiring control over their sexuality and gratifying his own desires by projective identification. He puts his heterosexual feelings into Roger and uses him to possess Goody and his feminine feelings into Goody, through whom he imprisons and entraps Roger. He gets his own sexual satisfaction, like a voyeur, through watching them, controlling them, and identifying with them. Their union results in a baby, but this is not allowed. For the baby dies and kills Goody in the process, and Jocelin thinks that it is his sudden appearance in Goody's room which brought about that death. The sexual parents, manipulated by Jocelin, are not allowed to build a baby; they are only allowed to build Jocelin's spire.

Jocelin's building of the spire is the building of a delusion—the delusion that the parents never had potency or creativity. (The "cellarage," as he calls it, of the cathedral contains nothing but dead bodies.) If the cathedral is Jocelin, the cellarage is his unconscious, containing nothing but a fantasy of dead bodies ("the cellarage knew").

Wherever the signs of sexual potency are found, they are destroyed anew, like Roger's and Goody's baby. Jocelin's aim is to be the only and wholly controlling partner of both father and mother; and only his spire is allowed intercourse with either. It pretends to be an offering to God, but it is only an offering to his own power. I said that the cathedral represented Jocelin himself, but this is only partly true. In fact, the cathedral was there before him, as Pangall bitterly reminds him: it represents also the body of his mother and the potency of his father which he ruthlessly destroys to create his own spire. The spire is supposed to be a completion of the cathedral, but in fact the cathedral is sacrificed to it. It represents a phantasy of taking over his mother's body and the sexual powers of his father to use them for his own needs, as he uses Roger and Goody.

This structure cannot be maintained for reasons of guilt and reasons of psychic and external reality. The basis of his structure is that there was no sex between the parents. When his aunt tells him how she and the king had chosen him, it represents to him the statement that he was not chosen by God but was born out of ordinary happy love-making between the sexual parents as represented by the king and the aunt whom he condemns and despises. Confronted with this knowledge, he realizes that the whole foundation of his inner world, represented by the cathedral, was false. He has to admit that the sexual parents existed and that it is he who has murdered them. The spire sways and threatens to collapse. Despair sets in. And the collapse of his omnipotent phantasy becomes the collapse of himself, since he had developed no other relation to his internal parents that he could turn to: "they never taught him to pray."

Described in that way, one could see the book as a case history of a manic delusion and its collapse. But of course, a good novel is never just that. It describes universal problems that can be seen from many angles. I think that in the author's mind, the book was to illustrate problems of true and false faith, as exemplified by Jocelin and Father Anonymous. But, as in every work of art, the novel contains also the story of its own creation and it expresses the problems, conflicts and doubts about the author's own creativity. The agonizing question that the artist poses himself is, "Is my work a creation or a delusion?" The story of Jocelin can be seen as exposing the common roots of delusion and artistic creativity and the differences between them. Why was Jocelin's spire a delusion and not a great artistic creation? Is it accidental that it is going to collapse? What did Jocelin have in common with the artist? And in what way did he differ? Jocelin exclaims at one point, "There is no innocent work." Is the artist's work different from Jocelin's? I agree with him that there is no innocent work, and the artist's work, in particular, has one of its roots in destructiveness.

In his book *The Invitation in Art* (1965), Adrian Stokes emphasized that at the beginning of every artistic creation is an act of aggression: the sculptor has to break and chip the stone, the painter and the writer feel that they defile the white canvas or paper with the first stroke of the brush or pen; and from that moment, they feel committed to the restoration represented by completing the work of art. In chapter 16, I put forward the theory that the artist's work is a way of working through the depressive position. This stage of development occurs when the infant begins to relate to his mother and soon to other people in his environment as whole and separate persons, in contrast with an earlier stage, where no such clear perception exists. Confronted with the wholeness and separateness of the parents, the infant, and later the child, experiences the impact of his own ambivalence toward them. In his experience of separation, jealousy and envy, he hates them and, in his mind, attacks them. Since the infant at that early stage of development feels his wishes and phantasies to be omnipotent, he feels that the parents thus attacked become fragmented and destroyed, and he introjects them as such into his internal world. This is one aspect of the infant's "cellarage." But since he also loves his parents and needs them, this destruction brings about feelings of mourning, loss, guilt and a longing to undo the damage done and to restore in his mind the parents to their original state. Reparative impulses come into play. When the child becomes aware of the parental intercourse and fertility, the reparation involves restoring to them in his mind their full sexual potency and fertility. It is in this situation, in the "cellarage," that are rooted the creative urges. The artist in particular is concerned with the task of creating a whole new world as a means of symbolic restoration of his internal world and his internal family. It is clear that the artist and the creator of the delusion are close to one another in the vividness of their feeling of the destruction of their whole inner world and their need to create a complete world anew. The artist's compulsion to create may at times be as overriding and ruthless as Jocelin's. There is a beautiful description of this aspect of creativity in Patrick White's *The Vivisector* (1970). His mother says of the young painter, "You were born with a knife in your hand, or rather in your eyes.

The artist, whatever his medium may be, creates an illusion, but at times it comes close to a delusion; his created world becomes to him as real, as in the famous story about Dumas, who rushed out of a room sobbing, "I have killed my Porthos," when he was describing the death of his hero. So both the artist and the person suffering from a delusion start with a common "cellarage": the destruction of the parent couple in their phantasy and their internal world; and both have the overriding need to recreate a destroyed and lost structure.

Here, however, the similarity ends and the differences begin. Jocelin does not aim, in his creation, at restoring any objects: what he is creating is an ideal picture of himself, including an omnipotent potency, at the expense of the parental figures. He seems to be serving God, but it is his spire, standing for a part of his own body, which is to reach heaven omnipotently. He bears an extraordinary resemblance to a patient I have in analysis who has a mono-delusion and has created in his mind an extraordinarily complex delusional system centering on his supposed "mission" but who in real life has achieved nothing (Segal, 1972). The artist, on the other hand, is concerned primarily with the restoration of his objects. Proust, for instance, has said that a book, like memory, is "a vast graveyard where on most of the tombstones one can no longer read the faded names." To him, writing a book is bringing this lost world of loved objects back to life: "I had to recapture from the shade that which I had felt, to re-convert it into its psychic equivalent, but the way to do it, the only one I could see, what was it but to create a work of art." Jocelin has some awareness of where he went wrong in his creation, when, toward the end of the book, he says, "But what is heaven if I can't reach it, holding them each by the hand?" He refers to Roger and Goody, destroyed by him and standing for his sexual parents, whom he never restored in his internal reality. This difference, restoring the object rather than the self, reflects the crucial differences between the artist's and the psychotic's relation to his creation and the means which each employs. To begin with, the creative artistic process lessens the guilt of the original destructiveness by real creation. When the artist in Patrick White's *The Vivisector*, (1970) is asked why he painted a cruel portrait of his crippled sister, he answered, "I had my painterly reasons: these come first, of course. Then I think I wanted to make amends— in the only way I ever knew—for some of my enormities." This answer expresses both the original attack and the amends, as does the picture itself in its cruelty and its beauty. This aspect of attack and reparation recurs constantly in *The Vivisector*. For instance, the painter's mistress died in an accident, probably due to his cruelty, and for years after her features reappeared in various forms in his work.

The delusion formation, on the other hand, perpetuates the guilt by repeating the crime, as, in Jocelin's case, his repetitive destruction of the parental sexual couple and their child.

Also, since the work of art primarily represents the object and not the self, the artist can visualize a separation between himself and the completed work. He can finish it and move on to the next one. An important part of overcoming the depressive anxieties and completing the reparation is to allow the object to be separate once again. This enables the artist to have a certain objective detachment from his work and a critical attitude to it. He is never completely identified with it. Very important consequences follow from this: unlike Jocelin, he does not become confused. In allowing the object to become separate he allows differentiation between his internal world and the external world and is therefore aware of what is phantasy and what is reality. In that way his work is not only not confused with him, it is also not completely identified and not confused with his phantasy objects. He can see it as a symbol, and as a symbol it can be used for communication. (This is elaborated upon in chapter 4.)

To Jocelin, the cathedral and the spire are himself. The artist is aware that his creations symbolize aspects of his internal world: they are neither him nor entirely his internal objects. This enables the artist to have a reality sense. If the artist succeeds and Jocelin fails, it is because the artist, as we know, is a supreme artisan. He does not confuse his wishes and his phantasies with realities; he has a reality appreciation of his material which Jocelin completely lacks. Where Jocelin relies on infantile omnipotence and magic, the holy Nail from the Cross, the artist relies on his reality sense. And by reality sense I mean reality sense in relation, naturally, to the external world, but also and primarily in relation to his own psychic world. Where Jocelin aims at maintaining an unconscious delusion that he is the source of omnipotence, the artist seeks to restore an internal truth. Jocelin, in his view of himself as chosen by God, is as blind to his own nature and his inner realities as he is to the material realities of the cathedral. When he feels threatened by the emergence from repression of the memory of what happened at the pit, the murder of Pangall, he flees up the tower where he recovers peace. His creation is an escape from realities, external and internal. The artist, on the other hand, is always in search of the psychic truth: he explores the world externally and, even more, internally, searches for the understanding of the cellarage, as Golding is doing in his book.

What is the difference between Jocelin, and William Golding who wrote the book? Jocelin must represent something of the author, in the sense in which Flaubert said, "Madame Bovary, c'est moi." The "cellarage," which represents Jocelin's unconscious, must be well known to the author, who can describe it with such feeling and depth. Yet Jocelin is clearly not all that there is to his author. The author must have fully encompassed and overcome that part of himself represented by Jocelin and seen it fully related to all his objects, past and present. Jocelin is but one part of Golding—it is the cathedral as a whole and the novel as a whole, which represents the author's internal world and its conflicts. Mason, the artisan and potent man in particular, represents both a potent internal father and the potent part of the artist. Father Anonymous represents the humility with which the artist views himself in relation to his task. Jocelin is wholly narcissistic; his creator is obviously aware of the reality of human relationships and capable of reintegrating what has been split and destroyed in the act of writing his book.

Where Jocelin's spire will soon collapse, William Golding's cathedral and spire stand complete, containing and bringing to life a whole new world in which we can become engrossed. But the theme itself which William Golding chose is significant: the collapse of his work is always a threat of which the artist is aware. And here Golding describes a particular threat which must be experienced by every artist. Artists are often accused of being narcissistic, which is a great misconception, but the particular kind of omnipotent narcissism represented by Jocelin must be a temptation that they probably have always to struggle with and to overcome.

References

Golding, W. (1964). *The Spire*. London: Faber and Faber.
Stokes, A. (1965). *The Invitation in Art*. London: Tavistock.
White, P. (1970). *The Vivisector*. London: Jonathan Cape.

18

Psychoanalysis and Freedom
of Thought

PSYCHOANALYSIS belongs to the great scientific tradition of freeing thought
from dogma, whether religious or arising out of an established scientific
tradition itself. In his *Introduction to the Study of Experimental Medicine*
Claude Bernard wrote that "an idea must always remain independent. It
must not be chained by scientific beliefs any more than by those that are
philosophical or religious." Such freedom, however, is hard to attain. In
any culture certain thoughts or ideas are inadmissible.

Copernicus's and Gallileo's work met with emotional resistance. It was
unthinkable that the earth should be anything but the center of the universe,
with stars revolving around it. Darwin's work was equally inadmissible. Of
course, I know that I am over-simplifying here. Copernicus, Gallileo, and
Darwin, like Freud, had predecesors. And in the case of astronomy there was
the added problem that its conclusions ran against the evidence of the
senses: the earth is flat. But be that as it may, however well-documented was
the evidence, their discoveries were resisted because they conflicted basically
with the accepted view of the place of God and man in the Universe. Before
Freud, it was unthinkable that incestuous wishes were part of human nature
and not the privilege of a few perverts. It was unthinkable that children,
even infants, had sexual wishes, fantasies, and activities. Even though, as
was not the case with astronomy or biology, much of the evidence was at

hand, both from observation and self observation. The notion of infantile sexuality was so unthinkable that Freud himself, when first coming upon the evidence, assumed that all his patients had been seduced in childhood by adults. Judging from a letter to Fliess, he was helped in allowing himself to contemplate the new idea because it released him from the burden of another inadmissible idea. In this letter, Freud said that when his views about childhood seduction were disproved by his own evidence, instead of feeling depressed about it, he felt surprisingly excited and relieved. The excitement was due to the feeling of being on the brink of a great discovery. The relief came from being able to discard another horrifying thought—namely, that so many respectable fathers, among them *his own father*, had been perverts. So his acceptance of one painful idea was somewhat facilitated by his relief at its freeing him from another. But it is important to note that while both thoughts were painful, they were not unthinkable to Freud. He could think about them and test them against evidence. The acceptance of the previously unthinkable thoughts about the child's sexual nature was a major breakthrough in his thinking. Before Freud, it was unthinkable that human beings regularly held not only incestuous but cruel wishes and death wishes against their nearest and dearest and that they invariably harbored death wishes against their parents. To make such unthinkable thoughts thinkable, it takes a genius and a hero of the stamp of Copernicus, Darwin, or Freud—someone of his time and yet stepping sufficiently outside what is thinkable in his time, to formulate hypotheses previously unthinkable.

Once such hypotheses are formulated, there is a long battle with emotional resistances and a long process of working through, overcoming first one's own inner resistances, then those of the scientific establishment, then of the world at large. Finally, these hypotheses may become part of accepted scientific thought, and eventually, of the general culture.

With psychoanalysis, however, it is not only a social problem. Even though psychoanalytic ideas have gained some general acceptance, the battle for the freedom of thought has to be fought individually with every analysand on the couch, as well as within oneself. And that is where it started. Freud did not set out to revolutionize culture, he set out to treat patients. Recognizing that the hysterical pathology hinged on the conversion into symptoms of thoughts which were not allowed into consciousness, he set about to free his individual patient's thoughts from inner resistances and prohibitions. His work—even the early work before his discovery of the psychoanalytic method—abounds in examples.

What is the origin of such inhibitions of thought? Most immediately evident is the fear of the superego. In the same way in which the fear of an external authority can make us afraid to speak, the fear of an internal authority can make us afraid to think. The superego, according to Freud, is the internalized parental figure, carrying the parental prohibitions, which becomes a structure in our unconscious mind. But while the external authority can forbid only actions, including speech, this internal authority can forbid thought. The prohibition may be directed not only at certain thoughts, say, hostile thoughts directed against the parents and siblings, it may also be against searching for knowledge and thought itself. The myth of the Garden of Eden lends itself to this interpretation: eating from the tree of knowledge is the first sin and leads to a fall from grace. In the myth of the Tower of Babel, the pursuit of knowledge of god is punished by an attack on on language, that is, verbal thought. The myth of Prometheus, involves punishment for seeking fire—light. One root of the inhibition of thought and the search for knowledge is the demand felt to emanate from the superego that it be deified. The superego becomes a god who cannot tolerate enlightment. When Oedipus finds the answer to the riddle of the Sphinx, the Sphinx has to kill herself. A god cannot survive being known too well. Such a god is also a terrible god. The Sphinx ate her victims. That aspect of the superego felt to be directed against knowledge and thought was particularly investigated and described by Wilfred Bion.

The superego is, however, a complex structure. It is more than the sum total of parental prohibitions and its savagery goes far beyond that of most parents. In his later works Freud expressed the view, partly in agreement with Melanie Klein and others who emphasized the point, that the superego is not only an internalization of parental prohibitions but is also and mainly a result of the projection into those parental figures of some of one's own impulses and phantasies. Both the ideal and the persecutory aspects of the superego have their roots in the infant's own impulses. Let us look at the case of the Wolf Man. If his superego was a wolf with staring eyes, we could now say that it was largely because he attributed to his internal parents his own biting and voyeuristic impulses. Similarly, the demand of the superego to be treated as a god, never exposed to critical thought, is rooted in the infant's own needs for such a perfect parent.

The prohibition against thoughts, which seems to emanate from the superego, is also in part a projection of the infantile self's own antagonism to thought. If we eat from the tree of knowledge of good and evil, we exile ourselves from paradise. Copernicus and Darwin dealt great blows to human vanity. It was not only the superego vested in religion and authority that protested against their discoveries but also human vanity and egocentricity. Man does not like losing his special and august place in the universe as god's elect. Freud referred to the blows Darwin and Copernicus dealt to man's self-love in several papers and he added: "But human megalomania will have suffered its third and most wounding blow from the psychological research of the present time, which seeks to prove to the ego that it is not even master in its own house." And the third blow is of a more personal nature. It is easier to accept Freud's theories in general than to accept the knowledge of one's self individually and specifically.

Thinking puts a limit on the omnipotence of phantasy and is attacked because of our longing for that omnipotence. For example, a patient dreamed that he was breaking the links in a chain with great fury. He associated to it that in the previous session the analyst referred to "a train of thought" and also used the expression "links" in pointing something out to him. When she said, "a train of thought," he had an angry thought which he hadn't verbalized:" it's not a train, it's a chain." He was in a temper after the session. He didn't want, he said, to be chained by his thoughts. He wanted to tear the chain apart and to be free of it. He felt his own train of linked thoughts as a prison and a persecution because it interfered with the belief in his omnipotence. It led him to realize things he didn't want to know. Paradoxically, the freedom of thought that gradually emerged in his analysis was felt by him as a chain on his freedom to think what he liked. The free thought became subject, for instance, to perceptual evidence, or laws of consistency, or logic.

I think that at this point I have to say something about what I mean by the terms omnipotence, omnipotent phantasy, and thought, and how they are related. In Freud's view, expressed most tellingly and succinctly in his "Formulations on the Two Principles of Mental Functioning," the emergence of thought is related to the loss of omnipotence, the experience of frustration and the move from what he calls the pleasure principle to the reality principle. The infant's peace of mind is disturbed by peremptory inner needs, such as hunger. His first response is by hallucinatory wishfulfilment and omnipotent phantasy of a need-satisfying object: a hallucination. His other response is by motor discharge, trying to rid himself of the experience by discharging it through muscular action. Eventually, however, he discovers that neither the hallucination nor the discharge satisfies the need. Freud concluded:

> It was only the non-occurence of the expected satisfaction, the disappointment experienced, that led to the abandonment of this attempt at satisfaction by means of hallucination. Instead of it, the psychical apparatus had to decide to

form a conception of the real circumstances in the external world and to endeavour to make a real alteration in them. A new principle of mental functioning was thus introduced; what was presented in the mind was no longer what was agreeable but what was real, even if it happened to be disagreable. This setting-up of the *reality principle* proved to be a momentous step.

To form a conception of the real circumstances and to endeavor to make a real alteration in them could be called a first step in thinking. It takes the place of the mindless motor discharge. Freud said, "Restraint upon motor discharge (upon action) which then became necessary, was provided by means of the process of *thinking*." According to Freud, it is thinking that makes it possible for the mental apparatus to tolerate an increased tension and to delay action. He called it "essentially an experimental kind of acting." Thus, thinking evolves in the gap between the experience of the need and its satisfaction.

On this hypothesis there is a distinction between hallucination and thought. I shall come back to that. A further extension of this hypothesis on the origin and nature of thought emerges from the work of Melanie Klein, particularly with very young children, and of Wilfred Bion, particularly with psychotics. In Klein's view the response to hunger is a hallucination of an all-satisfying breast, as suggested by Freud. But she added that when this cannot ward off the hunger, hunger itself is experienced also as the presence of an object, but a bad one, gnawing, tearing, attacking—a hallucinated bad object. According to Bion such an experience, felt to be a bad object, can only be dealt with by expulsion. I think that the motor discharge, as described by Freud, may be a way of dealing with bad hallucinations by an attempt to expel them. It is the realization that this discharge does not relieve the need, that brings in the realization that a need is not an object which can be got rid of, but is something intrinsic to the self, something originating within oneself; not a bad object, but the need for an object which is absent. The hallucinations are recognized as the product of one's mind. A phantasy of an ideal object or a persecutory one is recognized as a phantasy. So long as a phantasy is omnipotent, it is not a thought because it is not recognized as such. When a phantasy is recognized as a product of one's own mind, it moves into the realm of thought. One then can say, "I phantasied this or that, or I thought such and such." In that, thought differs from hallucination or delusion. Freud said that the reality principle is nothing but the pleasure principle subjected to reality testing. I would add that thinking evolves from omnipotent phantasy, and it is a phantasy recognized as such and one that can be subjected to reality testing.

Thinking first starts with, and then promotes, reality testing. It starts with the realization, "This is not what is, it is what I made it to be in my mind." But thinking also promotes reality testing in that omnipotent phantasy cannot be used for reality testing. Its very aim is to deny the reality of the experience. Thinking is not only an experimental action, as described by Freud, it is also an experimental hypothesis about the nature of things— a constant checking of what one phantasied against the evidence. Primitive thought starts at the preverbal level and is eventually encompassed in a word or a phrase, "Mummy—Daddy—Mummy gone." A word or a sentence encompasses a complex experience.

Both the omnipotent phantasy-hallucination and thinking enable one to bear the gap between need and satisfaction: the absence and the need for a satisfying object. But while omnipotent phantasy denies the experience of need, thought, which admits the need, can be used to explore external and internal realities and deal with them. But because thought springs from and admits frustration, it can be attacked at its very inception.

This hatred of thought processes, deeply rooted in the unconscious, can be active throughout life. For example, I had a patient who was highly intelligent and articulate in some ways, but certain areas of his personality were functioning on a very primitive level. He had psychosomatic symptoms—a gastric ulcer—and at times of tension, thinking was replaced by impulsive acting out. He had become aware in the course of his analysis of how he was obsessed with women's breast. Toward the end of one session, he reported a dream in which a woman was giving the breast to a baby. The breasts were so close to the patient that he could fondle them. Then the woman went away, but she left the breast with the baby and the patient, who continued the sucking and fondling. He added that the baby must also be himself, as it was so close to him. He started the next session with a great deal of irritation with himself. He said that he had plenty of important problems in his adult life which he wanted to talk about, but the moment he set eyes on the analyst he noticed she was wearing a white blouse and started thinking about her breasts and he said with exasperation, "I am not obsessed with breasts, I am mad. I am obviously mad about breasts." He then spoke of how he was always sucking something, like his toes and his thumb in his childhood, and now sweets, chewing gum, cigarettes, anything just to have something in his mouth. As he was talking, he was getting more and more dreamy and remote. I drew his attention to this and reminded him of the dream in which he, the baby, sucked and fondled the breast while the woman went away. He interrupted me angrily, saying,

"Don't make me think. I don't want to think. I want to suck. I hate thoughts. When I have thoughts, it means I have nothing to suck." My making the comment about his state of mind made him aware that what he was experiencing was a living through of the dream that he had possession of the breast, and made him aware of my presence. I was the woman with the white blouse, and there was a gap between us, necessitating speech for communication. The moment he became aware of that, he became aware that he was having thoughts, not a breast in his mouth, and he hated it. He hated the fact that he needed thinking to deal with this gap and with the problems he referred to at the beginning of the session, not the least of them being an impending analytic holiday.

The nascent thought conflicts with the illusion that the infant is merged with, or in possession of, an ideal breast. And disillusion must be tolerated for thought to develop. An element of this disillusion persists in sophisticated thought.

Toward the end of his analysis, another patient brought the following two dreams. In the first dream he saw himself. He was slim, but otherwise unchanged, a balding middle-aged man. On waking from the dream, he thought that his dream meant that being slimmer did not actually make him any younger. This patient, with a tendency to corpulence, would periodically diet and as he lost weight he used to become very manic. He had had a nearly conscious phantasy that being slim made him into an adolescent again, young and beautiful. In his association to the dream, he recognized with a certain sadness that it was no longer so. He was still pleased at having lost weight in the last week, but he couldn't feel as he used to, that it had changed him. His belief in the magic rejuvenating power of being slim and the elation associated with it had gone.

The next day he brought a more complex dream. He was saying goodbye at the door to an adolescent. He felt very tender toward him and sad at parting. In the background stood X, the adolescent's father, a cripple, and still further in the background, the patient's parental family. He had many associations to the dream. The first one was that the adolescent was himself and he was saying goodbye to his phantasies of still being an adolescent and goodbye to the picture of himself as still dependent on his original family. The associations to X were more complex. X was a rich, extremely mean, successful businessman, now crippled by a disease of the central nervous system. The patient himself had been a businessman, successful, mean to the point of ridicule and ruthlessly greedy. When he first came to analysis, being successful in business was equated with being not only omnipotently powerful but also very righteous. It was part of the culture he grew up in to believe that people were poor only because of their own fecklessness. Wealth was equated with godliness. Unconsciously, however, this greed and ruthlessness gave rise to a great deal of guilt, persecution, and feelings of emptiness which eventually brought him to analysis. In the course of his analysis, he recognized how crippling to his mental development were those attitudes. The cripple in the dream represented his past self and an aspect of his father, who had the same set of values in a less extreme form. In the dream he said goodbye, not only to the adolescent self, but to the set of values and ideas that he could no longer entertain. Now he was no longer free to think that being rich is equivalent to being righteous. Nor could he think anymore that that aspect of his father was admirable and to be emulated. So while analysis freed his perceptions and thoughts from the rigid set of values he was brought up in and which also suited his own greed and envy, he felt regret and sadness at the loss of another set of thoughts and beliefs belonging to the past. He mourned the lost idealization of his father and mostly of himself. Aspects of his personality which he used to think of as marvellous, he now thought of as crippling to his whole central nervous system. He could still think certain ideas but could no longer believe in their validity.

I am aware that I seem to be confusing here belief with thought, but among its other functions, thinking has that of examining belief. Thinking robs us of the luxury of blind belief. He could still think about the ideas he used to have and sometimes regret that he couldn't hold them any more as true, but he could no longer use them in thinking about the world and base his action on them. Similarly, once we learn that the earth is a planet revolving round the sun, we are not quite free to think that it is flat. Or rather, we can entertain such a thought as an intriguing phantasy, we can even, if we have the talent and inclination, write a science fiction novel about a flat world, but we have to recognize it as phantasy thought.

If thinking, as I suggested, is related to matching phantasies with realities, phantasies lose their omnipotent character.

The patient I referred to came to recognize that many of his views of himself and the world and his sometimes irrational actions which sprang from them were based on omnipotent unconscious phantasies. For instance, he had a phantasy that his feces had magic powers and were superior to mother's milk as a food and superior to his father's penis in potency. When this omnipotent phantasy had become a clear thought, he had to face his real feeling of helplessness and dependence as a child in relation to his parents, and now, as a patient in relation to me.

Freud linked thinking with "forming a conception of the reality circumstances in the external world." This involves forming a conception about one's self, one's needs, and one's impulses, that is to say, forming some conception of one's own internal world. The patient's belief in the magic of his feces had been linked with another omnipotent phantasy. He had a phantasy, amply illustrated in many dreams, that he had swallowed me up (as in the past, he had phantasied about his mother) and inside of himself, had emptied me of all my supposed riches and attributes, physical and mental. In his manic state, he felt the owner of all power and riches and contained me as an impoverished object full of greed and envy. This omnipotent phantasy underlay both his states of manic elation and those of persecution. This state of affairs was experienced not as thoughts but as a reality. Very schematically, one could say that there were three steps in his gaining of insight in that area. First: "My feces are everything (omnipotent)." Second: "This is so because my internal parents are empty and I have it all. That's also why they persecute me." Third: "This is so because I wished it so. In my mind I made it so by imagining that I swallowed them up and emptied them."

This third step brought him in touch with the fact that the state of affairs he experienced is something he phantasied because he wished it. He began to recognize that these were the thoughts he had, and he could no longer believe them as reality perceptions. The omnipotent phantasies turned into thoughts which could be expressed as, "This is what I wished, or, this is what I wish. This is what I thought I had done, or could do." At that point reality testing: "can I do it," begins to play a part in two ways. One is a reality testing of the omnipotence of one's wishes. For instance, the patient realized that it was a phantasy that he could possess himself of my attributes in that way. But another equally important element of reality comes into play. An internal reality testing occurs in relation to other feelings and wishes that one may have—as in the case of this patient, for instance, such feelings as love, gratitude, a wish to preserve inside himself a good perception of me, guilt about his greedy and envious thoughts, and concern about what this was doing to his internal world and how it was affecting his behavior in the external world. All these feelings were in conflict with his omnipotent megalomania.

I have been led by this example to bring in several additional problems: awareness of impulses, sense of guilt, the problem of values. Are they relevant to my theme? I think I have to introduce here the concept of integration and its relation to thinking. An omnipotent phantasy can, and indeed must, be split off from such perceptions, external and internal, which conflict with it. When a phantasy loses its omnipotent character and becomes thought, a hypothesis to be tested, or a wish recognized as such, it becomes integrated with other thoughts and wishes. Thought allows conflict and seeks resolution. I cannot here go into the difference between having thoughts and thinking. Suffice it to say that such an integration—comparing and matching and judging—is also a step from the state of having thoughts to the state of thinking. In the case of the patient, in a simplified way, a megalomanic phantasy lived as a reality began to give way to thoughts, to the appraisal of himself, me and the world and an appraisal of his contradictory wishes.

This was linked with a change in his sense of values because a sense of values and thinking are inextricably bound together. The sense of values naturally influences all thinking, but conversely, too, the sense of values is determined by what we think. Money-Kyrle explored this theme in his "Psycho-analysis and Ethics," and "Man's Picture of his World." My patient's view of the world was based on the phantasy that he had robbed his object, and therefore he feared that his object would rob and annihilate him. It led to a sense of values based on the idea, "You have to kill if you are not to be killed." With the emergence of integration and thinking and a changed view of himself and the world, his values unavoidably had to be altered. A paradoxical and complex situation arises in relation to the superego. When integration begins and thinking takes the place of split-off omnipotent phantasies, guilt is in some ways lessened and in others augmented. In my patient, the omnipotent phantasy of his superiority was linked with a terrifying superego, a parental figure stripped of all positive assets and seething with greed and envy. His thinking was not only constricted by the infantile need to annihilate any thought that would conflict with his own omnipotence; it was also under continuous attack by an equally omnipotent, envious, and hostile superego which did not allow him any real enrichment in feeling, thought, or knowledge.

When the phantasies are recognized as phantasies, they are allowed to exist in thought. The less the omnipotence, the more permissible a thought becomes, as it does not have the omnipotent power to change the object into a monster superego figure. On the other hand, this inner persecution by a monstrous superego is replaced by a feeling of responsibility for one's own thought and more conscious guilt, which I think in unavoidable, even if the thoughts are recognized as not omnipotent. In the case of the last patient I spoke about, the megalomanic phantasy and the accompanying fears mutilated his capacity to think. They were replaced by realizations that, for instance, there were people he depended on, that this often stimulated in him greedy, envious, and hostile thoughts and phantasies, and that the existence of those thoughts gave him some pain, guilt and disillusionment in his view of himself.

What then is the freedom of thought? Nietzsche says "The thought does not come when we want it, it comes when it wants." We could add: It is not what we want, it is what it wants. This, of course, is personifying thought as though it were a being with a will of its own. There is such a category of thought—those attributed to and felt as emanating from an internal object—as an inspiration or a persecution. But more generally, thought and thinking are the outcome of a complex interaction of our impulses, wishes, phantasies and perceptions. And, as such, it is not necessarily what we would wish it to be.

Freedom of thought—and at best, I think we still have a very limited freedom in that respect—means the freedom to know our own thoughts and that means knowing the unwelcome as well as the welcome, the anxious thoughts, those felt as "bad" or "mad," as well as constructive thoughts and those felt as "good" or "sane." Freedom of thought is being able to examine their validity in terms of external or internal realities. The freer we are to think, the better we can judge these realities, and the richer are our experiences. But like all freedoms, it is also felt as a bind in that it makes us feel responsible for our own thoughts.

And formidable forces, external and internal, militate against this freedom. The psychoanalyst sets himself the task to help the patient above all to recognize the immeasureable value of such freedom and how worthwhile it is to struggle for it, and to help him to achieve such freedom in a greater measure.

POSTSCRIPT 1980:
PSYCHOANALYSIS AND THE FREEDOM OF THOUGHT

This lecture was given to a mainly nonpsychoanalytic audience. Time did not allow me to elaborate on the passage from hallucination through omnipotent phantasy to thought nor to describe the role of projection and introjection in this process. It would have necessitated an account of Bion's work on the alpha function which appears in chapter 7.

I could also not go into the problem of unconscious and conscious thought and the role of symbolism and repression. These are described further in chapters 3, 4, 5 and 7.

Index

LaVergne, TN USA
15 January 2010
170094LV00002B/36/P